PORTALS

Published by
WINGS PUBLISHERS
1700 Chattahoochee Avenue
Atlanta,Georgia 30318

Book design by Melanie M. McMahon

Manufactured in the United States of America

10 9 8 7 6 5 4 3 2 1
First Edition

ISBN 1-930897-12-X

PORTALS

by
Betsy Gamble Hansen

WINGS
PUBLISHERS

Susan – Thanks
for everything you
& Bird always
do for the
Hansen.
Love.
Betsy

Dedicated to those I love,
including Pucho, Brandon and Ed.

PREFACE

One fall when I was recovering from a broken leg, my Aunt Mary Stuart sent me a box of books. On top of the books was a notebook wrapped in a plastic dry cleaner's bag. A note attached to the outside said, "I found this in my bedside table." There was no further explanation. Inside was a Blue Horse notebook. It was her personal journal for ten years. The events she recorded were unremarkable, just the comings and goings of her household, which included three generations, plus a Spanish-speaking housekeeper from Columbia, South America. The qualities that shone through so poignantly in the notebook were her strong faith and her steadfast philosophy of life.

As I looked through my aunt's journal, I was reminded that I had intended writing a book about my family. I had grown up with a large extended family of aunts, uncles and cousins. My mother and father had made certain we remained close by visiting both sides of the family and attending at least one family reunion each summer.

Now most of my relatives were dead, including my mother and father and sister. Somehow in all the hectic years of raising my own family, I had not managed to keep in touch as I had intended. My children, who were starting their adult lives, did not really know their relatives, did not know what my childhood was like and had never experienced the strong support of being loved by a large family.

This book is set in the period from 1940 to 1970. It is fiction, not about my family as I had thought it would be. But the two main characters, like myself, grew up when America seemed innocent. We sent our fathers and brothers off to World War II expecting their sacrifices to end all wars. Victory, however, was costly. When the Unites States dropped atomic bombs on Hiroshima and Nagasaki, thereby introducing nuclear weapons into the war, it opened the way for a nuclear arms race with Russia. At the same time our country was helping rebuild war-torn countries, it was forced to defend democracy against the growing threat of communism. In only four short years we were back fighting again, this time in the Korean War. Called the "Forgotten War," 159,000 Americans were wounded or killed. When survivors of this war returned home, they were ignored, and in some cases defamed, by people who had not supported the war.

Americans wanted peace. Our parents, survivors of the depression and WW II, wanted an easier life for their children. Our country moved into an unprecedented period of affluence. More people than ever before in our history received college educations and better jobs awaited them after graduation. But while the national mood was upbeat and full of promise, underneath was a current of unrest. All of our citizens were not living the American dream.

African Americans, who had been freed from slavery 90 years before, questioning the constitutionality of segregation, refused to accept the mediocre jobs and inferior social positions offered to them by their government and its citizens. Peaceful resistance in the form of protests, demonstrations and boycotts were organized under the leadership of Dr. Martin Luther King, the NAACP and the Southern Christian Leadership Conference.

By the sixties our national desire for change had erupted. Perhaps the civil rights movement added fuel to a general feeling of distrust for established institutions. Perhaps families who had lost relatives during WW II did not want their sons to go to another war. Whatever the reasons, when our government drafted young men to fight in the Vietnam War, many refused and chose to flee from their country rather than fight a war they believed was unjust.

College campuses, once considered safe havens, became battlefields where rioting students faced armed police. Students intent on controlling their own futures demanded that college administrators give them a voice in the type of education they were to receive. Three of our strongest leaders were assassinated, tragedies which cut to the very heart of our country. To this day the debate continues as to how and why and who directed these killings.

These decades, times of turmoil and change, are the settings for this book. The characters are not real, nor or their stories, but the emotions they stimulate are genuine. The book's events and themes could have played out in most any town or city in the South, perhaps your own.

My hope is that "Portals" will resonate with you. Perhaps through the stories set forth here, we may find glimpses into our own pasts and clues to our futures.

The space between memory and reality is as fleeting as a wisp of smoke. Some say it is self-indulgent. Others that it promotes melancholy. Reality, on the other hand, is in the moment and requires all a person's strength and attention.

Memory can be the backbone of an individual and the fiber of his soul, a portal through which reality can be viewed in a different light.

CHAPTER ONE

Spring 1970

At first the flashbacks came with the insistency of waves crashing on a deserted beach, breaking on a strip of clean, white sand only to recede back to the ocean, depositing broken evidence of past lives within the sea: ebony egg pods; fishing line tangled with sea weed; an oyster shell, ripped from its other half by an unseen predator, split, never to be made whole again; conch shells laced by worms, intruders who broke through the shell and invaded the perfect spiral within. Like a child gathering shells in his sand bucket, he picked in his mind at the objects, settling on the conch. It bore deep into his brain.

"Mace! Mace, is that you?" he called into the cool shadows of his bedroom. When the figure in his daydream stepped forward, it was not Mace, but Shaky Joe Potts. And the beach wasn't the sparkling beach of his childhood, but a dirty strip of beach in Wonsan, North Korea.

The daydream was wrong. Shaky Joe was trying to tell him something, whispering up close to his ear as if they were buddies. Mace was his buddy, not Shaky Joe. He and Shaky Joe didn't even like each other.

"Where are we?" Shaky Joe whispered.

"Korea. Behind enemy territory. You don't remember mine-sweepers clearing the harbor while we were stuck on troop carriers out at sea?" Shaky Joe's head wobbled like he was drunk. They were sitting on a log where the grass met the sand.

"I don't remember nothin'. Wait a minute. Sumpin's coming in...the gooks chased the gooks away."

He nodded, "Yeah, the South Koreans ran the North Koreans out of their own town."

"You know sumpin'?" Shaky Joe sat up straight and sober. "Sometimes I wake up in the morning and I can't think where I am. Then I remember. And I ask myself what the devil am I doing in this hellhole? We're gonna die, you and me, and it ain't even our war." His shoulders slumped forward again. "We're never going home."

"Don't worry, Shaky Joe. We'll go home. You and I won't get killed. We're both too mean to die."

✿

Davis Williams was coming home.

Josephine Scarborough was cleaning her kitchen in Matthews, North Carolina. It was a fair, April morning, and she had just sent off her husband, Michael, and their five-year-old daughter, Josie, when the telephone rang.

When Josephine answered it, she heard a distraught voice. It was her aunt, Ruth Williams, who lived in Bishop, a hundred miles away.

"Davis is coming home." Her aunt's voice was urgent.

"Aunt Ruth, what in the world are you talking about?" Josephine queried.

"I said 'Davis is coming home.'"

"Davis Williams? I thought he was committed for life!" Josephine began picking at a hangnail on her thumb. Davis was Aunt Ruth's nephew on her deceased husband's side of the family.

Her aunt was saying, "So did I, but that's the word in Bishop. Some new law. They say you can't keep a person locked up anymore in an insane asylum against their will."

Josephine's heart was flying. *Davis coming home!* Now of all times. "Aunt Ruth, I can't deal with Davis now. If ever there was a part of my life I want to forget, it's Davis."

"I know what you mean, honey. I'd like to be finished with him too," Aunt Ruth answered.

Things were already rough. In the last four years Josephine's parents and her only sister had died. Since then, at times painful memories consumed her, and no matter how she tried to focus on the present, she spent most of her time dwelling on the past.

The deaths of her family members were not the only problem either, and hearing Aunt Ruth's voice made Josephine want to open-up to her aunt. She couldn't think what to say. If only she could tell her about the vague, undefined tension that had been building between her and Michael, her husband. Maybe Aunt Ruth would understand. She had been like a mother to Josephine since her own mother died.

Josephine wasn't sure when or why the problems with Michael had started. They hadn't had a fight. In fact, a fight might be a relief. It was more that they didn't seem to care anymore. Whatever had tied them to each other over the past ten years of their marriage was eroding. They passed each other in the kitchen, hall, bathroom, even in bed, and didn't touch. Not even total strangers could live in the same house without constantly bumping into each other. Yet, they managed to *avoid* each other by sidestepping. How could she tell Aunt Ruth, or any one for that matter, nothing fit in her marriage anymore?

That wasn't all. Things were not going well with Josie, her daughter, whom she loved with all her heart. Just the other night, the two of them were tussling on the bed when Josie pushed away and said to her mother, "You over being sad, Mommy?" She had reassured her young daughter, but the flicker of guilt had remained.

Now this business with Davis. She hoped nobody, including Aunt Ruth, expected her to do anything about him. At the moment taking care of herself and her family was all she could manage, and she was doing a lousy job with both.

"Aunt Ruth," she said into the phone. "I'm shocked, but I don't know what to say except keep me posted."

"Sure," the older woman promised with a sigh. "And Josephine, courage. We'll get through this. We always do."

After she hung up the phone, Josephine poured herself another cup of coffee and took it to the breakfast table. She pushed aside the dirty dishes and dropped into Michael's chair. Usually the aroma of fresh coffee comforted her, but this morning she hardly noticed as she took a deep swallow from the cup.

It was hard to believe Davis was coming home after so many years. All the events that both bound and separated them swirled in her mind. The incident at the grapevine, the near drowning, the shooting, her fears—everything. Yet she had to admit to a strange fascination for him—a dangerous fascination that might pull her too close to the edge, like a mountain climber who continues to climb knowing one false step could plunge him to his death.

As children, her friends in Bishop felt it, too. Like Josephine, who was seven years younger than Davis, they had found him daring and good-looking. Sometimes her friends, dripping wet and giggling, huddled together near the back gate of Whitmire's swimming pool while they waited for him to arrive on his yellow motor scooter, his blond hair pressed flat by the wind, his blue eyes dancing. "Waitin' for me, gals?" he'd query as he pushed through the gate with that breezy air of his. Even though Josephine would never allow him to see her acting "stupid" over him like her girl friends, she knew he could charm anyone, even her, when he wanted.

But Davis had another side, and it was frightening. When he had headaches, *"blue ice headaches,"* he had called them, he was impulsive, and it escalated until he was dangerous and out of control.

Of course she had seen everything through the eyes of a child, at least in the beginning. Maybe she had distorted the

4

events, like a camera out of focus. But if that were true, she thought, she couldn't alter her memories now. They were too deep and painful.

What was it Aunt Ruth had said? "Courage." Where was she going to come up with that kind of strength?

The window above the sink overlooked the meadow. Lush spring grass covered the ground and ran up to the edge of a creek. Beyond the creek was a thicket of pines and hardwoods. They were thick but did not obstruct the early morning sun, which shone in dusty sheets from the sky to the ground below.

Most mornings Josephine watched as the meadow came to life. Birds marked their territory while Lady, the family dog, chased insects or nipped at the ponies' heels as they dipped their heads to graze.

But who could think of birds with the threat of Davis hanging over her head? For now, she had to clean up before Josie with her characteristic exuberance came bounding in from nursery school.

The leftover smell of bacon grease still rose from the frying pan. She emptied it and filled the pan with water and liquid soap. The soap floated on top in white, unbroken strings. She flipped on the kitchen fan to clear the air.

With automatic movements, she cleared the table, scraping bits of congealed egg and toast into the disposal. Then she ran the dirty plates under a stream of water and slid them into the dishwasher. She had never told Michael about Davis. She wasn't sure why. Embarrassment, she supposed but also some guilt.

Why did she feel guilt? She had never done anything wrong. Davis was the one who followed her practically everywhere as if he were her personal guardian. Finally, she lost track of him when she was in college. After she graduated, she never tried to contact him, or look him up. She heard he had enlisted in the Marine Corps and was sent to Korea. She was actually relieved he was gone. Later she heard he was married. After that, news of him was less frequent. When she asked Aunt Ruth questions about him, her answers were vague. She should have pressed for more details.

Now Davis was back, and considering her mixed feelings about him, plus the other questions that loomed in her life at the moment, it was best not to alarm Michael. Maybe it would blow over, she reasoned. Maybe Davis would not return to Bishop, and she could go on with her life without ever seeing him again. It seemed worth a try. For the moment at least, she decided not tell Michael.

After an early dinner that evening, Michael sat down at the kitchen table to pay bills, and Josephine settled in with the evening news. Josie was pretending she had kindergarten "homework." Her crayons and construction paper were spread across the table. As she bent over her work, her dark, straight hair swung out, hiding her face from Josephine, who was seated at the other end of the table.

Josephine watched her daughter out of the corner of her eye. *She is so innocent,* Josephine thought. *Her hair is like Momma's,* dark and sleek with the sheen of coal. Not like her own, which was pure Scottish. Wiry, reddish brown and fuzzy as a lion's mane.

Michael was getting the checkbook from the desk drawer. *He's going to pay bills,* she thought, her heart sinking. Josephine hated the monthly ordeal of paying the bills. Michael's inevitable questions about checks she had forgotten to record, or charges she had made, were upsetting. Always the banker, Michael had to be precise.

"Jo, you forgot to stub this check," he was saying, pointing to a place in the checkbook he had marked.

"Which one, Michael?" She tried to sound casual.

"I don't know how to tell you which one. Check 1101."

"What's before and after it?" She found the hangnail she had worked on in the morning and began rubbing her finger over it.

"Jo, that's no way to keep a checkbook. You have to write down every check." He sighed, then relented. "Before the grocery store. After the maid."

6

"Dry Cleaners. About twenty-five dollars."

"How can I balance the checkbook without the exact amount?"

"Twenty-five dollars will cover it. I don't remember exactly how much it was!"

Michael tossed his pen across the checkbook. It rolled toward Josie's crayons, startling her. She grabbed the pen before it reached her crayons.

"Can we finish this later?" Josephine said, gathering up the papers and crayons. She hated arguing with Michael in front of Josie. "Time for Josie to have her bath. Come on, Punkin."

Josie handed Michael his pen without speaking. Upstairs Josephine started the water in Josie's tub, and Josie began undressing. When she was ready, she stepped into the tub and squatted down, looking up at her mother.

"Daddy doesn't like checks," she observed from the middle of her tub.

"It's not Daddy's fault, honey. Mommy forgot to write down something important." Josephine shrugged her shoulders and rolled her eyes toward the ceiling like a comic. Josie laughed.

"What book shall we read tonight?" The mention of books sent Josie into a litany of her favorite books, and she seemed to forget the tension in the kitchen.

For Josephine, the incident over the checkbook lingered. She could not recall ever hearing her parents argue. Did they fight in heated whispers, sequestered behind closed doors in their bedroom? Or did her mother give in to her father, who had the stronger personality? Was she like her mother? If she gave in repeatedly to Michael would she loose some of her own self-identity? Daddy was easy-going, always smiling, joking, constantly telling Momma how pretty she was, what a good person, mother and wife. Did Momma give in because it was the easiest way to keep peace? Whatever had caused her parents not to argue, the results were that she, Josephine, felt uncomfortable with disagreements. Her parents, her role models, did not act like she and Michael.

After Josie fell asleep, Josephine settled down in bed with a book. When Michael came upstairs, he started in where they had left off in the kitchen.

"Each month we spend more than I make. We can't go on like this."

"I'm sorry, Michael. Of course we can't spend more than you make," Josephine replied. "We'll cut back. I'm thinking of going back to work when Josie goes to kindergarten next fall."

"You've brought that up before. I don't want you to work," he replied shaking his head.

"I can look for something during Josie's school hours. Besides I should be getting money from Dad's estate soon. I know it's not a fortune but it will help."

"That's another thing. Your dad should have done genera-tion-skipping." Michael had turned his back to Josephine. They had had the discussion before that over time the inter-est earned from Josephine's father's estate could have funded the taxes, leaving enough to pay for Josie's education.

"Michael, you discussed that with him long before he died. His lawyer said if he wanted me to have the money, he should leave it to me. Otherwise too many things could hap-pen. Is the cost of Josie's education bothering you? Do you want me to pay for it?" Josephine sat up abruptly causing her book to slip to the floor with a thud. "Is that what this is about?" She ignored the book.

Michael shook his head angrily. "No, I don't want you to pay for Josie's education. It wasn't a very good business move, that's all."

Josephine could feel her own anger rise. "Michael, listen to me. Daddy was a good businessman. Besides, I *want* that money! It's mine and maybe that's greedy, but it gives me some independence. It strikes me that's something I need right now."

"If it's independence you want, I'll......

Josephine jumped up from the bed and stepped toward Michael. The argument had escalated in a frightening way. It wasn't about recording checks and making ends meet. Not even about money. Something different was on the table now. What was Michael about to say? That he would leave her?

"Wait a minute," she interrupted. "I don't like where this is going. I LOVE you. It's not independence from YOU. I'm not really sure what I want. I feel—well—boxed in. I've quit growing. It has nothing to do with you."

He looked so fierce standing in front of her, yet as good-looking as ever. His black hair was straight and thick. His broad cheekbones promised the strength of his ancestors. And his thrusting chin, also a gift of heritage, gave him a determined demeanor. His eyes were dark brown and as fathomless as an ocean. A nerve under his left eye twitched, a quirk that appeared when he was nervous. She wanted to reach out and soothe the nerve with the tips of her fingers, but she resisted. She did love him but his unspoken threat lay in the pit of her stomach as if he had punched her.

A childhood memory filled her mind. She and Laura, her sister, were playing tag in their house. She was five or six years old; Laura, ten or eleven. Momma was in the breakfast room reading the afternoon paper and having a cup of coffee before starting dinner. Laura and Josephine started at the front door and ran through the living and dining rooms, hit the scatter rugs in the breakfast room and slid on them to the guest bedroom door. They continued through the guestroom into a small hall, through the den, ending up back at the front door. On one pass, when Josephine came through the breakfast room, Momma swatted her backside, laughing, "Hurry or Laura'll catch you!"

Josephine laughed but ran again out of the breakfast room, through the guestroom, and ducked into a coat closet located in the hall. She was careful to leave the door cracked. Seconds later when Laura came through, she unknowingly shoved the door shut, and Josephine was trapped inside. She tried to open the door, but her small hands could not twist the knob. She pounded on the door, shouting to her mother and sister, but there was only silence.

The small closet was black and crowded with coats that made her itch. They swept over her like monsters. She smelled the suffocating odor of mothballs, but she managed to push the coats aside and drop to the floor. There she waited. Minutes that seemed like hours went by. They had forgotten her, she thought, or they would have come. She was going to run out of air soon. Finally, she heard footsteps and the door opened. By then she was terrified and drenched with perspiration.

Momma and Laura pulled her out and carried her to the guestroom. They laid her on the bed, and Momma talked to her while Laura ran in the bathroom to get bath cloths. They wiped her face and arms with small rough, bath cloths until they were so hot they no longer relieved her. Then they shook them in the air and cooled them again. Even now, so many years later, she remembered the taste of her own salty tears.

Michael was standing in front of her, glaring at her. She felt the same sense of abandonment and panic she had felt in that closet so long ago. Only now there was no one to comfort her.

"Okay, you're right," Michael was saying. "We don't want to go there. Forget it."

Josephine wasn't going to forget it. Far from it. There was so much left—the old feeling of abandonment, the renewed panic. Why hadn't Michael engulfed her in his arms and pulled her to his chest the way Momma and Laura had done when they pulled her from the closet?

They kissed goodnight, a brief brush of lips that barely touched. Michael reached over to the bedside table and turned out the lamp. The sheets rustled as he settled in and then he rolled over on his side.

Josephine didn't move. Michael's breathing settled into a rhythm. She could have reached over and touched him, or curled her body along his back, wedging her legs behind his. Instead she stayed where she was, wondering what they had left unsaid and what there was left to understand. Why did she feel so far away and so alone?

During the night, the threads of a nightmare wound their way through Josephine's consciousness. She woke in complete darkness, her heart racing. A line of perspiration had formed under her chin and breasts. Shapes began to form in her mind like chips of glass in a smoky kaleidoscope. Davis was crouched at the side of a swimming pool. Josephine was under water, pushed there by Davis. Her hair floated in slow motion in streaming tendrils about her head and shoulders. As she tried to right herself in the water, the tendrils wound tighter and tighter about her face and shoulders.

Davis watched, detached and calculating, from the side of the pool. Each time Josephine tried to reach the surface, he leaned over the edge and calmly pushed her head under again, apparently intent on drowning her.

At length the struggle was too much and Josephine quit fighting. As her muscles relaxed, her body sank to the bottom of the pool. The change did not seem to disturb her. In fact she felt reckless, as if she wanted to giggle at an hilariously funny joke she had just told. Even the tiny bubbles that were slipping now out of the corners of her mouth and nose tickled her and made her want to laugh.

The scene changed. Josephine was on the side of the pool. She watched herself lean into the water and turn over what she believed was her own body. But the face had changed. It was Josie's. The shock of seeing her baby there in the water was terrifying. Josephine woke, gasping for breath, her heart pounding. She was dripping with sweat.

Her eyes could not focus clearly in the dark. Beside her, Michael's breathing was undisturbed. Around her, smoky shapes and shadows formed and then floated away. She felt nauseated, but she managed to throw back the covers and stumble out of her bedroom into the hall, where she could see more clearly.

Feeling her way down the hall, Josephine stumbled into Josie's bedroom. Her daughter was peacefully sleeping, bathed in a cool glow of iridescent light from a street light outside the house. The child sighed softly as Josephine straightened the spread about her.

On impulse, Josephine nudged Josie over. There she snuggled in beside her daughter and began to let the rhythmic breathing of her child's innocent sleep calm her.

Toward morning she woke, cold and stiff, in Josie's bed. She slipped out of her daughter's bed and headed down the hall to Michael's and her bedroom.

Michael lay on his side with his arm stretched out. The sheet lightly traced his muscles and the outline of his hip-bone. He looked boyishly inviting with his hair tousled and his T-shirt stretched tightly across his chest. She did love him and their argument of last night seemed foolish. She slipped into the crook of his body, not really caring that she would wake him.

"Where you been?" he whispered, half in the clutches of sleep.

"I fell asleep in Josie's bed. I had an awful nightmare in the night. I went to check her and stayed. Anyway, sorry to wake you."

"You're cold."

"Umm. Get me warm."

"Be my pleasure, ma'am. I aim to please."

"Sorry about last night."

"Forget it. I was a bear."

"I'll call the bank and find out when Dad's estate will be settled."

"Shh. All I want right now is your mouth."

"Well, I aim to please, sir."

She turned her face to meet him. Slowly, her muscles

began to relax. The bad thoughts of Davis and last night's argument with Michael were fading away.

Michael's hands began exploring her body, searching for familiar places; hers followed his lead. His tongue slipping down the smooth skin of her throat, up by her neck to her ear, around to her mouth. She copied his moves. They pressed closer with a new urgency, and she could feel his breath in her mouth and tasted it like food. They merged together without thought of last night's argument, only that they could suspend themselves for that brief time. In her mind Josephine wanted the singleness they were experiencing to continue, but their climax began to carry them over the edge, and they lay in each other's arms in quiet exhaustion.

By then early morning light was beginning to rim the edges of the curtains. She lay in her husband's arms, holding reality at bay, enjoying the beauty of the moment. Maybe everything would be all right.

CHAPTER TWO

Stateside
June, 1950

Panic prevailed in local recruiting offices. A general order had come down from Headquarters to press for recruits. Americans were mad. Nobody pushed the Yanks around, certainly not North Koreans. Yet the truth was American and Republic of Korea soldiers had been pushed all the way to the seaport at Pusan.

Recruits were called "Eight-Week Boy Wonders." Usually basic training was twelve brutal weeks of separating men from boys. Recruits were expected to arrive physically fit and leave combat ready. If they weren't, they were out.

At High Meadows Institute for the Criminally Insane Davis Williams lay on a metal cot in his room, clinging to the last traces of sleep. His sheets and army blanket were mounded up to his ears, covering his mouth, his own breath warming his face. Below his chin, his thin arms and hands clutched the covers to his chest like a baby.

Through the years, the mattress and pillow, skimpy at best, had become molded in the form of his body. His head rested in a hollow in the pillow. His shoulder, upper arm and elbow fit perfectly into matching holes in the mattress. Further down the bed, the largest indentation, the size of a shovel, comfortably fit his left hipbone.

Most mornings Davis dreamed of Celeste. The dream came between 3:30 and 5 a.m. in that space between deep sleep and first consciousness. She always wore the same gown, black velvet, and she floated across a smooth, black background, the gown disappearing in the darkness except for the sparkling rhinestones that bordered the top and ran down the front. The effect was stunning—her white body gleamed like pearls. Her arms reached out toward Davis. And, of course, she was singing one of her blues songs.

The first time, years ago, when he had this dream he was immediately aroused, and he let the dream run its course. He leaned toward Celeste, stretching out his hand to grasp hers, expecting a soothing caress. But when their fingers touched, her jewel face exploded into shards of glass, and her hair changed to crystal threads, which spun around her head like a fragile glass net. Davis grabbed at a single piece of jagged glass as it flew passed him, but it changed to liquid, running through his fingers and splashing, blood red, on the ground, which had turned as white as light. He must have screamed, because when he awoke, orderlies were on top of him, wrestling him into a straight jacket. That day he had ended up in a padded room.

This morning was different. He had "taken charge" as Doc Bostwick, his psychiatrist, had urged him to do. When the dream began, he willed Celeste to leave and, to his amazement, she faded away.

Usually the dream left him confused and disoriented but this morning he was energized. He had been victorious! Celeste had been tamed like a wild beast. And for a time, he lay in his bed vehemently turning the notion of his triumph over and over in his mind.

Except for those few lingering remnants of his dream, this hour before everyone awoke was his favorite time. By five o'clock the nameless night nurse on his ward would begin her quiet rounds. He could hear her from his bed as she moved from room to room, her crepe-sole shoes squeaking periodically over the asphalt tile floor. He could measure precisely how far away she was from his room by the grind of the metal door fittings as they yielded to the thrust of her shoulder against the door. He knew because he had slipped out of bed before and watched the way her shadowy figure moved against the light from the hall.

This morning he waited expectantly, like a lover hiding in the shadows, for her to approach his room. He anticipated the cool sweep of air from the hall that would announce her presence and the thin whiff of acrid odor that sometimes rose from her body. Once she was gone, he clung to the memory of the whisper of her uniform as she closed the door.

Doc Bostwick said Davis was transferring feelings for Celeste to the unidentified nurse, a thought Davis despised. How could the doctor compare Celeste to a ward nurse? He hated the doctor's incessant probing into everything he thought or did. After all these years, he continued to probe.

Doc Bostwick was right in one regard. Nothing was going to come of the early morning encounters with the nurse. Just as with the rest of his life, there was nothing to it. Absolutely nothing at all.

Still, these morning rounds puzzled Davis. What did the unnamed nurse expect to see? That a patient had escaped? Someone had fallen out of bed or died during the night?

Whatever the nurse's purpose, the results were that everybody on the ward began to stir. Davis's privacy, so coveted, would soon be gone. The craziness on the ward would surround him, seeping into everything he did or saw.

This morning, once the nurse had passed his room, Davis got up. It was Thursday, the day his mother drove up from Bishop in her black Cadillac, bringing clean laundry, toilet articles and best of all, cookies baked by Eula Mae, the family cook.

He went through his morning routine automatically, silently shuffling down the hall to the men's bathroom, showering and shaving, greeting no one, saying nothing. Afterward he returned to his room where he put on khaki pants, a white collared t-shirt, a navy sweater, and navy socks and tan crepe-sole shoes. Then he joined his ward mates in the common room for breakfast. When he was through, he returned to his room to wait for his mother.

At precisely ten o'clock he left his room and walked down the hall to the large window where he could watch the parking lot. He hoped his father wouldn't come today. Two years ago his mother had been diagnosed with cancer. On her bad days she sent his father, which lately had been more and more frequently.

When his father came, it was always the same. He sat on the edge of Davis's bed, hunched over his legs with his arms resting on his knees, twirling his gray felt hat in his hand. *"You all right, son? Anything I can get you?"* he'd ask.

It wasn't the questions Davis heard. It was the worry and unspoken disappointment in his father's voice. By the time his father left after these visits, Davis was exhausted with guilt. How could his father hope for anything different after all these years?

His mother, on the other hand, accepted him as he was. As if his failings made no difference to her, she simply moved forward with whatever was needed. Even when she was sick, she had a positive attitude toward everything. Just having her walk into his room made his day bearable.

Today he was not disappointed. When he spotted the Cadillac pulling into the parking lot, he could make out his mother's outline through the windshield. He returned to his room to wait for her. Within minutes he heard the elevator door open, followed by the insistent sound of her heels. He could see her in his mind. About five feet four, sixty-five, gray-white hair neatly curled, navy knit suit, white blouse, navy pumps—and her eyes, like his, as crystal blue as a cloudless sky.

"Knock-knock," she called from outside the door.

"Yeah." He smiled at her familiar greeting and opened his door. But when he reached out to hug his mother, he felt her ribs beneath her jacket. They were like tissue paper. He realized with alarm that she couldn't weigh more than 100 pounds.

She pulled away quickly, chattering nervously, and stepped toward his dresser. Holding the stack of his clean clothes in front of her body like a shield, she leaned forward to open a drawer with her free hand and was thrown off balance. She fell against the dresser, spilling some of the clothes. Davis rushed to help her.

"What's wrong, Mama?" When she turned to face him, her eyes were watery. For a second, Davis thought she might faint. He was about to ask if she wanted a glass of water when she spoke.

"I don't know how to tell you this." She stepped away from him. She was twisting a white handkerchief through her fingers. "Let's sit on the bed." When they were seated, she grabbed his hand and stared at it. "Davis, the cancer's come back, and Doc Abernathy's putting me on a new round of treatment. You know how that goes. One day okay, one day awful." Davis nodded, blinking.

"This is the last time I'll be able to come see you. I've worked everything out. Your father'll take over. He'll bring your clean clothes and toilet articles just like I do. And Eula Mae'll bake your cookies."

"Mama, for God's sake," Davis interrupted her. "It doesn't matter about the clothes and things. What's Doc Abernathy say?" As he spoke, he lifted her chin to force her to look at him, but she pulled away.

"He's optimistic, Davis," she was saying. "The chemo licked it once, he said, and there's every chance it'll do it again. But I'll tell you, honey, I'm tired, and I'm not anxious to go through another round of treatment. It saps my energy." She dabbed at her upper lip. "Do you mind if we don't talk about this now? There's something else I need to tell you."

He didn't answer. She was scaring him.

"For all your trouble, Davis," his mother went on, "I want you to know, I wouldn't change a thing about you. Oh, naturally I wish you hadn't been in this awful place so long, but I love you. You have to believe me. The things that happened, well, we can't change them."

"I've had to answer for them, Mama, but I'm sorry for the hurt I've caused you." He looked down at his hands. They were red and cracked.

"I know, I know," she said waving her hand through the air. "You paid dearly for everything you did. But I never believed you meant to hurt anyone. I want you to know that."

"What difference does it make?" he answered.

"A lot. You're not a bad person. You accidentally did some things that turned out wrong. There's a difference, you know."

"Will you just drop it, Mother?" His tone was sharper than he meant it to be.

She turned away, biting her lip. He had hurt her, like always, but she went on without commenting. "There's one more thing I have to say. Your problems, well, they're partly our fault, your dad's and mine. I know that. If I'd been a stronger person, not so namby-pamby." She balled her hand into a tight fist. "If I'd stood up for myself. And you, too." She wheeled back toward him. "Maybe things would have worked out better."

"I don't like your saying that, Mama. It wasn't your fault. Dad's either." He felt helpless. What were these words? Why wasn't she saying the things she always said?

"Anyway, enough of that," she continued. "Let's talk about good things. I have some good news. Dr. Bostwick and I've been working on a plan for you to leave High Meadows."

Leave! Had he heard her right? His eardrums were pounding. *Did she actually think he could leave?* Not his room. Not High Meadows. For sixteen years, it had defined the borders of his life and offered refuge from a world without controls. He hadn't considered leaving for years!

When he could get his breath, he said, "Mama, I can't leave here! Look around you. The window is covered with wire mesh. There're no lamps. No light bulbs or mirrors. No pictures. If I want to use a ball point pen, I have to check it out with the head nurse." A blood vessel at his left temple was throbbing uncontrollably. He put his hand over it to keep his mother from noticing it.

"Now, Davis, don't get upset."

"You can't possibly be serious, Mother. I can't put together two sane hours in a row. Out there," he gestured toward the street, "people drive cars. They go to work. Have families."

He began pacing between his bed and the window. His mother walked to the dresser and refolded some shirts. She was not paying the least attention to what he had said. "Laws for mental institutions are changing," she was saying. "Your father and I have set up a trust fund at Bishop Bank. The fund will pay for a house, everything. Somebody will live with you. It's the latest trend, outpatient care. Of course, you have to be approved by some state board, but Doc Bostwick says that's almost guaranteed."

Her words struck him like hot lava. He returned to the bed and dropped to the edge, sliding his hand across the bedspread as if it were a valuable possession. A wave of sadness flowed over him.

He *knew* this bed. Every inch of this room. He could walk it blindfolded. Four dingy light green walls. The far corner where he stuffed paper so the gray mouse that lived behind the wall wouldn't slip through. Eighty grayish asphalt floor tiles, cold to the feet even in midsummer. The dresser where his mother had just placed his shirts and underclothes. The brown stained door that the nameless nurse opened every morning.

He spoke slowly, "I appreciate your efforts, Mama, but I don't want to leave High Meadows. I'm safe here."

She sat back down beside him and patted him on the knee. "You'll be ready by the time it happens."

She rose quickly and spoke. "I have to go. My energy runs out on me." She picked up her purse from the dresser and handed him a thick envelope from it. "Here are the papers you'll need to get out. Dr. Bostwick's got a copy, and there's one in our safe-deposit box at the bank. Keep your copy in a safe place. Now, will you walk me to the car?" she asked. "I'm a little shaky."

Davis, not wanting to upset his mother, took the papers from her and put them on the dresser. He'd take up this crazy idea with her later. He put his arms around her and kissed her cheek.

They left his room together and walked through the activity room where patients were gathering for lunch. Now and then one of them reached a hand out to touch him or his mother as they moved through the room. Occasionally, Davis's mother nodded to one and called them by name.

From the kitchen, dishes clattered. Hot steam billowed out of the kitchen door and floated across the activity room. The air smelled of green beans, a thought that made Davis ill. He wanted to run back into the hall. Finally, they reached the elevator. Alone at last, Davis felt awkward. He had so much to say but his mind was blank.

When they reached the ground floor, they walked together to the car and kissed goodbye again. His mother settled behind the steering wheel. Davis put his hand on hers.

"I'm so sorry, Mama."

"There's hope for all of us, Davis," she replied. "There has to be."

"It's not good enough, Mama. Not for you."

"It'll be okay, son. For everybody."

"Don't go."

"I'm getting tired." She blew him another kiss, started the engine, and the car began rolling away. He watched as it left the parking lot and pulled onto the driveway, pausing at the automatic gate, then pulling out into the approaching traffic.

A light spring breeze showered apple blossoms from nearby trees across his shoulders and over the parking lot. He knew he should return to the ward where lunch was waiting. But he kept watching until his mother's Cadillac disappeared in the merging traffic. When he could no longer see it, he started walking slowly back to his dormitory.

Inside, he thought, everything was predictable. Hector would be finished with lunch and repositioned by the radiator, which he believed was his prison. He would pick up his wooden spoon and bang away. "Somebody let me out," he would say over and over. Angeline, held in her wheelchair by "humane ties," would be in the catatonic sleep of the insane.

Marteele, his lunch-mate, would be waiting for him. When he arrived, she would ask, "Who's gonna tell me to eat my peas?" "I will," he would reply. "Eat your peas, Marteele." Like a child, she would dutifully push the peas onto her spoon and shove them into her birdlike mouth. Once they were swallowed, she would drop her spoon on her plate and say, "I hate peas."

Inside life was predictable. But outside everything was different. Where would he go? What would he do? Unquestionably he would remember each event he had struggled so hard over the last sixteen years to forget. Korea, and Celeste, and how Mace came home, and all the promises Davis had made that he could never keep, like the one he made to Mace's mama.

Bishop, North Carolina
Early June, 1950

The young men in the bar pressed around Davis. He could feel the heat rising from their bodies, smell the beer drying on their lips. Two floor fans, which faced each other, cast broad bands of cool air across the room. A solitary couple gyrated on the dance floor to a bee-bop song. The floor was shaking with the beat.

It was June, 1950. Davis and his best friend, Mace Fuller, and two of Mace's friends from town, Shaky Joe Potts and Bobby Sagornian, were getting drunk, celebrating graduating from college. They were in the Blue Light, a dim, smoky juke joint in Bishop.

Somebody—*was it Mace?*—said something about the future. Without college deferments, the person commented, they'd all be drafted in the Army. It was just a matter of time.

Davis had never considered his future. The truth was he didn't think he had one. He supposed he'd work for his daddy in the family hosiery mill, but that was no future. Davis's father had made it clear he didn't want him there. He was too much of an embarrassment. If he had to end up at the mill, it would be more like an assignment, or a sentence, than a job.

The song ended and the record player whirred and hummed until a new record fell into place. The song was slow. The couple twined together as if they were made for each other. Their shadow, a single, black silhouette, fell across the dance floor and spread like black paint up the far wall of the bar.

They were living in the moment, Davis thought as he watched them change to the new tempo. He had learned to do that at Jellico Military School for Troubled Teens, but the lesson had not come easily. How could he understand at fifteen years old that comfort would come from relentless activity? Or that there would be victory in the mundane? All he understood was that time fell away when he was busy. It was as if he had found a vein of precious ore, or an underground river that was carrying him, safely cradled, through his days.

Oh, but there was a price to pay! The prize was peace, but the cost was freedom. He could no longer run free through the woods, catch a rabbit and hold it, trembling, in his arms until he released it back to the land, or track a quail back to its covey, and tossing a pebble, watch the birds quiver into flight.

Jellico was relentless. His routine began at 5:00 a.m. with calisthenics, followed by running the cinder track. Breakfast followed. Then chapel, classes, and lunch. Afternoons consisted of more classes, study halls, working with counselors, participating in athletic programs and dinner. Afterwards, study hall again, and finally, he fell, exhausted, into bed. No time to think about the past, or the future, or for that matter, anything.

The conversation between the young men around Davis had progressed to talk about the Korean War. Latest news reports said Red China was supporting North Korea with tanks and men. North Korean soldiers had been seen assembling at the 38th Parallel. The limited United Nations troops that had been assigned to South Korea, including Americans, felt they could not hold the Republic of South Korean Army's position on the 38th Parallel. Everyone, including people in the United States, were becoming more and more frustrated.

Mace was saying. "If we're about to be drafted, let's enlist in the Marines."

"I can't get in the Marines," Davis said, setting his empty beer bottle down on the bar and motioning to the bartender for another. Shaky Joe and Bobby were eyeing each other. They didn't like him, Davis knew. Mace was his only friend, and sometimes Davis liked to shock the two young men just for kicks. He said, "I just graduated from a college that had iron fences around it. Remember? Delinquents and misfits. That's who made up my graduating class! How the hell can I get in the Marines?"

Mace ignored Davis's reference to Jellico and plunged on. "While you were in college, did you get deferment notices from your friendly draft board?" He jostled Davis's shoulder.

"Sure." Davis nodded.

"Well, if the Army wants you, the Marines'll want you." Mace looked at Shaky Joe and Bobby. "Ain't that right, boys. They ain't gonna look up where you went to prep school and college, Davis. And you sure ain't gonna tell, are you?"

"Hell no!" Davis answered like a drill sergeant. Mace had a point. He was remembering the tight fit of his Jellico uniform. The way the gray-blue jacket hooked in the middle with smart, brass buttons. And how row after row of black braid running across the front made his chest seem wider than it was. The tapered waist, the flared hips—all emphasized his physic. Maybe the Marine Corps was like Jellico. Maybe he'd feel safe—even appreciated—there.

During a lull in the conversation, Bobby said. "My mom'd have my hide."

"You're over eighteen. She can't stop you," Mace replied sharply.

Mace was serious, Davis realized. The idea of enlisting was growing on him, too. "Wait a minute," Davis said. "If this is really something we're going to do, each of us has to decide for himself. Nobody can do it because of somebody else."

Shaky Joe answered, "But that's what happens. You join because of your buddies. Everybody does."

"Nobody joins because of me," Davis replied, bearing down on each word. "That means you, Mace. You hear me?"

"Christ, Davis," Mace turned toward his friend. "You don't have to get mad about it."

"I'm serious. Join because it's right for you, but not because it's right for somebody else."

Shaky Joe was looking out at the dance floor where the couple was still dancing. "Here's what I think," he said slowly. "About the only way my old man'll respect me is if I enlist in the Marines. He'd be so proud he'd bust. WW II Veteran First Marine Division Sergeant Alonso Joseph Potts' little boy Joe has went and joined the Marines. That's what he'd tell his buddies."

Davis was turning over in his mind how his parents would take the news. No doubt his father would be as pleased as Shaky Joe's, but he wouldn't feel pride. Just relief that Davis's future had been settled without any further trouble. And without disturbing his father's mill. As for his mother, she would withdraw a little the way she did each time Davis faced a crisis.

The young men were silent. The couple had moved to a booth, where they were necking. Shaky Joe drained his beer. Mace stared absently at the couple. Bobby was tapping his fingernail on the bar. Davis picked up his cap and started walking toward the door.

"Hey," Mace called after him, "where you going?"

"To enlist," he answered, pushing through the juke joint door.

That very evening the U.S. Marine Corps Recruiting Office in Bishop inducted four rather inebriated young men into the Corps—Mace Fuller, Davis Williams, Bobby Sagornian and Shaky Joe Potts. No one questioned where Davis went to college, or why, and all four young men passed their physicals with ease.

Their parents acted much as they had suspected but it was too late to stop the young men. In one week they were on a train for Yamassee, S.C., where they were met by drill instructors. They were loaded on buses and transported to Parris Island, where they would learn to be Marines.

Oddly enough, they arrived at Parris Island on the very day, June 25, that the North Korean People's Army crossed the 38th Parallel and invaded the Republic of South Korea.

From the beginning, boot camp came naturally to Davis. He was used to being awakened at 5 a.m. and put through rigorous physical training required at Jellico Military School.

His strongest assets, however, were his love of hunting and skill with firearms. These provided a base that put him above the other recruits.

Mace, on the other hand, had led the soft life of a college kid. He had a beer gut and no muscles, and soon he was struggling to keep up. He could not run 100 yards without getting winded, and his arms lacked the strength to climb a rope.

Davis helped his friend. He showed him how to break down his weapon and clean it. Spit-shine his boots. Make his bed tight enough to bounce a quarter. Roll his gear smartly and pack his footlocker so it would pass inspection.

While recruits were flunking out right and left, Davis rose to the top of his class. Mace, with his buddy's help, managed to stay unnoticed somewhere in the middle. Shaky Joe and Bobby, who had been assigned to another platoon, reported they were also surviving.

One day midway into the course, Davis was watching Mace run the obstacle course. His friend could rappel the tower and run a 100-yard dash in 15 seconds. Plus he was receiving passing marks on marksmanship. Still graduation was almost upon them, and Davis was worried about Mace. He wasn't picking up the skills he would need in actual combat. He lacked what their drill instructor called "killer instincts." Worse, he was developing a slack attitude.

Davis did not share his concern with his friend. Instead when Mace came off the obstacle course that day, Davis put his arm around his friend's shoulder. "Looking good out there, Marine. Loosing that beer belly, too." He slapped his friend in the midriff.

Several nights later Davis's worries erupted. A light outside the window was shining directly in his eyes, keeping him awake. It was unbearably muggy. His cot was too narrow. The sheets, damp to the touch from the humidity plus his own sweat, were tugging at his chest. Mental pictures clouded Davis's mind with horrible tragedies of war.

Explosions, lost limbs, gruesome details. Davis began thinking about Mace's chances of surviving once they landed in Korea. His friend would be over his head. When Davis couldn't stand his thoughts another minute, he crawled out of his cot and shook his buddy, whispering in his ear. "Mace, wake up. This is important, buddy. Don't you go dying on me. Once we get to Korea, don't you get shot up, or nothing. You got that?"

"Jesus, Davis, what the shit you talking about?" Mace muttered, coming out of his sleep, and rolling flat on his back. He raised his head off the pillow to look at Davis. "I ain't gonna die, okay. 'Sides, you don't *know* we're going to Korea."

"We're going all right. I've been nosing around. We're going to Twenty-nine Palms for cold weather training. Then on to Korea. You can make book on it. *You* just make sure you don't die. I don't wanna tell your mama I let you die."

"I ain't gonna die, Davis. If I do, I'll tell my own mama. Now just go back to sleep and quit worrying. Swear to God, you're the biggest worrier I ever seen." And Mace pulled his sheet up under his chin, rolled away from Davis, and went back to sleep.

Davis slipped away from Mace, and, glancing around to make sure no one had stirred, he went to his footlocker. Gingerly he opened the top and eased it back far enough to reach in and retrieve a pack of stationery. Then he tiptoed past his sleeping fellow recruits and entered the latrine. He leaned back against the cool tile wall across from the urinals and slid to the floor.

The fluorescent lights above him hissed, and the urinals breathed a sweet, acrid odor that stuck in the back of his throat, but Davis ignored the unpleasant odor. He composed the following letter to Mace's mother:

Dear Mrs. Fuller,

*I know you were upset when Mace enlisted in
the Marines. So was my mom but my dad was
pretty proud. I know Mace is all you have since Mr.
F. died. I'm going to take care of him and make sure
he comes home to you.*

> *Your good friend,*
> *Davis Williams*
> *Parris Island, S.C.*

Davis folded the letter and wrote Mrs. Fuller's address on
the front. He slipped back into the barracks and walked quietly past the sleeping recruits. He climbed into his bunk,
pulled the blanket over his head, and fell immediately asleep.

CHAPTER THREE

June 1970

The country lane broke away from Matthews at the edge of town, leaving behind a narrow rim of industrial plants and stretching out comfortably into farmland. The farms were large, well-manicured tracts of land. Occasionally a solitary figure on a tractor plowed an idle field, turning over the dark earth into neat rows that trailed off behind the machine. Except for a few small, white frame, or red brick houses, the landscape was green and brown. It spread over the hills as far as the eye could see. Where the farms began, the road became NC 16.

It was early June. Behind the wheel of her beige station wagon, Josephine was settling in for the two-hour drive to Bishop. There she and Josie would spend the night with Aunt Ruth before traveling to their summer home in the Blue Ridge Mountains.

Josie was on the front seat, chattering away to Pippi Longstocking, her favorite doll. Lady was asleep in back, sprawled between boxes and suitcases.

As Josephine drove, she thought back over the last six months. Winter had been difficult with its drab, gray skies, but spring had been a mockery. The bright daffodils and showy, pink Chino cherry trees that bloomed about their yard were normally sources of hope and renewal. This spring they had made her feel more depressed.

But today, what spring withheld, summer was offering. She was beginning to feel better. She cracked the window and the rush of moist air, scented with musk and fresh-cut grass, cooled her face. The countryside flashing by, even the sense of the speeding car, she saw as signs of better days to come.

It had been difficult to convince Michael that she and Josie should spend the summer in the mountains. For once, when he protested, she had not backed down. "I need it," she had declared emphatically. Everything would be okay, she reassured. "Besides, you'll come up every weekend." Michael had persisted, complaining about the house. "I'll arrange for someone to come in to clean," she retorted. Secretly she hoped distance would lessen the strain between them. She also hoped she and Josie would renew the closeness they used to share, and her grief for her parents and sister would diminish.

The farms on NC 16 began to fade away and were replaced by small foothill towns. Many of them were little more than railroad crossings that had sprung up on either side of the road.

Bishop would be coming up soon. Aunt Ruth was waiting there. She would rush to meet them, her flowered apron dancing about her waist, kitchen smells rising like feathers from her hands. Her hugs, pressing and urgent, would stir memories of the past for Josephine. Josie would have a doll tea party. They would eat finger sandwiches and sip tea on the screen porch and catch up on a year's worth of family news. Sometime in the leisured afternoon, Aunt Ruth would hint, as she had earlier on the phone, that she wanted Josie to stay on for a few extra nights. Maybe Michael could pick her up on Friday on his way to the mountains.

They could decide later. There was no need to rush. The entire summer with time for everything stretched out before them.

Josephine's wagon rolled to a stop in Aunt Ruth's driveway. Immediately the back door swung open, and Aunt Ruth ran down the stairs to greet them, her arms outstretched.

"You're feeling better since we talked on the phone," she said to Josephine as they hugged. "I can hear it in your voice."

Josie was tugging at her great-aunt's skirt, trying to show her Pippi Longstocking. Aunt Ruth took the doll and began talking behind its head as if it were a puppet. Josie howled with laughter. They grabbed hands and began walking toward the house. Aunt Ruth called over her shoulder to Josephine. "We're abandoning you! Can you manage?"

"Go ahead," Josephine replied. "I can get these." Their bags were light. Michael was bringing most of their things on the weekend.

As soon as Lady had a quick run in the woods, Josephine started for the house. By the time she had carried their suitcases inside, Josie and Aunt Ruth were already upstairs. Josephine paused in the front hall to catch her breath just as Josie's head appeared over the upstairs banister. She called excitedly to her mother, "Mommy, I'm sleeping in the snow bed!"

"Sleigh bed!" Josephine called back. The name brought back a flood of memories.

The bed, the size of a twin, was located in a small alcove at the entrance to Aunt Ruth's room. The ends were curved like a nineteenth century sleigh. On rainy days Josephine and her cousin, Petey, a year older than she, had played on the bed, fashioning it into pup tents or airplanes or lookout towers, whatever the favored war game of the moment.

"I'm gonna sleep in the sled," Josie repeated, drawing Josephine back to the present. Josie was at the top of the stairs. She squared her shoulders and marched past her mother, who was still wrestling with suitcases. Aunt Ruth followed Josie. As they passed Josephine, her aunt gave a quick shrug as if she had no choice but to keep up with the child. Josephine laughed, remembering the stubborn streak she had at the same age.

Josephine put Josie's things on the bed. She had always loved the small alcove. Everything looked the same. The French doors leading into Aunt Ruth's bedroom. Even Grandmother Yost's piecework quilt with the feather stitching still covered the bed and was tucked neatly under the pillow. Beyond the glass doors, she could see her aunt's massive double bed with its elaborate walnut headboard and carved posts. A gleaming white chenille spread was thrown over the bed. A shaft of sunlight from the window fell across the floor.

Once these familiar objects would have reassured Josephine. But today she was surprised by what she saw. Old photographs were scattered about her aunt's room. Snapshots were piled in cardboard boxes. They were stacked on Aunt Ruth's bureau and stuck around the mirror. There were World War II pictures. Family portraits. Several of Josephine's mother, Emma, and Aunt Ruth standing beside a high diving board. They wore old-fashioned wool bathing suits that almost reached their knees. They smiled coyly, their heads tilted to the side. She found one of herself, frozen in time, skinning the cat on the monkey bar in the backyard. Her hair was dangling over her head, and Laura was pointing to her head, laughing.

She felt certain her aunt had put the pictures out for her to see, but she wasn't sure why. Before she left the room, she absentmindedly picked up a photograph. Now, she glanced down at it. It was a picture of Uncle Jack, Aunt Ruth's husband, and Davis on the Catawba River. Davis's finger was hooked in the gill of a good-sized bass. Beside him, Uncle Jack, grinning widely, was wearing his canvas fishing jacket and holding a fishing rod. Behind them was a dock with a sign over it saying, "Hazel's Bait and Tackle Shop."

Josephine recognized the jacket. The last time she had seen it Petey was hiding in it. Her fingertips could almost feel the coarse canvas fabric. The smell of fish, which always lingered on the jacket, seemed to rise from the photograph. She remembered the jacket, but it was Daddy's black LaSalle that came to her mind.

It was summer, 1941.

Daddy had pulled the coal black car into the turn-around behind Aunt Ruth's house. Petey, eight years old, was waiting in the backyard, his dark eyes shining. A huge grin spread across his face.

"Uncle Nate, that car! What is it?"

Daddy pushed open the door, disentangled his legs, and rose from the car. He was a tall man with the agility of an athlete and the suave good looks of a movie star. He was dressed in his traditional summer cloths. Gray pinstriped trousers, white dress shirt, sky blue tie and black and white spectator shoes. Daddy sold cars.

"Finest car in the world, Petey," he said, straightening himself to his full height and adjusting his trousers. "It's a 1938 touring LaSalle. Goes 45 miles per hour on the highway. Real gas guzzler but quite a car. Yessir, quite a car." He ruffled Petey's hair and dropped his voice as if he were going to tell Petey a secret. "And if we go to war, this beauty'll likely end up a jeep." His voice returned to its normal pitch. "Where's your daddy?"

"Went to catch trout for our lunch."

Daddy nodded his approval, "How's your mother?"

Petey shrugged.

Momma and Laura piled out of the car. While Momma tried to grab Petey to kiss him, Josephine took her dad's place behind the wheel. Momma soon gave up on kissing Petey, and she and Laura headed for the house to find Ellen, Petey's older sister. Daddy followed.

Josephine called to her cousin from inside the car. "Get in, Petey. I'll give you a ride. " Josephine grabbed the steering wheel, twisting it from side to side while she bounced up and down. She had to peer between the steering wheel and dashboard to see out.

Petey let out a long, low whistle. He sauntered over to the car with his nose stuck in the air and stepped into the back-seat as if he owned it. Then he stretched his arms behind his head and extended his legs.

"Boy, this is the life." He leaned forward and ran his hand over the plush seat. He shook the tasseled window straps, pulled down the jump seats and pushed them back, and knocked on the glass partition between the two seats. "I never saw stuff like this," he said with admiration. Then he bolted out of the car and slammed the door. "Come on. I gotta show you something." He dashed toward the house, waiting for Josephine by the back door until she caught up.

They entered the house through the backdoor. The kitchen was semi dark and quiet. Josephine could hear voices talking in hushed whispers, but she couldn't tell where the sound came from. Petey grabbed her hand. His hand was hot and left a sweaty imprint on her hand, but she didn't pull away. Petey guided her through the front hall and up the stairs. His knickers rubbing together sounded like grasshoppers.

"Why's it so quiet?" Josephine whispered.

"Mama's been real sick."

They walked to the end of the hall and entered a small alcove. Against the wall was a bed made like a sleigh. "I'm supposed to sleep here while you're here," he whispered. "You're gonna take my room. We can trade off if you want."

Josephine nodded.

"Mama had her 'pendix out and 'bout died," Petey continued in hushed tones. "Doc Abernathy said it burst right in his hand like a hot balloon, but Mama still got sick."

"That's awful." Josephine's heart thumped with fear. Was her aunt going to die?

Petey pushed open the French doors.

"That you, Petey?" The words rose from the sheets.

"Yessum. I got Jo with me"

"Come kiss mama, sweetheart. You too, Jo."

Petey and Josephine tiptoed into the room. A nervous feeling was growing in Josephine's chest as she looked down at her aunt.

Aunt Ruth was surrounded by pillows and bed covers. Her pale face was heart-shaped like Petey's. Her skin, usually spotless and smooth, was marked with red blotches. Josephine wanted to say something important to her aunt, but the words in her mind were small and shapeless.

"I'm sorry you're sick, Aunt Ruth."

"Now that you're here I'm gonna get better. Give me a little kiss, and you and Petey go play," she whispered. Her voice was hoarse.

Josephine bent down to kiss her aunt. A heavy smell of medicine rose to meet her. When her lips touched her aunt's hot, dry face, a small burst of air flushed across Josephine's cheek. Her aunt was already asleep, snoring daintily.

Josie called from downstairs, bringing Josephine back to the present. "Mommy, we've got your favorite. 'Mento cheese."

Josephine was resting on the sleigh bed with her back to the wall. The photograph of Uncle Jack and Davis was still in her hand. She returned it to Aunt Ruth's bedroom and went to the bathroom to splash water on her face. When she examined her reflection in the mirror, she saw resemblance to both her mother and Josie. Her mother's smooth rounded forehead, the delicate eyebrows, and the fragile Grecian nose. But also, the thrust of Josie's determined chin, the plump, rosy flesh that bunched across her cheekbones like ripe apples. The sparkle in her eyes.

Josephine pulled back from the mirror. After looking at the family photographs in Aunt Ruth's bedroom, the similarities were more startling than ever. She had always thought of herself as an individualist, yet here was proof that she was a link between two generations. She wasn't sure she liked the idea that she and Josie were part of a long chain. Was her future predetermined for her? She shook the idea off and joined Josie and Aunt Ruth downstairs.

Josephine's aunt glanced at her as she entered the kitchen. "Gracious, Josephine. You look a little pale. Did you fall asleep?"

Josephine shrugged, brushing her hair away from her forehead. "All those photographs in your bedroom. I don't remember them. And the snapshot of Uncle Jack with Davis. Did you leave that for me to see?"

Aunt Ruth nodded, "I've been sorting through old pictures. When I ran across that one, I thought you might like to see it."

Josephine winced. "But on the phone, I thought we agreed we wanted to stay away from Davis."

Aunt Ruth picked up a plate of sandwiches and headed for the breakfast room. "I've been reconsidering. You remember Davis's mother, Grace. She's dying of cancer. High Meadows is almost ready to discharge Davis, by the way. I'm sure it's because of her. I just feel so sorry for all of them."

Josephine followed Aunt Ruth into the breakfast room. "Please, Aunt Ruth, I don't want to have anything to do with him."

"Who's Davis?" Josie piped in.

"Little pitchers," Aunt Ruth said, waggling her head.

"Somebody I used to know," Josephine replied to Josie and turned back to her aunt. "Let's just forget it, okay?" Her aunt nodded, and they all sat down to lunch.

That afternoon they took a leisurely walk through the neighborhood and ended up in the backyard, where Uncle Jack had cleared a play area for them when they were children. Josephine headed for an old oak tree. She stooped in front of the tree and began pushing aside leaves and twigs that had collected there. She pictured herself with her sister, Laura, and cousin, Ellen, as children. Ellen was kneeling on her hands and knees, much as Josephine was. Her wiry, dark hair surrounded her head like a halo, sunlight playing off its curly surface. Her hands were moving across the gnarled roots, searching out niches and inserting sparkling pieces of broken glass or buttons or tinfoil. She and Laura were watching. Kneeling in front of the tree, Josephine was overwhelmed with the thought that both Ellen and Laura had died of cancer.

Coming out of her sad reverie, Josephine called out to her daughter. "Josie, I want you to come see this." She had swept leaves and debris from the base of the tree, exposing the bare ground.

Josie appeared beside her. Josephine pulled her daughter close to her. "Here's where Ellen and Laura and I built fairy houses," she whispered.

Josie's eyes widened. "I don't see any fairies," she said softly, pushing back from her mother. A breeze stirred, and the leaves on the oak tree rustled.

"You can't see them," Josephine replied, her voice still low but firm. "But you might hear them."

Aunt Ruth spoke behind them. "Ellen used to say the houses had to be beautiful or the fairies wouldn't come," she said quietly.

Perhaps it was the nostalgia that had been building all morning, or the breeze that had picked up again, or the lump that had risen in Josephine's throat. Or maybe Aunt Ruth's words struck Josephine wrong. Whatever the reason, Josephine burst out crying. Aunt Ruth, realizing what was happening, steered Josie aside and spoke to her. "Josie, run over to the swings. I'll come push you in just a second." Josie did what her great-aunt said but gave her mother a puzzled look.

After Josie had gone, Josephine whispered as Aunt Ruth helped her up, "I can't help it. I hate crying in front of Josie, but you and I have lost so much. Ellen and Laura, and Uncle Jack, and Momma and Daddy. I don't think I can go on."

Aunt Ruth turned Josephine around and hugged her. "There, there," she said, patting her on the back as if she were comforting a child. "We *have* to go on. For Josie and Michael and Petey and all the people who love us. We go on because it's what we're meant to do." She pushed back from Josephine and pointed to the oak tree. "That old oak tree you've been admiring? Its roots grow all over this yard. Nothing can stop them. One time Jack and I drove a clothesline pole through a root. Split it in two but it just grew right around the pole." She pointed to the top of one of the trees. "During a storm, the entire top broke off that beech and left one limb barely hanging on. But it never fell. Just kept growing." She gave Josephine another pat. "You're going to be alright. It just takes time. Now why don't you run inside and get yourself together. I'll swing Josie for a while. By the way, you can always count on me and Petey and his family."

"I almost forgot Petey," Josephine sighed. "Good old Petey. He was the sweet one." When she returned to the house, she remembered something about Petey she thought she would never forget.

Petey was hiding. Nothing made sense. Strangers were walking around his house like they belonged there but they didn't. His mother was still in bed and Doc Abernathy was by her side. She had been the sick one, but his daddy had left last night in his truck to pick up Davis and never came back. Before he could get home, back in his bed where he belonged, his heart just stopped. One minute it beat. The next it stopped.

Josephine had been searching everywhere for Petey. In the basement, the fort in the backyard near the swings, behind the big leather chair in the den, in the pantry. He was nowhere. She was about to cry. Finally, in desperation, she ran upstairs and peered into his closet. There he was, huddled in the corner, draped in his father's canvas fishing jacket, holding a cap pistol in his hand.

"Halt or I'll shoot," he said sternly.

She whispered into the dark recesses of the closet, "You're not gonna shoot me."

"You may be a German spy."

"Where'd you get that cap pistol?" She whispered again.

"It was in Daddy's desk. He was gonna give it to me Fourth of July. He said so."

"That jacket stinks."

"It don't. Somebody was gonna throw it out, or give it away. I got Daddy's pipe too." Petey held up the pipe for Josephine to see.

"You gonna keep that jacket?"

"Yep."

"I'll get some papers. We can hide it in 'em."

Earlier that morning she had seen a stack of newspapers on the hall table. She darted downstairs to grab one. People were milling around, whispering, walking from room to room like they didn't know where to go. Laura and Ellen were in the dining room arranging sandwiches on trays. "What are you up to?" Laura hissed.

"Nothing," Josephine shrugged. "Aunt Ruth wants a paper."

"Momma told you to stay out of the way," Laura ordered, following Ellen with a tray into the living room.

Back in the closet with Petey, Josephine asked, "Where we gonna hide the jacket?" Petey tapped on a small door behind him. She handed him the paper, and he slipped the jacket from his shoulders. Tenderly, he folded it and wrapped it in the newspaper, opened the door and carefully tucked the package into the small inner-closet.

"You still got the pipe?" she asked. He nodded. "Maybe you ought to give it to your mama."

"Maybe," he said.

By dinner Josephine was herself again. After putting Josie to bed, she and her aunt decided to have a cup of coffee in the den. Aunt Ruth caught her up on Pete and Ellen's families. After Ellen's death, Aunt Ruth had kept in touch with her husband and children, who lived in Seattle. Pete, no longer Petey, was a professor of marine biology and lived on the coast. He and his wife had two small children. Josephine talked about Michael without mentioning the recent strain in their marriage. She remarked again how unfortunate it was that both Ellen and Laura died so young.

During a lull in the conversation, Josephine said, "Aunt Ruth, did I ever tell you how Petey saved me from a water moccasin?"

"Why, no dear," Aunt Ruth replied. "I don't believe you did."

"Well, the story goes like this…"

One day after lunch, two of Petey's friends came by to ask if he and Josephine wanted to go to the grapevine swing.

The boys were eight, and Josephine was seven and scared she couldn't keep up. They were going deep into the woods where she had never been. But she knew what it was like. She had seen it in a picture book, how the thick, dark leaves gleamed with sunlight that fluttered down like shiny coins. She knew how the woods smelled too, a musty smell that caught in her throat and wouldn't turn loose. And how it sounded, hollow as if two different objects clashed, leaving one sound shivering while the other grew and grew.

The path began just past the swings Uncle Jack put up last summer, the ones with monkey bars on them. Petey and his two friends, Jimbo and Donnie, had a head start on Josephine, and she had to run, or be left behind. The terrain was tricky, uneven. Roots of gigantic trees bulged up from beneath the ground, and rocks, exposed through long-forgotten rain torrents, protruded through patches in the worn surface. Her feet seemed to know the way as if she had run this path before. In reality, she had never been there; and if she fell behind, she would have to find her way back home to Aunt Ruth's alone.

She could turn back now, she thought quickly. She could call out to them and say she was going back, back to the cool safety of the house, back to Momma, who smelled like roses picked with morning dew still clinging to them.

In front of her, she glimpsed the boys as their clothes flashed through the trees beyond her. Banks of leaves speckled with sunshine lined the path. Occasionally branches whipped at her arms, but she couldn't take time to see if she were scratched. The boys talked, or laughed, but she could not hear what they said. The woods had noises of their own. As they ran, frightened birds scurried from under bushes. Leaves rustled, and twigs snapped under the boys' weight.

Soon the path opened into a meadow, and they continued through it. Here the sounds changed. A soft breeze rustled through the grasses and wild flowers. Grasshoppers leaped out of their way, and butterflies, startled by their presence, rose from the weeds like scraps of colored paper.

Beyond the meadow the path picked up briefly and then ended at the edge of Silas Creek. The banks were too steep to climb down. A grapevine that dangled over the creek was used to reach the other side.

By the time Josephine reached the boys, Donnie and Jimbo had already swung across, and Petey was holding the vine for her. The distance to the other side looked immense, higher than their garage back home, where she sometimes played. As far as she could see, trees grew up to the edge of the banks. Their roots dangled over the sides of the creek like fingers. Brambles sprawled everywhere.

"Hurry," Petey urged.

She looked across to the other side and shook her head. "I'll wait here."

"It's nothing. All you do is let go of the vine when you get to on the other side." He handed her the grapevine and, with an impish grin, said, "Besides, I dare you."

Josephine was trembling, but she never turned down a dare; and she certainly wasn't going to let Petey and his friends know she was afraid. She took a deep breath, a running leap, and she was airborne. The woods swirled past her. The water streaked below her like tinfoil.

A loud crack shot through the air, and the vine dropped several feet. It paused, then creaked and continued falling. Josephine felt herself crashing toward the creek. Strips of bark from the vine were falling around her. She screamed and landed with a thud, knocking out her breath.

For a moment the three boys on the bank froze. Then Petey took a running start and jumped off the bank. He landed with a splash in ankle-deep water, pitching forward. When he gained his footing, he scrambled over to Josephine. The other boys stayed on the bank, shouting encouragement.

When Petey reached her, she was gasping for air. He pounded her on the back. After what seemed an eternity, she began coughing. "You okay?" Petey asked nervously. "Stupid vine broke. It's too steep to climb up this bank. We'll have to follow the stream till there's a break."

Josephine didn't answer. She looked around. The trees above her looked menacing with their roots dangling over the water like writhing snakes. For the first time, she noticed how cold the air was. It settled on her skin and soggy clothes. She felt miserable. Her teeth chattered, and her leg hurt so much she felt sure a rock had gouged her.

"We gotta be careful," Petey was saying as he helped her up. "Cottonmouths live here."

"I hate snakes! I'm getting out of here." She started scrambling toward the bank. Petey grabbed her by the arm.

"I told you we can't get out here. Bank's too high and there are too many briars. Don't think about the snakes. Just watch for sticks in the water. That's what snakes look like." He added, "If you see one, holler!"

They picked their way over pebbles and rocks. The water tugged at Josephine's shoes, filling them with water each time she took a step. Donnie and Jimbo followed them on the path.

Finally, Petey stopped at a spot where the creek widened. He had picked up a large, Y-shaped stick, and he was squinting at it, rubbing his hand over the forked end. "We're almost there. We just have to get through the swimming hole," he was saying.

"Swimming hole?" Josephine asked with alarm. She wasn't a good swimmer.

"Spring-fed. Cold too," Petey was saying as he swung the stick toward the right bank of the creek. "See those holes? Cottonmouths' nests."

Josephine was stunned by his matter-of-fact tone. The sides of the banks were curved inward like spent apple cores, and they were pockmarked with dark holes.

"All of them?" She gulped nervously.

"Enough," Petey answered.

With Josephine in front, they waded into clean, ankle-deep water that gurgled playfully against their ankles. It was deceptively calm and gentle. But once the water reached the basin, it merged into murky, mud-red silt from the swimming hole. Nothing could be seen below the surface.

The water had risen to Josephine's waist. "We gotta swim from here," Petey explained. "Don't splash 'cause noise attracts snakes,"

"Petey, I can't swim that far!"

"It's not as far as it looks. I swim here all the time."

"What if a snake comes?"

"I'll catch him on my stick. You just keep swimming. Dog paddle if you have to. But don't make a lot of noise and don't act like a sissy!"

Josephine was halfway across the basin when she saw a copper shape slither out of a hole in the bank. It paused. For a moment it seemed suspended in time. Then it slid into the water and glided toward Petey.

"Petey!" she gasped, pointing toward the snake.

Petey extended his stick in the direction of the snake. The fork was hidden beneath the water. Then he motioned for Josephine to continue swimming. She pushed through the water quietly. Glancing back over her shoulder, she saw the snake inching toward Petey. Its long body trailed from a thick V-shaped head. A forked tongue flickered from the snake's white mouth. Once the snake reached the stick, it slid forward slowly. Petey remained motionless.

When the snake had crawled about six inches up the stick, Petey flipped the stick over, catching the snake in the angle. Quickly, he snapped the stick behind him and cast it like a fishing rod toward the stream they had just left. The snake hurtled through the air end-over-end, its pearly belly flashing against its copper sides. It plopped into the stream, and the water swept it down stream away from them.

Josephine kept swimming. When Petey caught up with her, they swam together toward the bank. Donnie and Jimbo were waiting to help them out of the water.

Halfway up the bank, they heard the sound of clapping.

"What the heck?" Jimbo asked, trying to locate the source of the noise.

"It's Davis!" Petey pointed to the path that ran beside the creek.

On the path above the creek a blond-haired boy about fifteen was sitting on a yellow motor bike. He was dressed in jeans, cowboy boots, and a striped T-shirt. The sleeves of his shirt were rolled up over his biceps and a pack of Lucky Strikes was tucked in the cuff. He was clapping his hands slowly.

Petey picked up a handful of dirt from the bank and threw it angrily toward the motorbike. Small pieces of dirt bounced off the metal fenders.

"Hey, don't throw junk at my bike!" The boy yelled sharply.

"You were sittin' up there watching!" Petey demanded. "How come you didn't help us?"

"Thought I'd see how you made out," the boy answered. "Water moccasin 'bout had you, didn't it," he laughed and glanced toward Josephine. "Who's the girl?"

"My cousin."

"I'm your cousin," the boy responded, touching his chest with his finger.

"So's she."

The boy patted the seat behind him, beckoning to her. "Want a ride home, cuz?"

She shook her head.

"Suit yourself." The boy turned the ignition key, and the motorbike roared away, spewing dirt. He yelled over his shoulder, "See ya', Petey."

"Who's that?" Josephine asked.

"My stupid cousin, Davis Williams."

"He act like that all the time?"

"Mostly."

The four children walked home silently. Josephine's clothes were still wet and she was shivering. Her leg stung, and she was covered with scratches and bruises. What was Momma going to say when she saw her? She might feel sorry for her and hug her. On the other hand, she might fuss at her for trying to keep up with the boys.

When they saw the rooftop of Petey's house, Josephine said, "Let's not tell about the snake. Momma can't stand snakes."

"Suits me," Petey replied.

As long as Momma didn't know, it was as if it never happened.

When Josephine finished her story, Aunt Ruth laughed. "Petey could get himself in more trouble, but I never knew you were involved in any of it." She added, "Your story points up something I told you this afternoon, which goes without saying. You know you can count on me and Petey and his family."

"Yes, I do know I can," Josephine replied. "And you can't imagine what that means to me."

Her aunt continued. "I was thinking of something else after we came in. Maybe you could renew some old friendships."

"Funny you mentioned that. I'm going to catch up with

my friend from Evergreen Camp, Angie Dennison. Her family lived in Rocky Ridge."

"Actually I was thinking about Davis."

"Davis!" Josephine was stunned. In her story she had stopped short of telling Aunt Ruth about the cavalier way Davis had watched them battle the water moccasin. "Aunt Ruth, I told you I don't want anything to do with him."

"What do you have against him?"

"My God, Aunt Ruth, you know what I have against him. You witnessed everything he did. I don't want Josie exposed to an unreliable person like that. Do you realize I was just two years older than Josie when it all began?"

Aunt Ruth shook her head. "Honey, the last thing I want to do is upset you. But Davis is family."

Josephine shook her head and chuckled, "Correction. Davis is your family. Not mine!"

Aunt Ruth replied, "Okay, okay. He's Jack's nephew. The point is we're all older now. And time and distance allow us to see things in a new light." After a pause, she added, "You know, sometimes we find solace in the most unusual places."

"Aunt Ruth, you know I'll never find solace in Davis. But don't worry about me," Josephine said, patting her aunt on the hand. "I'm feeling much better since I arrived. You've been great, and you mean all the world to me and Josie."

Josephine did feel better. Still, she was glad she had not mentioned hiding Uncle Jack's fishing jacket, or that Davis had seen the water moccasin come within striking distance of Petey.

Those secrets she and Petey should continue to keep.

CHAPTER FOUR

Davis had walked those halls the first time when he was under thirty years old. Sgt. Wilbur had brought him, ordered for psychiatric evaluation to High Meadows by the U.S. Marine Corps. The two of them had walked the distance of the narrow hall, almost marching, their shoulders brushing against each other with every step. Their shoes, shined to a glow, tapped across the asphalt tile floor.

They had driven in a drab, olive green military vehicle from Camp Lejeune, with an arranged stop in Fayetteville to see Father Kilpatrick. Father Kilpatrick, who performed the wedding ceremony for him and Celeste, was waiting for them. He held out a metal box trimmed in brass for Davis. "These are Celeste's ashes," he said reverently. Davis shuddered, recoiling from the box. He had not known Celeste was cremated. Even so, Celeste in a box? Absolutely not! Her beauty could never be confined to anything, let alone a box! Her songs belonged to the universe. They were riding the air somewhere above them. Hiding his emotions, Davis replied, "Will you keep them in a safe place for me, Father? Someday I'll come back for them."

It wasn't that Davis was out of sorts that June morning, although lately he often felt that way. It was Ranzoni, Davis's best friend at High Meadows. They were in occupational therapy. Ranzoni was running his mouth, going on about the smell of honeysuckle on a June day. Mrs. Sprinkle, the instructor, had opened the window, and a breeze was blowing the fragrant smell across the room.

Hector, Angeline and Marteele, plus a new woman named Pearl, who looked tentative and doe-like, were seated around a worktable. The table was covered with leather supplies. Davis looked out of the corner of his eye at Mrs. Sprinkle. If Ranzoni would hush, she was going to jump in and instruct them on how to make wallets.

Davis already knew how. He had made at least a wallet a year for as long as High Meadows had been offering occupational therapy. He had no interest in making another, and he certainly didn't want to listen to Ranzoni. He wanted to think without distractions through the events that had occurred since his mother's visit in April.

Although he had reluctantly accepted she was going to die, he desperately wanted more time with her. Still, sick as she was, she had managed to keep her word that his Thursday routine would remain undisturbed. His father had come in her place.

Their first visit was as awkward as ever. The clean laundry and Eula Mae's cookies were laid on the dresser along with a note from his mother. But the items his father brought—the cookies, the laundry, even the note—didn't bridge the gap between Davis and his father. They sat in awkward silence.

The second week his dad brought checkers. The two of them had set up the checkerboard on Davis's bed and played. Davis had won that day. The next time he won again. At the end of his third visit his dad said, "Checkers are too easy for you, son. Let's try chess."

The following week his dad brought a chessboard. They pushed Davis's desk chair over to the bed. Davis sat cross-legged like a kid. His dad sat in the desk chair, slumped over the board, studying it.

After a few moves, Davis's father looked up and nodded. "Not bad, son. Not bad at all," he said. Davis laughed. When his father left that day, he was smiling. Davis hadn't seen him smile for a long, long time. It was like the first light of dawn after a sleepless night, or coming out of a dark room into bright sunshine. Maybe leaving High Meadows was a possibility after all.

Today his head swirled with the idea of leaving. He had decided to buy a small house close to his mom and dad if they would help him pay for it. He would visit his mother daily and afterwards have lunch with his father at Lutz's drug store. In the afternoons he would take long walks on the land his family had owned on Silas Creek.

"Davis!" Mrs. Sprinkle was standing over him shaking his arm. "The loud speaker's calling you! Report to the Ad Building."

Davis came out of his daydream to find the people around the table staring at him. "The Ad Building?" he repeated slowly.

The loud speaker was seldom used, and the announcement chilled him. His mother must be dead, and his father was here to tell him. Her sufferings were finally over, and so were his second chances. He couldn't buy a house near his family or visit her everyday. Nor could he make things right with her.

"It's Mama." Davis said, rushing out of the room. As he ran, he heard Ranzoni call after him, "Want I should come wi'cha?" Davis didn't answer.

High Meadows used to remind him of a college campus, Davis recalled as he ran toward the Ad Building. Peaceful, secure, a place of learning. Nothing could be further from the truth. High Meadows was beautiful. But the lessons were too painful.

Now his mother was dead, and he had no idea what would happen to him. Would his father continue to visit him each week? His mother had been the one who kept him connected to the family. He had lived the same existence day after day, but the family had moved on. Whenever possible, she had kept him informed of their activities. Week after week, year after year, she had come to see him, never giving up, pecking away like a bird after a worm, bringing his supplies and news about the family.

Davis had crossed the quadrangle and entered the Ad Building through the backdoor. From the end of the hall, he saw two men standing in the lobby, their heads bent together. One of the men was his psychiatrist, Doc Bostwick. Davis expected the other man to be his father, but even at a distance he could see the man was too short to be his father, but Davis could not place who it was.

When he reached the men, Davis recognized the other man as his old nemesis from Bishop, Sheriff Dodd. However in his confusion, his mind couldn't take it all in. What was the Sheriff doing at High Meadows? Where was his father? Was his mother alive after all? Had the sheriff come to arrest him for a long-forgotten crime?

"Let me handle this," Doc Bostwick was saying to the sheriff as Davis approached.

"What do you want, Sheriff?" Davis asked, stepping toward the two men. "Where's my Dad?"

He turned toward his doctor. "It's Mama, isn't it, Doc?" he asked. His stomach tightened.

"I'm afraid we have bad news." Doc Bostwick fiddled with his glasses. "...Terrible accident last night, a fire."

Sheriff Dodd moved toward Davis. "Got there too late. Entire right wing of the house gone. That's where your daddy and mama were."

"Daddy and Mama?" He looked from one man to the other.

"Best we can tell," the Sheriff said, "your dad fell asleep with a cigarette. When the flame hit your mama's oxygen tank, fire went everywhere. Probably exploded. More than likely fire ran up the curtain to the ceiling and into her bedroom."

"There was a tank upstairs, too," Doc Bostwick said. "One of those tragic things. Just terrible."

"Fire? Not Daddy. Daddy's not dead."

"I'm afraid so, Davis." Doc Bostwick rested his hand on Davis's arm.

"Need you to identify the bodies...," Sheriff was saying.

"Out of the question," Doc Bostwick said. "It could be harmful to Davis's progress."

The two men argued back and forth, Davis between them, staring ahead. Their words stung him like darts but a deeper pain was forming, splitting him like a fissure in a rock and coming to rest deep inside where he thought only Celeste could resided.

The sheriff told Davis that Eula Mae had discovered the fire and called the fire department. She had Sundays off; and when she returned around midnight, she discovered flames shooting out of the roof. She tried to reach Davis's parents, who were in the den, but by then the entire room was enveloped in flames. All she could do was call the fire department and watch while the den burned.

The firemen managed to save the rest of the house but the den, where his parents were, and his mother's bedroom above, were burned to the core. The rest of the house, although damaged by smoke and water, was intact. Eula Mae, prostrate with grief, had been taken to the hospital for the night.

"Eula Mae," Davis muttered. In his pain he had almost forgotten her. Part of him wanted to turn and run back across the quadrangle into his ward where Marteele and Ranzoni and the rest lived, back into his room where he could close his door. There he could hide from the reality of what the two men were saying. But there was another feeling he couldn't ignore. He wanted to go home. He wanted to see Eula Mae, touch her face. Walk through the burned-out rooms. Smell the charred wood.

He turned to Doc Bostwick. "I want to go home," he said to his doctor.

Doc looked surprised. "You know other people can handle everything for you."

"I want to see Eula Mae. My house. I want to see my parents. Somebody from the bank can identify them. But afterwards I want to see them."

"Davis, I'm not sure that's wise. It will be very difficult."

"I want to see them," he insisted. "I won't believe they're gone until then. I have to make...the arrangements," Davis went on. "They'll help me at the bank. Eula Mae, too." He hesitated, unsure of the strength that seemed to be rising.

Then he added with his old, familiar skepticism, which felt far more comfortable than this new strength, "Besides you were going to make me leave High Meadows anyway."

"Well, I wouldn't put it that way, but yes, arrangements for your release are in place," the doctor agreed.

The doctor turned to the sheriff. "Davis has been approved for an out-patient program. Patients who qualify can live outside High Meadows if they follow a strict regime that includes medication monitoring and having an approved companion live with them."

The Sheriff nodded.

"Blackie Statton has already been approved as Davis's companion," Doc Bostwick explained.

The necessary arrangements were quickly made for Davis and Blackie to stay at his parents' house with Eula Mae. Davis went to phone her with his plans, hoping she was home from the hospital.

The sheriff drove Davis back to his dorm. On the way he said, "I'm going to assign a deputy to you. He can help you."

"What's the matter, Sheriff. Afraid I'll rape all the women and pillage the town?"

The Sheriff shook his head. "After all these years, you still have a mouth on you. I'll hand you that."

They were silent for several minutes. Then the Sheriff said, "It's not unusual to assign a deputy to the location of a fire. It keeps vandals out. Besides he can drive you and Blackie to Bishop and stay there until you can make arrangements for a car. Does that make sense?"

Davis didn't answer.

"Look," the Sheriff continued, "through the years you and I had our differences. I know that. But I am sorry about the fire. Nobody should die like that. I always admired the way your mama stuck up for you. And I'm not saying I always agreed with your dad, but everybody in town considers him a fair man. Never hurt a living soul."

Davis knew the Sheriff was trying to be kind but his comments struck a nerve. He and his father had made peace with each other but he wasn't sure his father never hurt anyone. As for the Sheriff, a few kind words wouldn't change Davis's opinion of the older man. He was an old enemy, and there had been many battles.

When they reached the dorm, Davis opened the car door. "Thanks," he said abruptly, jumping out of the car and slamming the door.

As the Sheriff drove away, Davis heard him mutter, "Sonofabitch."

It didn't matter what the Sheriff thought. Everything was too late now—his mother's hopes and dreams, his father's brief smile—all gone. Vanished like the smell of honeysuckle carried away by a breeze on a bright June day.

Davis was left with a future that was as uncertain as his past.

The Sheriff shook his head as he drove away. After all these years, Davis was *really leaving* High Meadows, he mused. Of course, once the news spread through Bishop, stories about Davis's antics were going to start up. The Sheriff had to laugh to himself, remembering the time he caught Davis and his friend, Mace Fuller, firing .22 rifles at a single engine airplane. "You do this, son?" he had yelled at Davis. Davis answered, calm as anything, "Sheriff, do we look stupid enough to shoot at a plane? We were knocking crows off a telephone line."

Then there was the night they hot-wired a '41 Chevy from the parking lot of Hazel's Beer and Bait Shop on the Catawba

River. When they accidentally backed the car into a ditch, they abandoned it on a dark country road, its headlights pointing to the sky. Later, the Sheriff found out Davis had boasted to a friend that he left the lights on so Sheriff Dodd could find where the car was parked.

Now, some twenty years later, Davis was returning to Bishop, and the Sheriff wasn't sure how he felt about it. For years, he had kept up with Davis through his mother and father. True, there had been bad blood between the Sheriff and Davis, but there was another side to their relationship. No matter what the Sheriff caught Davis doing, no matter where he found Davis and his sidekick, Mace, Davis's electric blue eyes would look at the Sheriff with the innocence of a newborn babe. Over twenty years, the Sheriff thought, most things, the innocent and the not so innocent deeds, could be forgotten.

There was one thing he could never forget. He had witnessed the encounter between Davis and his father the night Jack Williams died. The Sheriff had driven Davis home in the dark of night, waited while Davis turned the key in the lock, heard him call out to his father, listened while he told his father about the death of his father's baby brother. Sheriff Dodd was standing so close to Davis he could feel his hands shake, could see his neck muscles flinch. The father looked at his son with eyes as cold as steel. He didn't say a word, just turned on his heels and walked away. "Daddy, please don't walk away," the boy had pleaded. But the father kept walking, his heels clicking over the marble floor.

"You never cared about me!" the young man cried out to his father's retreating back. Then his voice dropped to almost a whisper. "Only Uncle Jack did." When Davis turned back to look at the Sheriff, the older man saw the pain and hurt in the young man's eyes. On instinct the Sheriff had reached out toward Davis, thinking he could comfort him, but the fifteen-year-old jerked away and ran out the door.

Funny thing, even way back then, the Sheriff knew he was seeing a turning point. One single event which placed a fragile boy on a different path to manhood. A moment in time when a young man's spirit was broken. The Sheriff thought of himself as a tough, even hard, man but being a witness to the breakdown of the relationship between a father and his son haunted him. Ever since then he'd felt a strange tie to Davis, almost like family. It had carried a responsibility that he'd never been able to carry out. At least up to now.

CHAPTER FIVE

Spring 1970

Nights were worst. The sweet peace of sleep was punched with gunfire from distant skirmishes, and dreams were layered with the whine of motor carriers grinding their way over unfit dirt roads, moving men or supplies to places they had never seen or been.

It was lonely. Even though the nights were getting chilly, most of the men rejected sleeping in their warmer tents, preferring to sleep on the ground. Sgt. Wilbur grumbled. "Some night the gooks are gonna slip into camp while you dumb-ass marines sleep and slit your god damn throats." Still he acquiesced and allowed the men to spread their bedrolls on the bare ground. Davis thought perhaps Sgt. Wilbur understood that from the soldiers's narrow perspective the stars up there somewhere were freeing them, were connecting them to an endless midnight sky, which led through time and space, to home.

There was no road out. As long as they were alive and could stand, their road would lead to a long string of battlefields from Bunker Hill to Heartbreak Ridge, marching one after the other as they cut across Korea while enemies appeared and assembled. Just battles to win or lose. And the knowledge that each day brought a new road, which went, only God knew, where.

✦

Eula Mae Dysart grasped the bottle of Early Times by the neck and poured three fingers of the amber bourbon into her empty glass.

"Want some?" she asked Davis, waving the bottle at him across the kitchen table.

They had both changed to comfortable clothes. He had on sweats. She wore a beige bathrobe and plain beige bedroom slippers. Blues were blaring from a radio somewhere in the vicinity of the kitchen sink. The smell of charred wood was overwhelming. Davis shoved his glass her way and watched while she poured a like amount of liquor for him. She looked exhausted. With sustained effort, she pushed herself out of the kitchen chair and went to the refrigerator where she withdrew a tray. "Ice?" she gestured. Davis held up his glass, and she plunked in a few cubes.

Smoke had caused Eula Mae's eyes to flush with red. She was edgy too. Davis supposed she was getting tight. Not that he blamed her. So was he.

He wanted to laugh. The irony of his having his first drink in sixteen years with Eula Mae was too much. They had spent a lifetime despising each other, and now she was his drinking companion, unaccustomed though they both were to drinking. Yet, the very morning when he had found out about the fire, he had desperately wanted to see her. This day had been the equalizer. It had reduced them both to their lowest point.

Since he had arrived that morning in Bishop, he and Eula Mae had walked the burned-out hull, which, only two days before, had been his mother's bedroom and his father's den. The upper room, including the bed with its flowered chintz spread, had collapsed into the den, where it burned to ashes. Den chairs, the sofa, books and built-in bookshelves, all were gone. Only his mother's closet was spared. Somehow, at the door, the fire had taken an unexplained change of direction, and now her personal effects and clothes stood like empty reminders of the tragedy that had taken place.

The deputy had driven him to the bank where he met

with Mr. Jarrard, the executor of his parents' estate. He listened patiently without absorbing any details to the plans his mother and father had laid out for him to leave High Meadows. Mr. Jarrard reminded him that he was "well-off," an ironic choice of words, Davis thought, considering the circumstances.

When Davis returned home, he and Eula Mae sat down in the living room to discuss the funeral. "No point in delaying it," Davis said sadly. "Aunt Ruth and Petey are the only relatives. I suppose a few town's people will come." He thought of Josephine but he quickly dismissed her from his mind, certain that she wouldn't want to see him.

Exhaustion began taking over. "Thursday should be all right, but would you mind making the arrangements?" He said, turning toward Eula Mae. "Suddenly it seems beyond me." She nodded and they went into the kitchen where she poured them both another stiff drink.

Perhaps the bourbon was mellowing Davis's attitude, or the smell of charred wood was getting to his brain, but sitting in his parents' kitchen, he began to feel closer to Eula Mae. She might as well be a relative. She had worked for his family for over forty years. During that time, she'd seen him at his worst, and he, at hers.

"Eula Mae, how come you stuck with this family all these years? I was mean enough to make enemies of a saint."

"Hump," she grunted. "Not 'cause of the likes of you. It was your mama, bless her soul. Now, there was a saint."

Actually, Davis knew very little about his mother's relationship to Eula Mae. He didn't know much about Eula Mae's personal life either. But he remembered her house like a photograph in his mind.

Until two years ago, when she moved into his parents' house to help care for his mother, Eula Mae had lived in a four room, shotgun house in Haytie, the black section of Bishop. The house was a small framed house, once white, but now flaking in sheets to the bare wood. There was a door on the right and two side-by-side windows on the left.

See-through lace curtains hung at the windows. Posts supported a flimsy porch that was surrounded by rickety railings. A limp swing, captured by chains, dangled from the ceiling.

Still, in a neighborhood where chickens scratched in bare dirt, Eula Mae's yard was a maze of color. It flourished with lush green grass and splashes of yellow hibiscus, red geraniums and pink roses. Flowers bloomed everywhere. In hanging baskets dangling from the porch beams, in clay pots placed on the porch and front steps, and in beds running down both sides of the front walk.

As a child Davis was embarrassed that Eula Mae worked for them. None of his classmates' families had maids. One day his mother made him ride with her to pick up Eula Mae. Children playing in the street stopped their games to stare at the spectacle of his mother's sleek, black car inching toward Eula Mae's. From the car window, he saw their blank, sullen faces. As soon as he and his mother passed, the children swarmed back into the street and continued their game. They acted as if the black car with Davis and his mother inside had never existed.

Watching the street fill up when he and his mother passed by had reminded Davis of a Bible story. Moses parting the waters of the Red Sea. But, looking out the car's rear window, Davis wasn't thinking of Moses. He was thinking of Pharaoh, wondering if he felt so betrayed when the waves crashed down, destroying him and his soldiers.

Davis shook away his memories and returned to the present where Eula Mae was making sandwiches.

"You remember that time Mama and I picked you up when Daydus didn't show?" he asked her. Daydus was Eula Mae's son.

She laughed. "Lord no, Daydus didn't show half the time. I was always hunting a ride."

Davis said, "Kids playing in the street laughed at Mama and me. I guess we looked stupid riding in that big black car."

She ignored him. "Tell you what I do remember. You was always in the woods. One day you brought home a wild rabbit. Told your daddy you wanted to keep it. He was madder'n a nest of hornets. You pitched a fit when he made you let it go. Kept saying that bunny had your smell on it."

He remembered. He had chased the rabbit until he cornered it between two fallen logs. When he retrieved the quivering animal from the undergrowth, he had cuddled it like a puppy to his chest where he could feel its heart beating. When he took it home, his father made him let it go.

"Once my smell was on it," he answered Eula Mae, "other rabbits would chase it out of the burrow."

"How come you didn't think of that 'fore you picked up that poor bunny? That's the trouble with you white folks. You just uses and uses and don't never think twice 'bout what you leave behind." Eula Mae's voice was breaking up. Davis suspected her outburst was really over his parents' death. He guessed she was as worried as he was about the future. If she cried, he couldn't handle it. Not now. Not when his own emotions were so shaky. He changed the subject.

"Eula Mae, Mr. Jarrard down at the bank told me this afternoon you'll never have to work again. Mama and Daddy left you money to buy a house and income for life."

"You're funning me."

"I'm serious. Mr. Jarrard called it a retirement account. Said daddy had been putting it aside since you first came to work for them."

"You don't say. Never work no more?" She put down the sandwich she was spreading and took a seat at the table. "Your daddy always was a fair man."

They both were silent. Then Eula Mae said, "Who's gonna look after you?"

"You didn't think you'd have to look after me? After all these years? I don't need you." He wished he felt as confident as he sounded. The truth was he felt certain he couldn't make it on the outside without Eula Mae. Two truths that every patient at High Meadows held to were the hope they would leave and the fear they would return.

"Where're you going?" She replied, arching her back. "This place won't be ready for months."

"The bank's going to sell the house. There's nothing for me here. Nobody in Bishop wants me back."

Eula Mae had returned to the sink. She was staring out the window that overlooked the backyard and the woods that bordered it. Her voice dropped, and it seemed to Davis that she was seeing passed the gathering twilight, passed the thicket of shrubs at the edge of the yard, deep into the woods.

"Reckon you wasn't more'n five years old," she began slowly. "Every time I turned 'round you high tailed it out that door and into them woods. It was like you owned 'em, like a birthright, or something. You wanted to know everything that was going on inside. Where to dig worms. How robins build nests. Why owls take nests hawks leave behind. How come snakes slept most of the winter. Seems like something inside your head was saying over and over that you and them woods belonged together."

Eula Mae was right. In the woods, he was always *safe*. He rose from the table and stood by her at the sink. Together they stared out into the woods.

"Yore mama never liked it, you know. Yore being out in them woods."

"Wonder why she wanted me to buy Granddaddy's house at Rocky Ridge? That's about as deep in the woods as you can get." Davis asked.

"I dunno, but when you was a kid, she thought it'd make you a loner," Eula Mae answered.

The Williams family had owned the land in Bishop for generations, and it passed to Davis's father and Uncle Jack when Davis was just a boy. It was a large, woodland track located on the northwest elbow of Bishop. The soil was rich and loamy, and the foothills of the Appalachian Mountains rimmed the horizon. An ambitious creek, Silas Creek, meandered through the property and eventually merged into the Catawba River, which flowed downward toward the town of Piedmont.

When Davis was eight, he and his dad and Uncle Jack camped out every possible weekend. They had the land to themselves, and never saw another person, only deer, rabbits, red foxes, birds including hawks, and snakes. And, of course, at night there were opossum and raccoons.

Just as Davis knew the terrain, he understood its animals. He could identify tracks and knew where deer watered. Several times, crouching motionless beside a stream, he had coaxed twin fawns to lick his hand under the alert eyes of the mother doe. The fawns were after the salt on his hands, and when they licked them, their tongues felt like sandpaper.

As Davis grew his father and uncle taught him more outdoor skills. He learned to thread a squirming worm on a fish hook. They showed him how to cast and where to catch large fish. At twelve, he received his first rifle as a Christmas gift, a .22. He named it "Belle."

Each year that passed, new feelings emerged. He wondered if his father and uncle could see the changes that he himself could not ignore. His voice wouldn't behave. The dark hair that sprang from his groin and chest itched like crazy. When he touched his penis, it flew up like a divining rod. His nights were full of weird dreams, and sometimes he woke in a cold sweat, milky sperm drying on the sheets and down his thighs. He developed headaches. He called them "blue ice" because of their intensity.

He was no longer the innocent child in the woods. When he chased a rabbit, a new surge of adrenaline spurred him on. After he had the creature cornered, he fired his .22, heard the crack of the rifle, watched as the rabbit flipped in the air from the jolt of the bullet and crashed, lifeless, to the forest floor. He felt no remorse when he picked up the limp, warm body and stuffed it in his pouch. He was a hunter now, he told himself, not a woodsman.

One day in the spring of 1940, he came through the back door into the kitchen. He overheard his father and Uncle Jack in the den talking. The gist of the conversation was that they were going to open a development and sell lots. They were discussing roads and sewer lines. Davis couldn't believe what he was hearing. His father would sell their land? Other people in his woods!

When Uncle Jack left, Davis stormed at his father. "This is your idea. Uncle Jack would never come up with this. You'll ruin everything!"

"Son, contrary to what you think, Jack agrees with me. We don't really have any other choice. Times are changing. My guess is that we'll be at war soon. Besides, we need the money."

Davis retorted, "Money! Is that all you think about? That land is more precious than money. It should never be sold!"

"Davis, the government wants our mill to make uniforms. We need new machines. You're old enough to understand men do what they have to. Besides, you can't spend your life running through the woods."

"What I understand is that I want my sons to grow up in the woods like I did. You're going to mess up everything with roads and telephone lines and sewers."

His father answered calmly, "Davis, there's plenty of land. This piece will never be missed."

"You don't know how wrong you are, Dad."

Davis turned and stomped out of the backdoor. As he left, he grabbed his daddy's keys from the table in the kitchen and headed for Mace Fuller's house.

The two boys drove to Hazel's Beer and Bait Shop on the Catawba River. At first they hung out at the dock watching pleasure boats come and go. Runabouts mostly with 35 horsepower motors and flashy paint jobs. Everybody, including Uncle Jack, claimed runabouts weren't good for much but water skiing. Real fishermen, his uncle claimed, came to the River before dawn and used flat bottom boats with small motors. But Davis was thinking how his uncle was letting him down by selling their land. He was thinking that his uncle wasn't always right. A speedboat might be a whole lot of fun.

When Hazel's neon sign came on out front, and jukebox music floated out to the dock, Davis and Mace went inside. Beer and liquor were being poured freely, and they both ordered beer and helped themselves to one of the baskets of french fries, which had come steaming hot out of the kitchen.

Hazel had two rules at her bar. Everybody, young or old, had to have a good time. But if they got too rowdy, she'd call the sheriff. That night Davis and Mace went over the line.

By ten o'clock, Sheriff Dodd called Davis's parents to say that he and Mace were in jail drunk, and Mr. Williams's car was in a ditch on Catawba River Road. That was the only time Hazel called the cops on the two boys. After she found out Davis was the nephew of her high school boy friend, Jack Williams, she called his uncle when Davis was in trouble.

Still, the support of Uncle Jack and Hazel could not stop Davis. After his argument with his dad over the land, everything went down hill for him.

By the time Davis was sixteen most people in Bishop, including Sheriff Dodd and the Bishop County school system, had decided Davis's behavior had gone far beyond prankish. He was smarter than most of his teachers and better read. He was handsome with thick blond hair and brilliant blue eyes, but with the chiseled look of a statue, a look that left young girls swooning, but timid.

At times he was moody and defiant, complaining of severe headaches. Sometimes he was rakish and self-confident. And constantly he questioned the boundaries adults wanted to impose on him.

His bewildered parents turned to doctors for help. They traveled to hospitals around the south. The prognosis was always the same. There was no clinical reason for the headaches. Davis would outgrow the erratic behavior.

Only Jack Williams and Hazel Forts believed the doctors. They insisted Davis meant no harm. "Have you forgotten?" Jack chided his older brother when the two brothers discussed Davis's problems. "Everybody in Bishop thought the same thing about me when I was Davis's age."

Then, one starless night in June, 1941, when the sky was so black it seemed to disappear, Hazel received a call from one of her regulars, a dispatcher for the Sheriff's department. Sheriff Dodd, the caller said, was going to raid Hazel's establishment sometime after 10 p.m.

The first call Hazel made was to Jack. "Come pick up the boys," she said when Jack answered the phone. Mace and Davis had started hanging out at Hazel's every night.

"They drunk?" Jack asked.

"Naw. I'm getting raided. Better hurry. The boys'll wait at the back door."

"Be right there."

Hazel hung up the phone and motioned to Mace and Davis to meet her in the room behind the bar. The two boys followed her. She closed the door and in the dim light whispered, "Your uncle's picking you up. Go through the kitchen to the back hall. Back door's at the end."

"I'm not ready to go," Davis said indignantly.

"Listen, just do it. I'm gettin' raided but keep it to yourselves."

"I left my red Yankees cap on the bar," Davis said.

"Forget it. I'll keep it for you." She shoved them toward the kitchen.

"We owe you one," Mace said clumsily.

"If the Sheriff gets here before Jack, you run like hell. Hear me?" She jabbed her finger at Mace.

Davis, realizing the situation, changed his attitude about leaving and answered, "Me and my big mouth. Sorry, Hazel.

And thanks." She nodded, pushing them through the kitchen door.

The two boys ran through the kitchen, which had closed down for the night, and into the back hall. They stood on either side of the back door, peering out into the darkness, waiting for Uncle Jack. They could hear the muffled sound of the jukebox and occasional laughter, but their own nervous breathing drowned out most other sounds.

In less than ten minutes, an eternity to them, they saw pinpoint headlights in the distance.

"What if it's the Sheriff?" Mace asked.

"Like Hazel said, we'll run like hell."

The two boys burst out of the back door and darted toward the lights, which turned out to be Uncle Jack's pickup truck. The truck circled around the dirt lot and pulled up beside them. They jumped in and immediately broke out laughing. Uncle Jack threw the truck in gear, and they scratched off toward the road. When they were less than a hundred yards from the roadhouse, they passed Sheriff Dodd's patrol cars speeding toward Hazel's.

After the boys settled down, they bantered back and forth with Jack, talking about nothing in particular except the fish Jack and his friend, Joe Buella, had caught that morning. Davis noticed his uncle repeatedly clearing his throat.

"We get you out of bed?" he asked.

"Naw."

"You okay?"

"Got a pulled muscle in my shoulder."

"You're holding your chest." It was true. When Jack mentioned his shoulder, his right hand had gone to his chest. He was rubbing it with circular movements.

Suddenly his uncle lurched toward the steering wheel and let out a low, guttural moan. His uncle must have tried to hit the brake and instead stomped on the gas because the truck sped up and careened out of control. Davis, who was sitting next to his uncle, pulled him away from the steering wheel.

"The brakes, Uncle Jack!" he shouted. His uncle's head rolled to one side against the seat, and he groaned again.

"Do something," Mace yelled. Davis managed to push his uncle's foot off the gas and then maneuvered his own foot to hit the brakes.

The truck jolted to a stop, and Davis turned off the motor.

"What's wrong with him?" Mace asked.

"What's the matter, Uncle Jack?" Davis asked. Then he motioned for Mace to get out of the car, saying, "Let's get him out."

The two boys scrambled out of the car and raced around the truck, pulling open the door and easing Jack out. They stretched him out on the road.

"Can you hear me, Uncle Jack?" Davis was asking. His uncle moaned again. "Where do you hurt?" His uncle weakly motioned toward his chest.

Davis dropped down to the asphalt road. He slid his arms under his uncle and pulled his upper body onto his lap. The car headlights were still on, and they threw angled beams into the darkness.

"Mace, run back to Hazel's for help. I think he's having a heart attack. Maybe there's a doctor. But bring somebody. The Sheriff if you have to."

Davis watched his friend disappear beyond the headlights. He dropped his voice to a whisper, "Stay with me, Uncle Jack."

"I'm here," his uncle responded.

"Does it hurt?" Against his legs he could feel his uncle's back shaking.

"Better," the soft answer came back. "Heart," he added.

"You're going to be all right. Mace went for help."

"Davis, tell Ruth I love her."

"You'll be okay. I can feel it. Just hold on. They're coming."

"Hot inside." He waved his hand, and it fell like a weight on his chest. A silence followed. In the distance sirens began to wail, and thin ribbons of light bore down on them. "The Sheriff's coming," Davis told his uncle.

"Look after Petey and Ellen for me," he whispered.

"You're not going to die, Uncle Jack."

"Believe in yourself," he answered softly. "Always believe." Davis felt a long shudder run through his uncle, and then his muscular back went slack against Davis's legs.

The cars had screeched to a halt around the two men, their headlights still blaring. Car doors burst open. Men erupted from everywhere. Mace came running toward them with Hazel, the Sheriff and a stranger, who turned out to be a doctor.

"He's passed out," Davis said to the approaching crowd. He couldn't consider that his uncle was dead.

"Get out of the way, Davis, so the doctor can examine him," Sheriff Dodd ordered.

The Doctor waved the Sheriff off. "He's okay, son," he said to Davis, resting his hand on the boy's shoulder. "He's comfortable." He knelt down and unbuttoned Jack's shirt, slipping a stethoscope against his chest.

An ambulance approached from the opposite direction and two attendants emerged with a gurney and raced toward the group. Patrons from the bar had collected around them, and the ambulance attendants had to push the crowd aside to get through.

Hazel was crying. Dew had fallen. And as the doctor bent over Jack, his breath collected around his mouth in foggy, gray puffs. After the doctor tried several pressure points, he folded his stethoscope into his left hand. Then he reached for Davis's arm. "You his son?" Davis shook his head.

"Nephew."

The doctor replied, "There's nothing, son." Then he looked up at the Sheriff. "No heartbeat."

The two ambulance attendants reached down to pull Jack off Davis's lap. "No," Davis said sternly. The sound of his voice echoed through the silent crowd while he cradled his uncle protectively.

"Son, we have to take him," the Sheriff said.

"Leave us alone," Davis cried angrily. "Go away."

The two ambulance attendants stood back and watched while the Sheriff stooped down beside Davis and spoke. After a time, the Sheriff stood up again and nodded toward the attendants. Davis dropped his arms and the men lifted his uncle off his lap and stretched him out on the gurney. Then they spread a white sheet over Jack and anchored it under his body.

Davis's eyes never left his uncle as the ambulance attendants pulled the sheet across his uncle's body and over his face. The wheels of the gurney ground across the road, and Davis began to cry. The Sheriff put the two boys into his patrol car and drove them home.

When Davis's father heard the shocking news that his younger brother was dead, listening with disbelief, after all the details had been given and the explanations made, he assumed that Davis was somehow responsible. And in the spacious entrance hall of their home, the father and son stood facing each other, Sheriff Dodd as a witness. This terrible hurt they both were enduring stood between them. And the one person in all the world who could smooth over their rough spots, the one who could cajole them when they were angry, love them both enough to overlook their weaknesses, this person was dead. He could never jostle his brother's shoulder again saying, "Don't you remember? I was just like Davis." Or put his arm around Davis and whisper to him, "You have to believe." Now, with that person gone, how could the father, or the son, without that one person, reach out to the other? The father looked with eyes as cold as steel at the son, and he turned his back and stormed out of the room.

For years after, a red Yankees baseball cap hung on a nail behind Hazel's bar. Hazel never told anyone whose it was, and no one ever came to claim it.

Their buzz had worn off, and Davis was left with a tired sadness that dredged up memories of his Uncle Jack. "Whatever happened to Hazel Forts?" he asked Eula Mae.

"Dunno," she mumbled. "People don't fish the river no more. Too many pleasure boats."

"I left my red Yankees cap at her bar."

"Hump." Eula Mae reared back and cut her eyes at him. "More'n likely that won't all you left there."

"I'll ignore that remark and change the subject. Did my old rifle burn in the fire?"

"Belle? Nope."

"Where is it?"

"Under my bed," Eula Mae replied, the light splaying off her tilted chin.

"What'd you needed it for?"

"Protection."

"From what?"

"Saints and sinners," she replied quietly.

"How can you tell the difference?"

"They knows. They knows all right," she answered with a deep sigh that echoed through the room long after they both were silent.

CHAPTER SIX

As Josephine Scarborough pulled off Highway 321 onto Main Street in Rocky Ridge, she was surprised by the brisk activity. She remembered a lazy street lined with no-nonsense stores, businesses that moved from winter to summer with a fresh coat of paint and little fanfare.

Today people and cars were everywhere. Delivery trucks lined both sides of the street, making it difficult for her to steer her car through. Workmen in orange Parks and Recreation coveralls added to the confusion by attempting to install large planters on the sidewalks. By mid-July the planters would be a stunning addition to the atmosphere of the town, but, for the moment, the installation crew was causing traffic to go at a snail's pace.

Only the park in the center of town remained unchanged. As Josephine passed by, she felt the same nostalgia return she had felt at Aunt Ruth's. She chuckled to herself when she saw the split rail fence where she and Laura had tied their ponies when they were children. Momma sent them off in the mornings with a sandwich and drink. They rode the short mile to the park, tied their ponies, then scouted the area for new vacationers, or old friends. Often their cousins, Petey and Ellen, were with them. Sometimes, when Davis didn't have anything better to do, he would join them as well.

Josephine remembered Davis with irritation. Why had Aunt Ruth urged her to renew contact with him? She had despised him because he picked on her. It had started with the water moccasin incident and continued to grow.

"Wanna frog?" he'd ask innocently with that smirk of his.

"No!" she'd retort, trying to scramble away, yet knowing what was coming. Of course, he managed to grab her arm and poke his raised knuckle into the soft flesh of her upper arm, making a knot rise on the muscle. She winced remembering the sting the bump made on her arm. By the time Josephine reached the far end of the park, she spotted her destination, a Victorian house. She forgot about Davis and the traffic.

Her good friend, Angie Dennison, worked in the house, which served as a real estate office. Josephine was anxious to see Angie. She had grown up in Rocky Ridge. Her parents owned the Sunshine Inn. The two girls first met as eight-year-olds when they attended Evergreen Camp and became fast friends. They remained in touch through the years, but lately their contact had been business. Angie managed the rentals of the house in Rocky Ridge that Josephine had inherited from her parents.

Josephine pulled into a parking place in front of Angie's building. Lady began to whine, and Josephine took her for a quick walk. Then she tied her to the porch railing and entered the building. Inside a youthful receptionist greeted Josephine and announced her over the phone: "Angie Dennison, Josephine Scarborough to see you."

Angie had come into real estate in Rocky Ridge at the perfect time. The agency she worked for catered to new, young families who loved the out of doors and brought an influx of money into the region. Younger clientele adored Angie. She was the perfect female realtor, a petite blonde with a perky personality and an energy level that never quit. She could see possibilities in a dump, any dump. Josephine had always thought that went for the men she dated, too. In the office her associates called her the queen of "just a little

paint." They claimed with a face like hers, she could sell
Grandfather Mountain to the Cherokee Nation.

Angie emerged from a corridor behind the receptionist's
desk. She was wearing blue, a good color for her, and her
hair was curly and blonde. The women embraced, and Angie
guided Josephine toward her office. Soon they were laughing
and talking at the same time. For Josephine the years seemed
to melt away. The warmth she felt toward her friend was just
as strong as if they had just stepped off the bus from
Evergreen Camp.

"I thought I'd grab a hamburger at the Antler's,"
Josephine said when they sat down. "Can you join me?"

Angie shook her head. "I have to appraise a couple of
large tracts of land over in Tennessee. In fact I'll be tied up
until Thursday afternoon. Tell you what, how about meeting
me Thursday night at the Mountain Trout?" The Mountain
Trout was a favorite restaurant in town.

"Sure," Josephine answered, disappointed that Angie
couldn't have dinner with her until Thursday. It was her own
fault. She had not called to say when she would be arriving.

"I just thought of something," Angie was saying. "Let's
make a night of it. A group of people from work are going
square dancing Thursday. If we eat early, we can do both.
What do you say?"

"I'd love to," Josephine smiled. They agreed on a time,
and Angie added, "By the way, somebody's making inquiries
about the property next door to you."

The house had been vacant for two years. Angie rummaged through the piles of papers on her desk and came up
with a scrap of paper. "A bank in Bishop inquired about it. I
seem to remember one of our agents showed it to a Williams.
Know anybody by that name?"

"That's my aunt's name and she's from Bishop."
Josephine frowned, puzzled by the name. "I can't imagine
anybody in the family looking for a house."

Angie shrugged, "We may never hear from them again."

Josephine remembered Lady was tied to the porch and

excused herself. Angie seemed genuinely sorry to see her go.

"Jo," she said wistfully as she showed her to the door, "I'm glad you're here. I've missed you these last years. I'm sorry about tonight, but I can't wait to catch up on everything on Thursday."

Josephine nodded, feeling suddenly overwhelmed with emotion. It would be good to renew her ties with her childhood friend. By Thursday, she hoped to have the house in order, and she'd be ready for a relaxing evening without responsibilities.

On the way to her cottage, Josephine stopped at the Antler's Restaurant for a takeout burger. She placed her order, picked up a *Charlotte Observer* and headed for a booth to wait for her order. As she was skimming the paper, she noticed a small article at the bottom of the front page. The headline read "Elderly Couple Killed in Bishop House Fire."

She began reading. "An early Monday morning fire has resulted in the deaths of prominent Bishop residents, Robert Emerson Williams and his wife, Grace Ripley Williams. Local police are investigating the origin of the fire, which allegedly began in the den and spread into the bedroom directly above. The Williams are survived by their son, Robert Davis William, and a sister-in-law, Ruth Warner Williams."

Stunned, Josephine scrambled from the booth and located the proprietor. "Something has come up," she told him. "Just give me a cheese sandwich. I'll pay for the burger."

"Forget it. Dollar fifty for the cheese sandwich. Cook'll eat the burger."

"I'd like the paper, too."

"Quarter for that."

Josephine paid the man, and he returned with her sandwich. She rushed out and hurried to her house. As soon as possible, she wanted to call Aunt Ruth.

When Aunt Ruth answered the phone, Josephine said, "I'm on my way back to your house."

"No, no," her aunt replied. "We're okay. Josie's going to stay with the little girl next door. I'm getting ready to go over to see Davis and Eula Mae right now."

"I can be there in two hours. I'll bring Josie back with me."

"Don't come unless you want to see Davis," Aunt Ruth answered. "I'm fine."

Josephine sighed, "Aunt Ruth, it's you I'm worried about. Not Davis."

Her aunt answered. "Petey and his family will be here tomorrow. Josie'll be entertained by her cousins."

"I don't think I can handle another funeral right now."

"I understand. We're okay."

In the afternoon Josephine aired and cleaned the cottage. After being closed for the winter, the house was full of spiders and dead crickets, and a trail of black ants had managed to slip under a crack at the back door. To make matters worse, Josephine found mice droppings throughout the kitchen cabinets. Disgusted, she attacked pots, pans and dishes, loading everything washable in the dishwasher, scrubbing kitchen shelves, and setting mousetraps.

Bad as cleaning the kitchen was, she had trouble keeping her mind off the shocking death of Davis's parents. It was making her tasks of tackling her parents' bedrooms even more difficult. Everywhere she looked were painful reminders of her family. Her father's bedroom was located at the end of a central hall. Each time she walked through that hall, she imagined him asleep in his bed, his back to the door, the yellow and white woven spread pulled across his shoulders.

When she could not avoid that part of the house any longer, she took a deep breath and walked directly to the maple chest of drawers in the far corner beside the windows. Opening the drawers, she discovered white dress shirts still wrapped in dry cleaner bags. She pictured her father standing in front of the drawer lifting out one of those shirts. She hurriedly shoved the drawer shut and headed for the bath-room. There she found his plaid bathrobe, hanging on the bathroom hook. His smell, the musty, acrid smell of a tired old man, still clung to the material. She hung the robe in his closet and closed the door, thinking she'd have to pick up boxes from the Dollar Store to pack things away.

In her mother's room, the dressing table caught Josephine's eye. In one of the drawers she found a box of old bobby pins with strands of silver hairs still clinging to the metal. She remembered her mother kept her face powder and rouge in the center drawer, and sometimes she let her play with it. Josephine opened the drawer and to her delight there was the powder and rouge. A picture came to her mind. She was sitting on her mother's lap looking at their reflections in the mirror. Her mother rubbed the puff in the well of rouge and handed it to Josephine. Josephine smeared it across her checks. Her mother laughed and grabbed a tissue, dabbing at Josephine's cheeks to remove the excess. Her mother kissed her, and the picture in her mind faded away.

Next she tackled her mother's closet, intent on collecting old coat hangers and dry cleaning bags from the top shelf. Reaching into the back left corner and sweeping her hand forward, she brushed against an object. She felt a sharp prick, and when she pulled her hand away from the shelf, a small bead of blood had formed on the end of her finger. Curious, Josephine dragged over the dressing table stool and climbed up to find a small black metal box. She guessed it was a doc-ument box because it had a slim metal handle on one end. She ran her hand over the top. The paint had flaked in spots to the tin, but she could still make out gold and red detailing. Puzzled, Josephine turned the box over in her hand. *Funny that I've never seen this before*, she thought. *I could have sworn I knew every item Momma owned.*

Josephine carried the box into the dining room where she placed it in a sunny spot on the table. The box seem dingy and insignificant resting in the sunlight that fell across the maple dining table. She pressed the lock to see if it would open, but nothing happened. She recalled seeing a set of keys on the telephone table in the living room and rushed to get them. She inserted one key after another until one clicked into place and the lid sprang open.

The box was full of old letters tied with a faded pink ribbon. Most of the envelopes were blue gray, printed on the edges with red and blue slanted lines and marked "Air Mail." All were marked with the standard West Coast wartime return address "in care of the Postmaster, APO San Francisco, Calif." No other identifying marks were on the envelopes, but Josephine guessed they were from her mother's three brothers, who served in the Navy in the Pacific Front during the war.

As Josephine untied the ribbon and pulled the first letter from its envelope, she hesitated. She was invading her mother's privacy. Surely she was going to discover things she had never known, but what purpose would be served if she returned the letters to the closet unread? Someday Josie would find them. Besides, her curiosity was getting the best of her. If her mother had something to hide, Josephine wanted to find out what.

Just as Josephine suspected, the letters were from her mother's three brothers. They wrote of shipmates, landings for repairs, running into friends, loneliness and infrequent liberty. Each letter was stamped "censored" across the front. Words had been cut out, leaving thin rectangular holes in the body. Missing were any hints as to where they were, or what battles in which they might have engaged. The letters were intriguing, but she pressed on, thinking there was more.

The last two letters held the secrets she suspected her mother had hidden. One she knew. The other left her shocked and confused by events her parents had never revealed.

The first letter was from her sister's college roommate. Debbie Partain. The letter began, "Dear Mrs. Broughton, I feel awful telling you but I know my mama..."

Piedmont, N.C. 1946

It was a bleak, January Sunday. The sky was blanketed with thick clouds that never moved, nor yielded the rain they held. Josephine was thirteen years old, in limbo, suspended like the clouds that encased her world. The year was 1946, and she was on a midwinter break from school, dying of boredom.

Her mother and father were in Los Angeles, California, attending the national automobile dealers meeting. They planned to extend the trip an extra week to visit her mother's brothers, all of whom lived near Los Angeles. Mrs. Saffrit was sitting with Josephine. From the first day, Mrs. Saffrit had made it clear that she preferred staying with newborn babies who smelled like talcum and didn't "run around."

Josephine, similarly, decided she despised the squat woman with the flat nose and stringy white hair, which was twisted in a tight knot on top of her head. The truth was Mrs. Saffrit was the nervous type. Every time Josephine left the house, the silly woman stood at the corner window in the living room, watching until Josephine returned, even if it was hours later.

Ten days into the trip, Daddy had called to say they would be delayed. Momma was in the hospital.

"What's wrong with her?" Josephine asked her father, uneasiness stirring.

"Female trouble."

That could take ages, Josephine thought, her concern rising. Sometimes Momma was in bed with female trouble for *weeks,* but she had never been in the hospital. "She's gonna be all right," Dad added as if he sensed Josephine's concern. "But she's not up to a train ride right now." He didn't sound like himself.

Josephine cupped her hand around the phone so Mrs. Saffrit couldn't hear. "Daddy, let me stay with Cookie, *please.* Mrs. Cook would *love* to have me. She practically said so." Cookie was her best friend.

"No, Josephine. Mrs. Saffrit has already canceled her next appointment. Use the extra money I left you if you need to."

"Daddy, *please!* She *broke* the frying pan the other day, and all she can cook is fried chicken!"

"That's an iron skillet," her father signed. "It can't break."

"It did. She poured ice water in and the side popped. Split a *whole* inch. I swear, Daddy, it did."

"Don't swear, young lady," he chided, adding, "all right, you cook. You can do that."

"I can't cook," Josephine muttered, but she knew her father was already signing off.

"Laura's coming after her exams to stay with you for a couple of days. Mrs. Saffrit has some business to take care of."

"Daddy wait!"

"Jo, I have to go. You be a good girl and mind Mrs. Saffrit."

Her father's voice was gone. Disappeared through miles of telephone line that ran across the United States. And she, Josephine, whose mother said her name meant strong woman, was left with Mrs. Saffrit while waiting for her sister, Laura, to come from college and save her. Worse of all, she hadn't told Momma she loved her. Momma was sick *in the hospital,* and Josephine had forgotten to ask Daddy to tell Momma she loved her.

Around three o'clock a car pulled up to the curb of the house, and Laura emerged from the back seat. She was laughing and tugging on a small suitcase. Josephine dropped the afternoon newspaper she had been reading and watched her sister from the den window. Laura waved to her college friends as they drove away. She was still laughing.

Even in a sunless sky, Laura's auburn hair had managed to pick up light. To Josephine, it gleamed like fire. But when the car turned the corner, Josephine noticed her sister's manner changed noticeably. Her shoulders dropped and she looked tired and listless.

Laura must know something about Momma, Josephine thought, and she hurried out of the house to greet her sister.

After they hugged, Josephine blurted out, "You heard anything about Momma?"

"Momma's fine. Don't worry about her."

They walked arm in arm to their house, meeting Mrs. Saffrit with her suitcase in hand coming out of the front door. Josephine introduced them. After a brief greeting, Mrs. Saffrit indicated she had called a cab and would wait for it on the sidewalk. Laura reminded her to return by Wednesday lunch.

Once inside, Josephine grabbed her sister and danced around.

"I'm finally free of the old buzzard!"

"Not so fast," Laura replied. "Don't forget she'll be back on Wednesday."

Wednesday was eons away.

Their first dispute came over which bedroom Laura would occupy. Josephine was counting on sharing their room as always, but Laura said she needed privacy. She would stay in Momma and Daddy's room. Josephine said it was disrespectful, and if Laura wasn't going to share *their* bedroom, she should stay in the guest bedroom. After all Mrs. Saffrit was gone.

Laura held her ground and carried her bag into their parents' room. After she was settled, she called Josephine in to talk. Still miffed, Josephine stalked in and collapsed on their mother's faded red velvet chaise lounge.

Laura was holding a silky, blue nightgown in her hand. The gown didn't look like it belonged to a college kid. Surprised, Josephine raised up from the chaise and asked, "Where'd you get *that* thing?" Laura shrugged. The gown fell through Laura's fingers like liquid and rested on the bed.

They chatted pleasantly for a while, Laura asking questions about Josephine's school. Josephine was beginning to think her sister was avoiding something. Without knowing why, she blurted out, "Heard from Tony Sparks?" During World War II, Tony Sparks served as a paratrooper. After the war, Tony decided to accept a GI Bill to attend college. He showed up at Blue Ridge College, where Laura went, supposedly to look at the college but decided not to stay.

Josephine might as well have thrown water on Laura. Her sister became visibly shaken, the color washing from her face. "What's the matter?" Josephine asked.

"Daddy said you had extra money," Laura was saying. "I need to borrow some."

"Daddy said it was okay?" Josephine suspected her sister wanted to buy a new sweater.

"I didn't ask him," Laura replied. "I have to borrow some of it, and I'll have most of it back in a week."

"It's for food," Josephine protested.

"Daddy said you had two hundred fifty dollars. You can't possible use that much for food. I only need 100 dollars."

"Hundred dollars! M'gosh, Laura, what the samhill you need that kind of money for?"

Laura was twisting her hands. "I need your help, Jo. I'm in trouble."

"What's the matter?" Josephine repeated, her stomach flipping over.

"I'm pregnant."

"Pregnant!" Josephine bolted out of the chaise, a bad taste filling her mouth. What was her sister saying? Bad girls got pregnant! "How could you be? You wouldn't let a man put his...his *thing* in you!"

Laura, who had been pacing back and forth in front of the bed, stopped and turned to face Josephine. "Jo, it isn't like that. Someday you'll understand. The whole thing just happened. Anyway, I've found somebody here in Piedmont who'll do an abortion."

Josephine couldn't believe her ears. Her sister wasn't

making sense. "First you say you're pregnant. Then you say somebody'll do a…a what? Abortion? What's THAT?"

"A doctor removes it." Laura hesitated. "In his office. With an instrument."

Josephine's eyes were burning. She was going to cry. She *knew* she was going to cry, and that was the last thing she wanted to do. Her sister needed her. Really needed her, maybe for the first time in her entire life. She swallowed hard and blurted out, "How come you just don't get married?'

"The man doesn't know."

Questions swirled in Josephine's head. It was all too much. Too much to ask. To know. To think through. Still, she adored her older sister. And if Laura were in trouble, Josephine would go to any lengths to help her. That was the real point, wasn't it? That and the fact that if their parents found out, they'd kill Laura.

"You'll put the money back?" she asked, tilting her head up to look at Laura.

"I'll have fifty this weekend."

Josephine looked away. She didn't know what to say. She turned and silently walked back into the bedroom the two of them had shared until today. As she opened the door and entered the closet, a wave of her smell, the warm earthy smell of a child's sweat, rose to meet her. Inside, she lifted her cheerleader sweater out of the way and reached for her favorite white socks, which she kept beside the sweater. From the toe, she pulled out the money and counted out five twenty-dollar bills. For a moment she held the remaining money, wondering what Mrs. Saffrit would say if they ran out of money. Then she shrugged, replaced the sock and returned to her parents' room. She handed Laura the money. Her sister tried to hug her, but Josephine backed away.

"You can't ever tell Momma and Daddy," Laura said sharply. Josephine nodded. "And there's one more thing. Somebody has to go with me." Josephine nodded again.

"Thank you," Laura said, sighing. Josephine turned to

leave the room. "Jo," she called after her sister, "please don't hate me."

Josephine stopped in the doorway. "I could never hate you, Laura. I love you. I'm just sorry, that's all."

Laura hadn't told her who the father was, and Josephine hadn't asked. But she remembered how Tony had looked at her sister when she was only sixteen years old. Back then he had come for lunch every Sunday. It was part of the war effort to match lonely paratroopers who were in training at Fort Bragg with families who wanted to help. Josephine's family had signed up, and Tony and his friend, Frank, were assigned to them. Every Sunday they arrived on a liberty bus from Fort Bragg. Daddy picked them up at the bus station and brought them home.

When the war was over and Tony had mustered out of the paratroopers, he turned up at Blue Ridge College. Laura had told Josephine he came to look at the college, but Josephine guessed he was there to visit her sister.

Through the doorway, Josephine looked back at her sister. She was still sitting on their parents' bed, fingering the blue gown and staring into space.

Things would never be the same between them. Laura would never sleep in their room again. She should have fallen for Frank Charmaine. He never made it back from the Battle of Normandy.

Next morning Josephine rose in predawn darkness and, preferring the dark, she fumbled about her room. She knew precisely where her clothes were. They were laid out neatly on the chair. She could barely make out their shapes. Her navy blue skirt with knife-edge pleats had seemed perfect last night, and now it looked like part of a cheerleader outfit. She looked over the other items. The gray sweater with the Peter Pan dickey already attached. Not dressy enough. Her nylons and first heels, which were all of 1-inch high. Not grown-up enough. She had rolled her hair on bobby socks to make it curl in a pageboy. Her hands flew up to touch the makeshift curlers. If one curler had fallen out in the night, it would leave a bump in her hair. It didn't matter, she thought with irritation. The whole outfit was stupid. She was going to look like a baby.

Laura emerged from their parents' bedroom. She was wearing a trench coat over loose sweats. "You awake?" she asked, and without waiting for an answer, she said, "How come you're in the dark?" She reached out and turned on the light switch. Light flooded the room, and Josephine, further annoyed by her sister's intrusion, mumbled a reply and yanked at the underclothes she had laid out.

They didn't talk. Laura lit a cigarette. She inhaled deeply and allowed the smoke to flow out of her mouth and into her nostrils. It was called French inhaling.

"You want some juice?" Josephine asked her sister.

"God, I'd love a cup of coffee, but I can't have anything." She went into the bathroom and flicked an ash into the toilet. Josephine went to the kitchen for juice and returned.

Sunlight was beginning to gather outside. It looked weak against the bright, artificial light inside, but it was still going to be the prettiest day they had in weeks. On the first sunny day in ages, plus a school holiday, Josephine thought, and she was going to be inside.

Laura returned to their parents' bedroom to dress. When they both were ready, Laura called a cab, and they gathered in the living room to wait for it. Laura chain-smoked. She opened her pocketbook, withdrew her wallet and fingered the money. Josephine stood by the front window, where Mrs. Saffrit always stood, and watched for the cab.

"There he is," Josephine cried when she spotted a yellow car turning down their street. She grabbed her coat and hurried out the door, waving at the driver, leaving her sister to collect her things and lock the door.

The ride was uneventful. Their cab driver dropped them at an address on High Street in a mixed commercial and residential neighborhood. It was on the edge of town across the street from the high school. The house was a Victorian style, freshly painted white. A black iron fence circled the property.

"Not bad," Josephine said, trying to be cheerful. Laura gave her sister a disgusted look. She paid the cab driver and stepped out onto the street. Josephine followed and the cab drove away.

Laura pulled up the collar of her coat, hunched her shoulders forward, and started up the walk. Josephine fell in beside her. Halfway up the walk, Laura stopped. "If anything...well..." Josephine threw her arms around her sister.

"Please, let's get out of here," she begged. "Dad and Mom will help us."

"Josephine, you can never tell Mom and Dad. Promise me that, do you hear?"

Josephine's eyes stung. "Please, Laura."

Her sister pushed and took hold of Josephine's arms, shaking them. "This is the best way. Believe me. I don't want to loose Momma and Daddy's respect." Then she held Josephine's hand and started walking. When they reached the massive oak door. Josephine reached out and rang the bell. Her finger was shaking.

From inside they heard a woman's voice call out, "coming," and a pleasant-looking woman, wearing an apron and holding a dishtowel, answered the door.

"You're here for the doctor," she said, smiling. "Top of the stairs."

The two girls stepped into the entrance hall and waited for the woman to close the door.

"Wonderful to see the sunshine today, isn't it," she said, closing the door. The girls nodded. "Straight up the stairs. Doctor's waiting for you."

The woman acted as if the girls were going upstairs for a haircut, but Laura didn't seem to notice. She started up the steps, and Josephine followed.

At the top, Laura faltered, leaning back momentarily against her sister. Josephine steadied her. Laura straightened her shoulders and pushed open the door.

Just then a calico cat ran up the stairs after them and brushed passed Josephine's leg. They stepped into the room and the cat slipped by them and ran down a corridor.

The waiting room they entered was orderly and smelled of antiseptic. Post-war blonde furniture with flowered cushions lined the walls. Coffee tables, neatly stacked with magazines, were placed in front of two sofas. Overhead bright fluorescent lights gleamed over the room.

A reception area was located at the right. Behind the counter, a wiry woman, wearing horn-rimmed glasses, dressed in a nurse's uniform, spoke. "Norma Smith?" The woman frowned as she called the name.

Laura answered. Josephine winced at her sister's lie, but she said nothing.

"Fill out these papers," the nurse ordered, removing her glasses and extending a folder to Laura. The woman looked toward Josephine, and Josephine straightened her back. "This your attendant?" she asked, tilting her head toward Josephine.

"Yes." Laura was sorting through the papers and spreading them on the counter.

"She's too young," the woman said with a shrug. "We usually have somebody older."

"She's my sister."

"You can take care of her?" The woman stared at Josephine as if sizing her up.

"Yes, m'am. I can do what you tell me to do." Josephine decided the woman was mean.

"Let's see the money." Laura pulled a wade of bills from her pocket book and counted five twenties on the counter, which separated them from the nurse.

The nurse ripped a receipt from a pad and thrust it toward Laura. Then she rose from her desk and pointed toward the waiting room. "You wait there," she said to Josephine, motioning toward the sitting area. "You follow me," she said to Laura. "It'll take about an hour," the nurse called over her shoulder as she pushed open a pair of swinging doors that opened into a dusky hallway.

"Good luck," Josephine whispered as Laura followed the nurse like a zombie through the swinging doors. Josephine wanted to run after Laura and tell her the whole thing was wrong. Mom and Dad would help them. There were other—better—answers. They could...but Laura was gone. The doors closed behind her, and Josephine was alone.

For what seemed like hours, Josephine paced back and forth in the small waiting area, imagining what was going on. Where was Laura? What was the operating room like? Was she spread-eagle, her knees in the air, like Josephine had seen in that stupid movie in health class? Josephine could hear her heart beating. How could she have been so stupid? Why had she agreed to this? They should have told Momma and Daddy and let them figure out what to do.

Exhausted, she dropped into a chair. If only her mother were here to help them, she was thinking when she was distracted by sounds coming from outside. A car started. A dog barked. Shrill laughter broke out. She turned around and sat on her knees to look out the window. A school bus was dropping students off at the school across the street. It struck her that the sounds outside weren't connected. They fell like raindrops in a puddle and then were lost. But inside it was different. Everything depended on something else. The sweet lady who opened the door. The mean nurse who was with her sister. The unseen doctor who was willing to break the law. Laura and even her. Each of them was connected by a single deed.

The cat jumped from nowhere onto the back of the chair, blocking Josephine's view. "Hey, cat. You're in my way." But instead of pushing the cat away, Josephine picked her up and turned around with her, cuddling her. The cat began kneading Josephine's thighs. "You're gonna run my nylons." The cat ignored her protests, and Josephine was too glad for the company to dump her on the floor. The animal finally tucked its legs under its body and curled up in Josephine's lap.

Automatically, Josephine began to stroke her, and the cat purred contentedly. The warmth from the cat's body began to sink into Josephine's legs and her shoulders began to relax. A wedge of sunlight spilled across them.

"Do you have kittens, Miss Kitty?' she asked the purring animal. "I'm never going to have children."

The hall doors opened and the nurse swept through, approaching Josephine.

"It's over. Your sister's waking up from the ether. It'll take about twenty minutes." Her rubber heels squeaked on the tile floor as she returned to her desk.

Josephine dumped the cat on the floor and followed the nurse to her desk. "What do I do with her?" Josephine asked, remembering she was going to have to take care of Laura.

"She'll sleep it off. I've got pills for her. One for infection and one for pain. If she hemorrhages, call us."

Josephine stared helplessly at the nurse. Hemorrhages! That was bleeding! She was going to cry.

"She'll be all right," the nurse answered sharply. "It happens more than you'd believe."

Josephine felt a shiver run down her spine. For a moment, she could see what lay ahead for her and her sister. For Laura, the abortion was like the sounds Josephine heard outside the window. Here one moment, gone the next. Raindrops in a puddle. But not for Josephine. No, she would always bargain with life. Planning, calculating until one thing led to the next. And all of them, good and bad, she would carry with her like baggage.

The cat had followed Josephine to the nurses' station and now she was rubbing against her legs. Josephine turned away from the nurse and stooped to gather the cat into her arms. She whispered in its ear. "Do you really have nine lives? I wish I did." The cat squirmed out of Josephine's arms and leaped to the floor, swishing her tail at Josephine. Then she began her regal cat walk under the swinging doors and down the hall where abortions were performed.

Josephine fell back against the dining room chair. The letter, which had prompted her memories, slid out of her hand and came to rest on the table.

It said:

> Mrs. Broughton,
>
> I feel awful telling you but I know my mama
> would want to know if it was me. Anyway there
> have been rumors around the sorority house that
> Laura is pregnant. I've been telling everybody
> they're dirty lies and people are just jealous of Laura
> cause she's so beautiful. I just hope it's not true
> cause Laura is in big trouble if it is. And so am I for
> sticking up for her.
>
> > Hoping for the best,
> > Debbie Partain.

Her parents knew? Why hadn't they said so? Why had they let her and Laura bear all the pain of that horrible event alone?

The next letter held the answer.

At first Josephine thought the two papers belonged together. On closer examination the second paper stood on its own. It was a birth certificate. In tall letters at the top of the page were the words: State of California, City of Los Angeles. Under the heading was an infant's footprint, not two inches high, stamped in black ink

The certificate read:

> Be it known to all parties that on January 23,
> 1946, a premature son was born at Los Angeles
> General Hospital to Emma Elaine Warner
> Broughton and Alfred Nathaniel Broughton. The
> infant was christened Alfred Nathaniel Broughton,
> Jr. The infant subsequently succumbed.

Josephine had a brother, the son her father always wanted. His namesake, Alfred Nathaniel Broughton, Jr. While her mother was losing a son, she and Laura were terminating a pregnancy.

The birth certificate explained so much. Her mother's melancholia. Her father's attempts to assuage her by buying gifts, each more lavish than the last. Her rejections of Josephine's efforts to engage her in something useful, anything, even classes at the local college. The way her mother dropped out of her clubs one by one, and her friends quit coming by in the afternoon to have a glass of sherry. Mrs. Hazelhurst no longer planted the flower beds. Her mother wore the same dress day after day. The sheen left her hair, her beautiful hair.

For every answer the letter and certificate explained about her family, a question arose for Josephine. Had she failed her mother by not seeing and understanding what was really happening? And hadn't her father been incapable of dealing with her mother's distress? Wasn't the real truth that she and her father both wanted life to go on as before?

If she failed her mother, she also failed her sister. She had been so busy judging Laura as irresponsible and promiscuous, declaring that she would never be like her that she had not tried to understand her, reach out to her.

Were these revelations the reasons she could not stop grieving for her family? And was that in turn why she and Michael weren't getting along? That she had unfinished business from the past?

She slipped the birth certificate back beneath the letters and returned the metal box to the closet. Then she walked out on the porch overlooking the gorge and dropped into one of the Kennedy rockers. She was still holding the letter from Debbie Partain.

A haze had settled on the mountains, capping them so that all the peaks and valleys were wiped away. Only the middle ground remained. The outcroppings and trees were hidden just like the secrets her family had kept. But the weight of secrets was still there, just as the rocks and trees were hidden behind the haze.

If only she could spend an hour with Laura and Momma. Just an hour. Sit with them and tell them her regrets. Hold them. Pat Momma's hair. Put her arms around her sister's waist and tell her she understood. If she could just do those things, maybe she wouldn't feel this remorse.

She rose from the rocker and tore Debbie Partain's letter to pieces and threw the scrapes of paper in the air. The wind lifted them toward the gorge, and soon they disappeared into the landscape.

CHAPTER SEVEN

At seven-thirty Thursday evening Josephine pulled into the parking lot of the Mountain Trout on Highway 321. The parking lot was almost full, a good indicator in a town where restaurants had difficulty surviving winters.

The building was rough, gray-stained lumber. Its most notable feature was a sign, attached with rusty chains to a beam, hanging over the entrance. In the middle of the sign, an artist had carved a striking mountain trout. Its body was a blackened gray; the lower part of its sides, bright yellow and freckled with brown dots. In the setting sun, the colors shimmered, giving the fish a startling, life-like appearance.

Inside, the restaurant was surprisingly elegant. Tables and booths were covered with white tablecloths. Candles, reflecting warm light in their globes, sent inviting shadows across the room. Customers gathered in parties around their dining tables. They were young and attractive, and their laughter filled the room.

Josephine felt her spirits lift. It would be good to leave behind the shocking discoveries of her week and let herself become part of the crowd.

Angie was waiting for her at the bar. As her friend crossed the short distance between them, Josephine felt a twinge of envy. Her friend was smiling, her blonde hair bouncing across her shoulders. She was wearing a low-cut dress the color of summer raspberries. It had been a long time since Josephine had looked that good.

When they were settled in a booth, Angie plunged in enthusiastically, "So, what's been happening the last two years?"

Josephine laughed, an edge in her voice. "I don't know where to start. I've left Josie with my Aunt Ruth, but some of her relatives were killed in a tragic fire in their home. Plus, I've had a disturbing week packing Momma and Daddy's things. It's the first time I've been to Rocky Ridge since they died. I feel like they're following me around all the time. It's weird, like I'm stuck in the past "

"God, that's spooky. I'm so sorry."

"Michael thinks I'm nuts." Josephine shrugged. "Maybe he's right. Anyway, I decided to come up here this summer with Josie and see if the mountain air won't do the trick." She added hastily, "Michael will be up on weekends."

Angie patted her hand sympathetically. "Sorry about your family. Hey, you want to join my bridge club for the summer? You used to beat the pants off everybody in cards."

"I can't stand cards anymore. I go stir-crazy waiting for somebody to decide what to play next."

"Not even gin?"

"Gin was the first to go." A waiter came and took their drink orders. When he left, Josephine picked up their conversation. "When I started dating Michael, one night he lost about twenty-five bucks to me. I was about to scoop the money up when I looked at him. He was flabbergasted."

The waiter returned with their drinks. Angie reached for hers and took a swallow. "I knew if I took the money," Josephine continued, "I could kiss him goodbye. I made a quick attitude adjustment. I handed him the money and said I'd keep a running tab. Course, we never played again. Not till after we were married." She looked down at her drink. "Funny thing, I can't beat him now for anything. It's like I gave my luck away."

Angie laughed and raised her eyebrows. "That's quite a story. You guys are still okay, aren't you? How's Michael?"

"Oh, sure. He's okay. We're okay." She swished ice around in her glass. "How about you?" she added, looking up at Angie. "When I saw you last, you and Charlie were married. What happened?"

"That jerk. He couldn't keep his hands off other women. Finally I got sick of it and divorced him. He's over in Mountain City selling cars. I got into real estate. It was a great trade-off."

"How'd you pick real estate?" Josephine felt envy creep back. Angie seemed so competent.

"Women are naturals. It's the best fit in the world. Think about it. When I show a house, the man wants to know what's wrong with it. The woman, how it flows. I'm bound to hit with one of them. You ought to consider it when Josie's older." In her wildest dreams, Josephine had never considered going into real estate. Teaching school, maybe. Real estate, never.

The waiter returned with their entrees.

Angie fluffed her loose curls. "A minute ago you mentioned 'attitude adjustment.' Funny, that's what Michael said when he called me."

"Michael called you?" Josephine's fork slipped out of her hand and hit her plate. She felt incredulous. "What did he want?"

"Asked me to keep an eye out for you."

"And he said I needed an attitude adjustment." Josephine said flatly.

"It's not a big deal. I just thought it was strange that you both said the same thing."

"I was talking about playing gin. A long time ago! Believe me, that's not the way I'd describe my summer in the mountains. Taking some time off. Grieving for my family. Figuring things out. That's what I'd say I'm doing." Josephine flew on. "It frosts me to think Michael called you to check on me." Her voice echoed loudly in the restaurant, and she suddenly was aware other diners were staring at her.

"Hey, keep it down." Angie glanced around nervously. "People are looking at us. I have to live here."

Josephine lowered her voice. "He's out of line to call you, Ang. And it makes me mad as hell."

"Okay," Angie said with some irritation. "I'm sure he didn't mean anything. He's worried about you, that's all. I certainly don't want to make you mad. Let's change the subject." Angie pressed her napkin into the corners of her mouth. There was an awkward silence. Then, she dropped her napkin back in her lap and snapped her fingers as if she just thought of something. "Hey, you haven't told me about Josie. I've never even seen her."

"I forget we haven't been able to get to the mountains much. I was pregnant with Josie when Momma and Daddy got sick."

Angie asked, "And your sister? Didn't she die of cancer?"

Josephine nodded. "April a year ago. It hit me hard, too. Maybe worse than Mom and Dad. We used to say our day would come, but it never did."

Angie reached across the table and squeezed Josephine's hand again. "I thought we'd grow old together," Josephine said with a sigh.

They finished their meal with scattered conversation. Afterwards Angie excused herself to go to the ladies room, saying, "Why don't you order a brandy to calm your nerves? I won't be long." Josephine watched her friend walk away. She had no intention of ordering a brandy. Michael wasn't going to boss her around and neither was Angie. She was in the mountains to take charge of her life. She signaled the waiter for coffee.

When Angie returned, her friends from work had arrived. They were assembling in the bar where Josephine and Angie joined them. Josephine was beginning to waver about going square dancing. She pulled her friend aside and said, "Ang, I'm done for. I think I'll call it a night."

"Oh, no you don't. This is the Nashville Five. You hear live music like this once in a lifetime!"

Josephine looked at her watch. "I'm just worried about what time we'd get home."

"I promise I'll get you home by midnight." She put her arm around Josephine. "The stuff with Michael? I hope you're not mad about it."

"Forget it." Josephine answered. "It's just one of a long line of problems for the week."

They settled the check and caught up with Angie's friends, who were already leaving the restaurant. As soon as they were in the parking lot, Angie began organizing every-one into cars. Watching her friend, Josephine felt her envy creep back. Angie had taken charge effortlessly. She was free to do, or be, anything she wanted, Josephine thought. By contrast, she allowed circumstances to control her life. She might as well be a speckled trout, like the one carved on the sign in front of the restaurant, being swept toward the river by the currents of a high country mountain stream.

Angie drove her jeep northwest, leaving Green Mountain and Rocky Ridge behind them, the sun setting in their faces. They were heading for Tammy and Tom's Square Dance Pavilion in the portion of the mountains called High Country, near the North Carolina-Tennessee line. Josephine had never been to that section of the Blue Ridge. When she was a child, there was so much to do her family seldom left Rocky Ridge.

As Angie maneuvered the jeep through one curve after another, they moved from shadow into sunlight and back again, depending on the position of the sun. Each time they rounded a new curve, Josephine felt her stomach rise as if she were on a roller coaster. She managed to peek over the edge of the road and was shocked by the steep plunge into the valley. Angie was taking the curves skillfully, yet the combination of the queasy stomach and the sheer drop made Josephine feel lightheaded. The drive was dangerous, yet she felt exhilarated as if she were living without regard for past or future, only present. Time seemed suspended, and her confusion over the week's discoveries diminished. Even the fact that Michael had asked Angie to check on her seemed less important.

What would her life be like if she could let loose? Could she live in the moment like Laura? Was this what Michael meant when he said she needed an attitude adjustment?

Lulu and Bryon, Angie's friends from work, both in their twenties, interrupted her thoughts. Josephine looked back at them. They were sitting in the backseat giggling. The sides of the jeep were up, and the cool mountain air whipping across them cast their hair about like scarecrows. Suddenly they broke into "Country Road." When they finished their song, Bryon called out to Angie, "Hey, Ang, how s'about we bust open a beer?"

"Nothing doing," Angie called back. "If I loose my license, I don't eat. Wait till we get to Tammy and Tom's."

Bryon and Lulu returned to their songs, this time, "Proud Mama."

At length Angie pulled off the highway. She down shifted and steered the jeep up a steep dirt road. They were driving through a stand of conifers, which gave the woods a bluish green color and gave off a clean, fresh smell. Even though the needles of the trees were light and airy, the stand was so dense only small patches of light came through.

At the end of the road, the landscape opened up, revealing a panoramic view of the Blue Ridge Mountains and its surrounding valleys. The western sides of the mountains were still in sunlight. They threw off a yellowish-green hue that reflected on the craggy rock outcroppings. The eastern sides of the mountains, however, were bathed in cool, midnight blue shadows. The shadows had the effect of wiping away distinguishing features and created a striking comparison between the two sides of the valley.

Angie steered her jeep left into a field where people were parking. Once their cars were parked, everyone was walking toward an open-air pavilion, apparently where the dance floor was located. The sound of country music rose from that direction and spread over the parking lot.

The rooftop of the pavilion was visible from the field. It was octagonal shaped and its cupola ended in a sharp point. It reminded Josephine of an old-fashioned garden house. The building, stained a natural color, was surrounded with banisters. Sweeping grass tiers sloped down to the pavilion and served as seats or steps, whichever was needed. Broad wooden steps led from the grass to the actual dance floor. Beyond the pavilion, trees had been cut down to expose the same mountain view as the parking lot.

By the time they reached the grassed tiers where everyone was sitting, the sunset was in its final stages. It was sending long, flaming streamers across the sky.

The four of them found a spot on one of the grass tiers. They set the cooler of beer down and Lulu and Bryon flew off to dance. Josephine said to Angie, "Go on. I'll watch a minute until I catch on." Angie joined her friends, and Josephine was left alone. She popped a beer can and sat down to watch.

Angie, Lulu and Byron had quickly blended in with the dancers. Josephine was surprised at how skillful they were. Still, the dances didn't seem hard, and most didn't require partners. By the third dance, when Angie came back, Josephine was ready to join them.

She danced several numbers, swinging from person to person, when a Texas two-step, which required a partner, started. Josephine was headed for her seat beside the beer cooler when a man stepped up to her.

"Can I have this dance?" he asked.

Josephine glanced up to see a wiry man standing in front of her. He wore blue jeans and a plaid cotton sports shirt with a black bolo string tie, with silver tips. As he moved, the shiny tips of the tie bounced against his shirt.

It hadn't occurred to Josephine that someone might ask her to dance, and she quickly scanned the crowd to find Angie and seek her advice. But she was across the dance floor ready, to dance.

"I don't know how to do a two-step," Josephine said.

"Don't need to. Just follow me." Before she could protest, the man slipped his arm around her waist and guided her toward the dance floor.

He wheeled her through the steps as if she were a feather, and soon she was comfortably following him through twirls and turns. One dance ended and another began, and they continued. Once he danced in place, continuing the rhythm, while sending her spinning, holding only the tips of her fingers. As he twirled her, he cocked his head to the side, speaking to her, "Looking good, darling."

Josephine couldn't believe her ears. Was he getting fresh with her?

"Don't..." she stammered, "say that to me."

"Which," he replied. "Lookin' good or darling?"

"Both. You don't even know my name!" She tried to move away but he pulled her back against him and held her with such a grip she could do nothing but follow him.

"I call 'em like I see 'em," he chuckled, dancing on, not seeming to notice Josephine's shock. "Well, what is it, your name, that is?" he added.

"Josephine," she answered, blushing.

"Nice," he nodded, continuing to dance.

Finally the music stopped. Josephine escaped as fast as possible and returned to her seat. *How dare he get fresh with me!* Upset, she reached into the cooler for another beer and took a long, slow swallow.

"You doing okay?" Angie called from the edge of the steps.

"I'm sitting this one out," Josephine called back to her friend and waved her on. Angie returned to the floor.

The man was leaning against the banister watching Josephine. It was unnerving, She kept looking in the other

direction, but her eyes were drawn back to him. She finished
her beer and reached into the cooler for another. He was still
watching her.

Angie appeared again and began motioning to her from
the dance floor, calling out, "I want you to meet some folks
from work."

Relieved to escape the man's intense stare, she hurriedly
joined Angie. Angie led her to a small group of people, introducing them. One of the men, Howard, asked her to dance,
and he steered her onto the floor. They had danced several
numbers, including a conga line, when a slow dance came on.

Josephine was just beginning to relax when the man with
the western string tie cut in. Before she could protest, he
grabbed her and glided over the dance floor with her. He
was holding her too tightly, and she squirmed away, pushing
on his chest with one hand. He ignored her movements and
collected her back to him. They were so close she could feel
his breath on her ear. The heat from his legs was seeping into
her jeans. Again, she managed to push away to a comfortable
distance. At the end of the dance, she broke away and
headed toward Angie on the other side of the floor.

When Josephine caught Angie's attention, she motioned
for them to meet on the stairs.

"Who was that man I was dancing with?" Josephine
asked.

"T.J. Butts."

"You know anything about him?"

"T.J.? Oh, sure. He's an eastern cowboy."

"What's that?'"

"You know. Frustrated. No steer to herd, or ranges to ride.
He and his mama think he's God's gift to women and the
most misunderstood man alive." They laughed.

"I don't think I like him," Josephine replied with a gri-
mace. Truthfully, Josephine was shocked by her own reaction.
Although she hated to admit it, the man named T.J. Butts
seemed exciting, somehow dangerous, and she was flattered
by his attention.

On the way home Angie told Josephine she looked up the name of the man who asked about the house next door to her.

"Who was it?" Josephine asked.

"Davis Williams," Angie replied.

"You are kidding! Davis Williams from Bishop?" Josephine threw back her head. "No way! Not Davis! That man's a lunatic!" By now the curving road and the beer she had consumed, were making her lightheaded. She started laughing.

"What is the matter with you?" Angie chided.

"He's crazy as a loon! Been at High Meadows Mental Institute for sixteen years. And he's going to live beside us at Rocky Ridge? Not beside me and Josie. No way."

Her laughter resounded in the darkness through the turns and curves of the car. For the life of her, she couldn't think why she was laughing because it wasn't funny at all.

CHAPTER EIGHT

D reams were mixed that night and characters traveled from one to another without regard for events that spawned them. Once, Josephine woke, startled by the feeling that someone or something, was watching her.

She listened, frozen in her bed, to the sounds of the night. Was someone on the catwalk that ran from her house to those beside her? Leaves brushed against each other, and branches snapped under the weight of something, or nothing, and left her heart flying to a new tension. Was it incidental or a warning?

Down in the valley, a dog barked and another answered. A pack of hunting dogs picked up the scent of a coon, or 'possum and treed him, and they bayed the exciting news across the valley. She remembered a night long ago when thundering hunting dogs had chased some poor creature until they were captured in the crawl space under the porch. The dogs yapped in an explosion of sound and the house rattled with their noise. Surely they would rip the poor creature to pieces. Bedroom doors opened, and everyone, bewildered by the noise, emerged from their bedrooms. Daddy had grabbed a walking stick and hammered on the floor with it until the frightened dogs ran away.

Beside her Lady growled, bringing Josephine back to the present. Was the dog being sensitive to Josephine's fear, or was she, too, startled by an intruder nearby? Josephine longed for dawn when trees would shed the dew they collected during the night, and sun would flood the valley once again with morning light.

What was she doing here, she wondered, self-doubt taking over. She shouldn't have gone square dancing with Angie and her friends. She had actually danced with a stranger. He held her so tightly she could feel the heat from his legs through his jeans. Surely that was a betrayal of Michael's trust in her.

How she wished tomorrow would come, bringing Michael and Josie with it. She missed them more than she dreamed possible. It had seemed so important for her to come to grips with herself. Maybe Michael was right. She only needed an attitude adjustment.

She curled up into a ball like a child. Exhaustion was taking over. As she began falling back to sleep, she remembered Davis was buying the house next door. He was coming home. Everything would start over again. He would spy on her, and she would be as helpless as a child. Had it already started?

Next morning Josephine woke with Lady barking and someone pounding on the front door. She grabbed her robe and stumbled into the living room, Lady at her heels.

Dutton Spikes, the caretaker who looked after her house, was standing on her front stoop. Lady nosed her way passed Josephine and quickly sniffed Dutton's leg. Then the dog proceeded to leap by Dutton, still barking, and rounded the corner of the house.

"Dutton, what are you doing here?" Josephine asked as she opened the door. She clutched her robe to her chest and tried to smooth down her wild hair. "Is something wrong?"

"Well now, 'ats jest what I was agonna ask you," he

answered removing his cap and scratching his head. "Heard you was up to Tammy and Tom's last night, and thought I'd best see if you was okay."

By mountain traditions a caretaker was not only responsible for a house but also the family who owned it. As soon as Dutton spoke, Josephine began moving through a series of emotions from brief amusement to discomfort and finally alarm. Had Dutton heard something about the man who flirted with her?

"How in the world did you know that?" she stammered.

"Word gets around," Dutton replied, nodding.

Her mood shifted to defensiveness. It wasn't any of Dutton's business. Still when she spoke, she tried to sound casual. "I went with Angie Dennison and some people she works with."

"There's some mean 'uns hangs out at Tammy and Tom's. My missus and me steers clear of 'em."

Josephine leaned her head against the door. Dutton was getting out of line now, and she was about to say so when Lady came running back around the house with something in her mouth.

"What's Lady got there?" Dutton tried to grab the dog as she ran by, but Lady veered away a safe distance and crouched down on her front paws, ready to spring again if Dutton moved.

"I'll get her," Josephine motioned to Dutton. She stepped barefooted out on the cold stone stoop and into the wet grass. "Come here, Lady," she called, patting her leg. "Give me that." Lady trotted to her mistress and dropped a slobbery object on the ground at Josephine's feet. It was a tan work glove. When she picked it up, she caught sight of a pack of cigarettes stuffed inside.

"Dutton, there're cigarettes inside. Winstons." She held the glove out for Dutton to see, and as they examined the items together, Josephine confessed she thought she heard someone outside her house last night. They agreed that Dutton should examine the catwalk and around the house.

When he returned, he was carrying two cigarette butts.

"Found 'em on the catwalk all right. Side by side. Ground out in the boards."

The catwalk was a plank and rail walk that ran from Wilderness Trail to Lover's Leap. It ran across the properties between those two points, Josephine's lot being one. Through the years, the owners of the lots the catwalk crossed had used them for quick access to their neighbors, or to Wilderness Trail and Lover's Leap

Staring down at the cigarette butts in Dutton's hand, Josephine bristled with alarm. Someone had been on the catwalk last night. She took the cigarette stubs from Dutton's outstretched hand and clenched them in her fist as if they held the secret of who had watched her and why.

After saying goodbye to Josephine, Dutton Spikes steered his truck up her driveway. The incline was steep, and when he reached the hairpin turn he had to shift into second to keep the truck's gears from slipping.

"Com'on baby," he muttered, pressing down on the gas and easing back on the clutch. No way he could afford an overhaul, he was thinking, let alone replace his clutch. While the truck inched forward, he held his breath. It felt as if the vehicle were going to break away and careen back down the mountain, crashing into Josephine's house.

Once he safely reached the top, he looked over his shoulder. He could see Josephine's gray shingle rooftop some sixty feet below. The house seemed to float in a sea of dark shadows and green leaves. To say the least, it looked isolated and vulnerable.

Through the years, even though this location had the best view on the mountain, development had favored the other end of Rocky Ridge. These nine houses, three on this ledge and six on the upper one, had become more and more isolated, a fact that troubled Dutton.

This morning Dutton was asking himself what a good-looking woman like Josephine was doing stuck out on the ledge by herself. Further, why was she, a wife and mother, at Tammy and Tom's last night with the locals? The information about the square dance had come straight to Dutton early this morning from his cousin Zeke. Nothing got passed Zeke. Summer residents never went to the square dance pavilion, which was known for attracting a wild crowd who liked to drink and party all night. He had been serious when he told Josephine she should stay away from them.

The troubling presence of the glove Lady found was another matter. He had played it down, but he was concerned. He failed to tell Josephine he found fresh boot marks on the catwalk. The marks had been clear despite last night's heavy dew, indicating someone had been there after the dew fell. He hadn't told her about the marks because he wanted to spare her. Now he was thinking she had a right to know, and he was feeling guilty for withholding this important piece of information. The truth was Dutton felt responsible for Josephine's safety. He needed to protect her, some way or other, just as he needed to repair her house, or get rid of a nasty varmint. Exactly how, he wasn't sure.

On top of his concern over a prowler, Dutton couldn't get a reading on where Michael fit into the picture. Josephine hadn't mentioned him, which seemed strange. Something was not quite right, and Dutton couldn't put his finger on what. Michael probably would be up on weekends, but why hadn't Josephine just told him so?

The distinct feeling Dutton had was that Josephine was alone and isolated and vulnerable. And, of course, all those notions struck a cord with Dutton because he could end up looking very good in her eyes—something he had waited for since he was eight years old, and his dad had dragged him over to meet her. After all the years in between, he could still remember the humiliation he had endured that first day. He had stood on the same cold, stone stoop, the one he had stood on this morning, his tweed wool hat in his hand, the hat he was so proud of until he found out mama bought it second-hand from the Women's Exchange. He could still feel the flush of shyness spread up his chest and neck when "Mr. Nate" said, "Wait a minute, I'll call Josephine." He was remembering his cowlicks and yellow teeth and elbows and thumbs that stuck out everywhere and how mama made him wear knickers that day. When he walked they sounded like running water, and his brogans squeaked if he shifted his weight.

And how Josephine had stepped out on the stoop in shorts and a shirt so white and clean they seemed to burn in the sunshine. Her hair hung in two orange braids—except for the bangs, which bunched out like fluffy clouds. Way back then, he had thought she was the prettiest thing he ever saw. He'd been so stupid. He'd actually thought he had a chance with her. Funny how life works out. Here she was on the mountain without her husband, and he was married with four kids and a pregnant wife. His dad and her dad were both dead, and he was the one left to look after her and her house.

He glanced at his watch and realized with irritation that he had taken too much time. It was going to make him late for work. He gunned his truck forward onto the road. All the same, he thought pulling away, it was going to be one hellava summer.

As he drove by the house next door to Josephine's, a young man was taking down a For Sale sign. Dutton waved and the young man, whose hands were both full, tilted his head back in a makeshift greeting. Except to note that the house had been sold, Dutton paid scant attention to the young man. In fact, he was already forgetting the man and Josephine and focusing on getting to work at Padgett State Park, where he was a park ranger. He glanced down at his trousers and noticed some dirt. Tromping around on the cat-walk had messed up his uniform, he grumbled, brushing away the dirt.

In the park Dutton was an authority figure. He was proud of his job, loved the olive green twill uniform he wore, and the cap with a real leather band around it. He liked for his uniform to be neat and crisp. Furthermore, contrary to what his daddy always said, he had finally found something at which he was good. Dutton knew the forests and trails, the lakes and trout ponds, the camping sites and picnic grounds—at least as much as anybody could know forty-two hundred acres. People respected him, too, especially park visitors, who stopped to listen attentively to what he had to say about the park and its animals.

Dutton drove into a deserted stretch of road nicknamed the "wilderness." Since he was a little boy, this section of road had frightened him. The heavy vegetation made the road dark and gloomy. There were no houses for a mile and a half. On the left side, solid rock stretched to the upper level, which made the road seem more narrow than it actually was. On Dutton's side the shoulder plunged straight down the mountain. Except for a dirt road called Wilderness Trail, which followed the contour of the mountain, the landscape was thick with underbrush and old forest growth.

Out of the corner of his eye, Dutton noticed a run-down red Camaro approaching him from the rear. The car began tailgating his bumper and bouncing up and down. After several moments, the driver darted into the left lane and zipped passed Dutton. Instinctively Dutton jerked the wheel to the right. The front wheels spun off the shoulder. Rock and gravel slid out from under his tires, and the backend of the truck fishtailed sharply. It was all he could do to hold the heavy truck on the road.

As the car passed, Dutton recognized the driver as the young man in the yard taking down the sign. Dutton stuck his head out the window and yelled at the man, "Sonofabitch." But the Camaro rounded the curve and was disappearing out of sight.

Damn fool! He passed on a blind curve, Dutton muttered to himself. The incident was over before he had time to be frightened, but now his heart raced and perspiration flooded his armpits. His uniform was getting spoiled. If another car had come from the other direction, all three cars would have plunged into the ravine.

What a way to start the day. Now he would have to face the park visitors with shattered nerves and a dirty uniform. That's what he got for trying to be neighborly. The young man repaid his kindness by almost running him off the road. Now he was shaken and old doubts that his dad had managed to hammer into him about his abilities were creeping back. Maybe helping Josephine wasn't such a good idea. It never paid to get too close to outsiders, even ones as pretty as Josephine.

In the distance Josephine heard shouting and a horn blowing, but she was going over the things she had to do before Michael and Josie arrived, and she took no particular notice of the noise. She wanted to go to the farmers market before the fresh vegetables and baked goods were gone. First, before the sun was too hot, she needed to cut flowers from the garden, and she had to straighten the house.

The morning air was chilly. She pulled on a sweater and retrieved the garden sheers from the closet by the front door. Armed with her clippers, she stepped out onto the stoop and into the grassed yard.

A stacked stone wall surrounded the garden. On the left, the wall rose thirty feet, providing the foundation for the parking area above. Stone steps led down from the parking level, and larger stepping stones ran across the grassed area to the front stoop. Flowerbeds bordered the wall.

The garden reminded Josephine of an English garden. It was charming, and despite two years of neglect, the small beds gave a quaint, intimate feeling to the space. White and blue Dutch iris bloomed together in the bed on the right. Rugosa roses cascaded with ivy from the parking area above. More rugosa roses bloomed at the end of the garden near a birdbath. Josephine loved their color, soft magenta, a color she had never seen in any other rose. Her mother had told her the bushes were planted in 1920 when the house was built. Somehow they had survived each cold winter since.

A picket gate, flanked by stone columns, was located in the right wall. More stone steps led through the gate and down to the lower level of the house and its unused rooms. Beyond the steps and down the mountain, the land was over-grown with weeds and gigantic hydrangeas and rhododen-drons. The shrubs were swollen with bright green and hot pink buds.

Josephine spread a newspaper on the ground to collect the flowers. As she cut, she imagined how the garden could look. On the right, mountain phlox was about to bloom, but there were several open spots where annuals could be added for a splash of color. Also the stone wall would make a strik-ing background for brightly colored dahlias like the ones her mother used to plant there.

A sound from the house next door startled her. She was so accustomed to having the house empty that the thought of someone there was surprising. She rose to look and saw a man, not more than forty feet away, emerge through the basement door. He was intent on negotiating the door while juggling a shotgun and a shoebox, and he seemed unaware anyone was watching him.

Josephine was more curious than concerned, even when she noticed the gun. Since he was carrying a box, she assumed he was about to clean the gun. Still, when he stepped away from the house, the terrain sloped sharply, and he seemed so unsteady on his feet that she felt sure he would slip, accidentally discharging the gun. After looking around a moment, he worked his way to a level place where he set down the gun and box. Then he returned to the house, retrieved a folding chair and dragged it to the spot he had selected. He unfolded the chair, secured it and sat down.

Josephine inched forward to see if she recognized the man. Maybe he was a workman but he seemed too frail for that. Regardless of why he was there, it seemed strange that he was cleaning a gun.

Spellbound, Josephine watched as the man lifted up the gun and lay it across his lap. Then he selected a rod, which she had not noticed. Next, he tore a small square off of a rag, dipped it in a can of oil and threaded the rag into the end of the rod as if it were a needle. Once the rag was secure, he inserted the rod in the barrel of the gun and pushed it up and down in the gun.

Watching, Josephine sensed a familiarity about him. His long arms and legs, the shoulder slope, the way his head pitched slightly, the razor-like edge of his chin. A memory flashed through her mind. The dream she had before coming to the mountains. At first she was in a pool, and someone on the side repeatedly pushed her head under water each time she surfaced. The dream became more terrifying when the person she thought was herself turned into Josie, and the other person turned out to be Davis.

Now, concealed by the rose bushes, she watched the man next door in shock. She studied his lanky frame sitting on the chair cleaning the rifle. She imagined him sitting at the edge of the swimming pool just as the person in the dream had done. She visualized his hands pressing the top of her head. Shocking as the idea was, Josephine realized she was watching Davis, her cousin, who had been in an insane asylum most of his adult life. Angie had been right. He had bought the house next door.

Josephine grabbed her flowers, bunched them in the newspapers, and ran inside her house. Once the door was closed, she pressed her back against the cold glass panes of the front door. *What if he had seen her!* Her heart was pounding. She was acting silly, she kept telling herself. She had to act like an adult.

When she could catch her breath, she twisted the rusty skeleton key in the front door lock and slid the extra deadbolt in place. Then one by one she moved to each window, pulling down the umber shades against the growing sunlight, shutting out the remains of the puzzling scene she had just viewed.

Her flowers lay abandoned in a pile on the easy chair by the front door.

She sat in her living room scarcely breathing, watching shapes form and disappear behind the amber window shades. After a time, she managed to drink several shaky cups of coffee and talked with Angie on the phone. Every time she let her mind wander memories connected to Davis at various periods throughout their childhood floated like a dream into her mind. The shotgun episode, maybe the very one she saw him cleaning. Uncle Jack's heart attack, which Davis witnessed. The woman he married but never brought home. The unanswered questions about why he was committed to an insane asylum so young, and why he was being released now after all these years.

After a warm shower, she coaxed herself into her clothes and began to feel better. It was useless to worry about it, she told herself. *Finally* she managed to organize herself, retrieve the flowers she had cut and collect Lady. Soon she was heading for the Farmers Market.

When Josephine pulled into an open field that served as a parking lot for the Farmers Market, the lot was beginning to fill and groups of people were walking toward the open-air market. She found an empty parking place and pulled in. Lady had settled down in the back of the wagon and was watching the scenes outside the car. The field had been recently mowed, and a heavy thatch of grass was spread across the lot.

As Josephine drove in, a young man jumped out of the car on her left and ran around to the passenger's side to let out a young woman. The man was dressed in jeans and a sweatshirt, and as he ran, he drew his hand through his hair to brush it off his forehead. But as soon as he withdrew his hand, the hair fell back, giving him a boyish look.

Josephine stayed in her car to give the couple enough room to get out. They seemed to be in no hurry. The two cars were close, and she could hear them laughing, but they were oblivious to her.

The young man drew the girl's hand to him and kissed it. Then he pulled her out of the car and wrapped one arm around her and lifted her chin with the other to kiss her lightly on the lips. Finally, he steered her away from the car, his right arm sliding around the back of her waist and coming to rest comfortably on her hip.

Their moves were so intimate that Josephine felt like an intruder. As they walked away, she could hear the muffled hum of their words. Their faces were so close they were almost touching.

Her thoughts veered away from Davis and her troubling morning and went to Michael. How long had it been since he had touched her like that? She thought back to the first years of their marriage. The delight she had felt each time Michael came through the door. When he touched her, the thrill that rippled through her. The deep ache that stirred. She had actually believed they were the only two people who could experience the bliss of knowing the delicious secrets of dissolving completely into each other.

Annoyed with herself for having such thoughts, she collected her pocketbook, adjusted the windows for Lady and locked the car.

Farmers from all over the mountain brought homegrown produce to the market. They set up their goods in bins, or stalls, in an open-air pavilion. The stalls were lined up back to back down the center of the structure. A couple of breaks in the line of bins provided lanes to both sides.

Josephine went straight to the far end where baked goods were sold. In this section tables with checked tablecloths were covered with pies, cakes, cookies, candy, loaves of bread, jellies, jams and pickles. Delicious smells rose from the tables. They seemed refined next to the heady smell of fresh-cut grass, which covered the ground.

As Josephine moved from table to table, women greeted her, urging her to taste their samples and buy their goods. She tasted a pecan pie, but she knew what she wanted. Michael's favorite—strawberry pie. Plus two loaves of sourdough bread, red plum jelly for breakfast, another favorite of Michael's, and oatmeal cookies for Josie.

She found the baked goods she wanted and was headed toward the vegetable bins when she saw T.J. Butts coming from the other direction. She quickened her steps to avoid him. Her morning had been unsettling enough without seeing him, she thought. Maybe she could miss him if she hurried. Before she could get out of the pavilion, she heard him call.

"Hey, pretty lady," he yelled. "Where you going?" He quickened his pace.

"I'm just leaving," she called over her shoulder. He was already at her elbow. She shifted her packages in front of her, but he reached out to help her with them. She pulled back from him. "Look," she said, dropping her eyes, "I'm married. I have a five-year-old daughter."

There was a long pause. Then he laughed, "Hey, I won't tell if you don't."

"No, you don't understand." She shook her head, her eyes still on the ground. "I shouldn't have gone with Angie square dancing. I'm not available." She looked up at him. His eyes were two intense grayish green ovals, which seemed to be bottomless, and his hair was tussled in the casual way she liked, just like the young man's in the parking lot. She could feel her body quicken, her pulse, her heart, even a warm feeling in the pit of her stomach. She tried to ignore her feelings and will her body to behave. *Don't feel anything,* she was saying to herself. *Don't react.*

"Just friends." He put his hands up as if she held a gun on him. "Promise."

Then he reached in her arms—more gently this time—and took the packages from her. "Let's get a peach basket for these." And he led her back the way she had come. "By the way, I don't know your last name."

"It's Scarborough, Josephine." It sounded hollow to her, as if something—*wood maybe*—were striking tin.

He picked up a peach basket and carefully laid the baked goods in it. They began strolling through bins of vegetable, Josephine making selections as they went. From time to time he would half sing, half hum a song, imitating the Shirelles. *Josephine—Jo-se-ph-i-ne, prettiest girl I have seen."* When he hit "ever seen" he crescendoed and twirled the basket around. In no time she was laughing, not thinking, or caring, what might happen to the strawberry pie.

"Like barbecue?" he asked her casually. She nodded. "Best in the world. Right over here. Sourdough rolls and slaw." He steered her over to a picnic area where an open grill was smoldering. A rotund man with stained white apron and a chef's cap jammed on his head was chopping barbecue. Beside him, two assistants were heaping mounds of the pork on plates and passing it to the people in line, who moved down to help themselves to rolls and slaw.

When Josephine and T.J. had filled their plates, they slid into a bench at a picnic table. People began stopping by to say hello to T.J. He attracts them, Josephine observed. Each time he introduced her it sounded as if he were saying her name for the first time, as if it were a delightful surprise to him.

Despite all the warnings she was issuing to herself and the reprimands she was repeating in her head, she could not stop her mounting attraction to him. His subtle messages were flattering. She moved away from him a little, distancing herself as if an accidental brush of their hands, or arms, might be dangerous. He didn't seem to notice and continued chatting comfortably.

When they finished eating, he picked up her vegetables, and she took the peach basket, and they walked together to her car. When she unlocked the car door to set the basket on the floorboard, Lady began to growl.

"What's the matter, Lady?" Josephine asked the dog, reaching back to give her a reassuring pat. But the pat had the wrong effect on the dog. Lady lunged over the seat toward T.J. but couldn't squeeze past Josephine. T.J. moved back from the car, but Lady kept advancing, barking ferociously and curling her upper lip back in a way Josephine had never seen.

Just as the dog was about to leap out of the car, Josephine grabbed her collar. It took all her strength to restrain the dog.

"No, Lady," Josephine ordered sternly. Again, the sound of Josephine's voice seem to urge Lady on, and she thrashed and struggled trying to break free and go after T.J.

"Back, Lady," Josephine commanded again. "I've never seen her go after anybody. I'm sorry," Josephine said to T.J., trying to turn toward him. "I can't imagine what's gotten into her." The dog began settling down.

T.J. shrugged. "Can't blame her for trying to protect her mistress," he said with a smile.

"She didn't bite you, did she?" Josephine asked apologetically.

"Naw, don't worry about it."

"The sandwich was delicious." She started to reach out to shake his hand but pulled back. "Guess I'd better not shake your hand. Lady would probably start up again, but I do thank you."

"My pleasure." He moved back, and as much as the grass would allow, he clicked his cowboy boots together and turned to leave, shoving his hands in his jeans pockets and walking away. Lady growled again as he was leaving.

Josephine walked to the driver's side of the car and opened the door.

"What in the world was *that* about, Lady?" The dog took Josephine's words as praise and began licking her mistress's hand. Josephine pulled her hand away and settled into the driver's seat.

She turned the car around. As she was pulling away, she glanced in her rear view mirror. T.J. was standing in the parking lot, talking to a man. The man shook his fist at T.J.

and ended by shoving his shoulder. T.J. lowered his head and raised his open hand to the man, keeping his head down.

Josephine thought T.J.'s message was clear. If the man shoved T.J. one more time, T.J. was going to level him. He didn't seem like the type to get shoved around.

CHAPTER NINE

Davis's problems started the moment he stepped into the living room of his new house on Valley View Trail and saw the expansive view of the Blue Ridge Mountains. It was overwhelming. With absolute certainty he knew the great hulk of mountain in front of him, framed by the picture windows that ran across the front of the house, had the capacity to suck him straight through the glass and launch him into the valley like a missile.

The early sun was part of the problem. It came from the rear of the house, splashed over the rooftop, and flooded the valley with shattering light. Davis was forced to squint, narrowing his eyes into a thin line, to protect himself from the pure power of the sun.

He and Blackie had arrived that morning. Blackie had gone to the hardware for light bulbs, a suggestion from the realtor since the house had been empty so long.

As soon as Blackie left, Davis rushed to close the living room curtains.

Of course, he didn't tell Blackie the mountains and sun were more than he could handle. He could not allow Blackie to see craziness seeping back over him. He was proud of the way he had gotten through his parents' death. The funeral itself had proceeded without incident. Doc Bostwick had complimented him on his control. So had the High Meadows staff members who attended.

He had come too far to allow paranoia over the mountain to ruin everything.

Back in April when his mother first had the notion he should leave High Meadows, she had suggested this house. Davis would feel *comfortable* there, she had said at the time as she ticked off the reasons. He had grown up on this mountain. His grandfather had owned the house. His uncle, the one next door. Relatives still lived close by.

His mother had arranged an appointment with Mr. Jarrard, and he had looked at the house but never followed through. Actually, he hoped his mother would forget her silly plan and he could stay on in the secure isolation of High Meadows. He *hoped*, that is, until his parents died, and Eula Mae had made him take stock of his situation.

Of course he remembered the house had a view, but that day last spring when he and Mr. Jarrard came, everything was blocked by fog. How could he guess the view would give him vertigo? Even so, the house in Rocky Ridge was clearly his best choice. Now that the living room curtains were closed, the room was flooded with warm, umber shadows. His mother had been right. He *was* comfortable, at least with the curtains closed.

Arrangements had been made easily. He had called the realtor to see if the house was still available. Papers were signed, and a check was delivered. Final paper work was completed and the house was his. At least on paper.

Given the warm shadows, the reassurances of his mother, and his other alternatives, there was one additional point that swayed him. This spit of land, running from Wilderness Trail to the end of Lovers' Leap, was considered sacred Indian ground. Local historians claimed this ledge was used as a lookout for the entire valley. Indian chiefs and medicine men held ceremonies at Lovers' Leap to receive wisdom to lead their tribes.

As a child, although his blond hair and blue eyes betrayed

his dreams, Davis had fantasized he was part Indian. His love of the mountains. The virgin forests. The soft green moss he loved to lie on and the black, raw dirt where grubs and worms moved through life cycles. All these things gave him a kinship with civilizations that lived in harmony with nature.

Now, he couldn't wait to get back to the woods. He wanted to feel the rugged terrain under his feet, see the trees speckled with sunshine, smell the rich odor of pines, hear the birds twittering the arrival of an outsider. He scribbled a note telling Blackie where he was and left the houses through the basement door.

The hill was steep. The incline looked gradual, but the minute he started down the hill, he realized he had to move from tree to tree to keep from plummeting down the hill. At length he ran across a gravel road, Wilderness Trail, he vaguely remembered. The road cut across his property and that of the two houses next door.

He followed the road through a hairpin curve and came upon a hog pen. The stench was awful. It reminded him of Korea. On the edge of every village had been a hog pen where villagers tossed their daily scraps for feed. When the hogs were big enough to slaughter, everyone shared the meat. The memory sickened him and he rushed passed, covering his nose, and wondering if the animals would cause him problems.

The road turned right at the hog pen and he continued following it until it dissolved into a creek bed. If his memory was right, the creek fed into Wilderness Falls and flowed all the way down the mountain to the Boone River. He continued making his way toward the northwest where the mountain received the most severe weather.

He traveled for some time in the flat creek bed and at length reached what appeared to be the point of the mountain. There the land turned sharply to the right.

The terrain changed dramatically. To the right was a solid rock cliff, which he judged was the base of Lover's Leap. In front of him were stunted pines shrubs. On the far left, a lush bog. The house he had just purchased was above and slightly east of where he was standing.

He stepped forward cautiously, looking around. The land seemed stuck in time as if the world had passed it by. The smelly hog pen. The stunted pines. The soggy terrain—all were reminiscent of Korea.

He had come to the mountains for solace. Were they going to be constant reminders of Korea?

Korea
15 September, 1950

They had landed in Korea at Inchon Harbor as the right flank of a three-prong attack.

Harbor was a misnomer. There was no beach, only mud flats at low tide. When the customary thirty-foot tide roared in, the water crashed with thundering force into a solid stone seawall, making landing on the beach almost impossible. Peak tide was required to allow time to offload troops and equipment from the convoy to amphibious troop carriers.

For two days before the landing, as a diversionary tactic, the Navy mercilessly shelled the island of Wolmi-do. In addition the ships in the convoy blasted the harbor so steadily that a fog of gunpowder floated between the convoy and the target. When the Marines finally traversed the mud flats, scaled the wall with ladders brought in for that purpose and secured the wall, they had met little resistance. The real fighting took place in the town of Inchon and the surrounding countryside. By the time they had obtained their objective, they were exhausted to the last man.

After Inchon, the Marines advanced toward Seoul on the Inchon-Seoul Road. They encountered heavy resistance from the North Korean Peoples Army; and by the time they reached Seoul four days later, they were experienced and battle tough.

When Seoul was secured, the next large objective was Wonsan, a port on the east coast, north of the 38th Parallel. Rumors were circulating through the troops that Red Chinese were crossing the Yalu River to join North Korean soldiers.

For Davis, Mace and the soldiers in their company, the Red Chinese seemed too far away to worry about. The enemies at hand were a greater threat. Everytime the U.N. and Republic of South Korean forces secured a position, North Korean soldiers would slip behind their lines and retake it. The Americans were learning the hard way that except for the uniform, one Korean looked like another, and sometimes innocent-looking civilians held grenades behind their backs.

One September day, Mace and Davis were on a patrol with their squad. They were ordered to sweep an area ten miles southwest of Seoul to make sure no enemy stragglers were hiding in the woods. Sgt. Wilbur was their squad leader. They were divided seven and seven in two columns with bazooka teams in the middle. Mace and Davis were scouts, out it front of the column. The back-up column was 100 yards behind.

Mace and Davis traveled about fifteen minutes with their rifles drawn without seeing or hearing anything. Suddenly gunfire erupted and bullets sprayed everywhere.

"Hit the deck!" Sgt. Wilbur shouted. Everyone fell to the ground and crawled on their bellies for the best cover they could find. Davis and Mace dove into a low bunker and slid to the bottom. The bunker was mounded in front to a height of about three feet but dropped in back.

"How many you think there are?" Mace whispered.

"I think we're surrounded," Davis said. "Keep your head down 'til we know."

Mace positioned his rifle on the edge of the bunker. "Guess nobody was hit. I didn't hear 'em yell." After a pause, he added, "What's the plan?"

"Lay low and wait."

The woods were quiet. Davis's muscles were cramping. He looked toward Mace and whispered to him. "I think the shots came from dead ahead. We're pinned down and these scrawny pines are no cover. I'm gonna crawl to the edge of the bunker to see if I can tell where everybody is."

Davis pulled himself up by his elbows and slid to the right edge of the bunker, slowly raising his head. Immediately gunfire erupted and exploded in the dirt around them. Davis ducked back into the bunker about the time he heard the twang of a bullet striking metal. He jerked around to check on Mace, who was sprawled against the backside of the bunker. His arms were flung across the dirt as if he were sleeping.

Davis crawled over to Mace, grabbing his arm. "I told you to keep your head down, Mace, god damn it! You didn't get hit, did you?" He shook his friend's arm. "How're we gonna get you out if you're wounded, you dumb Marine!"

Davis leaned over his friend, pulling his arms to a more natural position. "Answer me," he urged with irritation. "Where you hit?"

A small dent showed on the front of Mace's helmet, but there was no sign of a wound. When Davis saw the size of the hole, he sighed with relief. The helmet must have deflected the bullet, and Mace was simply knocked out. He shook him again. This time his friend slid further down in the bunker, causing his helmet to roll off. Behind the helmet was a small, neat bullet hole in the middle of Mace's forehead.

At first, Davis couldn't put it together. The dent in the helmet. The hole in his forehead. The lack of blood. What was going on? He pressed his ear to his friend's chest. The warmth from Mace's body spread across his ear, but there was no thump. Still he clung to the hope that Mace had only passed out.

He slipped his hand over the artery in Mace's neck the way he had seen in the movies. Nothing. But when he checked the back of Mace's head, he discovered a collection of crimson liquid. Slowly his mind began tracking the bullet through Mace's helmet, into his skull, until it exploded out the back. He began to shake.

"No, Mace. No," he whispered. "I told you not to die."

Not a sound could be heard. No rustles of birds or insects in flight.

Panic crept over him. Slowly, he understood. Wilbur and the others were dead. All of them. Otherwise he would have heard from them. He alone was left, and he was surrounded by North Koreans.

He had not fired a shot. No one in his squad had. Yet Mace, *his best friend, his only friend, was dead!* Instinct told him to jump from the bunker and run. *Let the bastards kill him, too. Then it would all be over!* Another part of him wanted to lie down beside Mace and accept whatever happened. Still another part, and the most convincing, wanted to kill whoever fired the gun that killed Mace.

Davis had to think, to sort things out. When the patrol started out, it had a mission. If he were the only one left, he had to carry it out. They were to kill, or capture, stragglers. Otherwise, Mace would have died for nothing. He had to come up with a plan.

First, Davis removed the I.D. tag from around Mace's neck and stuffed it in his fatigue pocket. Then he eased himself out of the bunker, expecting any second another round of bullets. Nothing. Then, he crawled toward the scrub pines. Nothing.

Once in the pines, he positioned himself in the center of the trees. When he felt safe, he cut off a few pine branches and stuffed them for camouflage into the netting on his helmet.

When he was ready, he began crawling in the direction of the gunfire. A hundred feet from the bunker where Davis and Mace had landed, Davis spotted a single North Korean soldier manning a foxhole. *Were there others?* It didn't matter. Whatever else happened, this one was his.

He planned to attack from the rear, which meant he had to distract the soldier. He collected rocks and dirt clods and piled them by his knee. Then he watched and waited.

The soldier was less than twenty-five feet away. He was

dressed in the ordinary green fatigues of any soldier. When he moved his head, his straight black hair swirled around his head like a coolie hat. In his hands was an automatic weapon. Davis knew he was so nervous he would fire at any sound.

Davis picked up a rock and lobbed it over the solider's head. It landed with a thud about ten feet beyond the nest. The soldier swung his weapon toward the sound and fired. Bullets exploded into the woods.

Davis continued throwing rocks. While the North Korean's back was turned, he sprinted toward the foxhole. His knife was grasped in his right fist, unsheathed and ready. The blade flashed in the late-day sun.

Davis was out of breath, but he managed to drop into the foxhole before the soldier realized what was happening. Davis's arms brushed against the man's back. The sudden contact with his enemy was disarming. Still, he thrust his hand tight under the soldier's chin, realizing it was far too late to change his plan now. He forced the soldier's head back against his own chest, where he held it until he drew the knife across his neck. The soldier screamed and twisted trying to squirm out of Davis' grip. But the soldier was small and no match for Davis, who held the man in place until his jerking and twisting stopped.

When the man was motionless, Davis dropped him. Davis's hands were covered with blood. He shook it off, splattering drops across the foxhole. He tried to wipe the rest off on the back of the soldier's fatigues. But as he did, the head rolled back, revealing his face. He was a kid! He didn't even have a beard! Davis drew back in horror. *He had killed a boy,* no more than eighteen, and maybe younger! The soldier should be vicious and mean. But he wasn't. Then he remembered this "boy" had killed Mace. And he had paid with his life.

Davis fell back against the foxhole. There was no thought in his head, nothing that called him to action. And he remained motionless—he didn't know how long—until he heard a weak cry, "Semper Fi." Then another followed,

"Semper Fi." And he whispered, "Semper Fi" and crawled out of the foxhole and began walking toward his comrades.

There were no other North Koreans in the woods. Only the one machine-gunner who killed Mace. Now he was dead.

Scully came running to meet Davis. "You got the son of a bitch. He had us pinned down. Christ, if you hadn't taken him out, I don't know what the hell we'd a done."

"One of you would have charged him. Where's Sarge?"

"Down."

"Dead?"

"Wounded."

Sgt. Wilbur was shot in the leg. The corpsman bound the wound and radioed for an ambulance to meet them on the road. Two soldiers carried Wilbur, firemen's carry, off the field. Davis carried Mace out over his shoulder.

When they were loading Sgt. Wilbur in the ambulance, he motioned for Davis and Scully to lean over so he could talk to them.

"Good job, Williams. You saved us. I'm recommending you for a bronze star. You're a witness, Scully. "

"Not Mace, Sarge."

"No, not Mace," Wilbur said, reaching out for Davis's arm and squeezing it. "But I'll recommend him for a posthumous purple heart, for whatever that's worth."

Mace was going home in a pine box with a purple heart, Davis thought.

He couldn't think straight. Thoughts swirled in his head. Why was a kid fighting a man's war? And the automatic weapon he had used. It was deadly accurate at 100 yards. Chances were either he or Mace would get it because they were in front. Why had it been Mace? It could just as easily been Davis. None of it made sense.

"It's not worth shit, Sarge," Davis muttered under his breath. "Not the bronze star or the purple heart. But Sgt. Wilbur never heard him. He had already been loaded into an ambulance and was speeding toward a triage center.

CHAPTER TEN

It was six o'clock and Josie and Michael had not arrived in Rocky Ridge. Josephine, on the verge of falling asleep on the couch, got up for a drink of water. They should be here by now, she thought, concern mounting. Michael had said he would leave by three. Too agitated to sit, she began pacing the length of the small living room. The evening news blared out, unnoticed, over the TV.

The afternoon had seemed an eternity. After she returned from the farmers market, she began cooking dinner. All the puzzling events of her morning kept running through her mind. The results were that she attempted to rationalize about all of them.

How could she possibly have been bold enough to have lunch with T.J.? What if someone had seen them and told Michael? "Friends" was what he had said. "Just friends." But Josephine didn't feel like a friend. She felt flattered by his attention. Even attracted to him in a strange way. But she *wanted* Michael. She wanted to rekindle the intimacy they had in the past, the same emotions she had seen in the young couple at the farmer's market. That's why she had spent the afternoon carefully planning and cooking their dinner. Even the Chardonnay, cooling in the fridge, was a favorite. That's why she had showered with extra care, splashing on Michael's favorite perfume and putting on her new linen slacks and shirt. He should fall in love with her again the moment he saw her. Everything had to be *perfect!*

And then there was Davis. It seemed an impossible twist of fate for him to move next door to her, but nobody ever said fate was fair. She would have to tell Michael about Davis this weekend. Of course he would insist she bring Josie home, which presented still another problem. The *last* thing Josephine wanted to do was put either of them in danger, but she had made up her mind to stay in the mountains all summer. She wasn't going to cave in because of Davis. She would tell Michael the entire story, but she would have to convince him that she could handle Davis. Something she herself knew was questionable.

Josephine had decided something else. Disturbing as Davis's presence and T.J.'s attentions were, discovering the glove was more alarming. She could think of *no* logical reason why anyone would be spying on her last night. It had to be Davis. There was no other explanation. He had found out that she owned the house, and he had come to—she didn't know what. But it certainly was not reassuring that she had caught him cleaning his shotgun. She definitely would *not* tell Michael that. Dutton could find out who had been on the catwalk last night. In the meantime the glove was safely hidden in the back hall closet behind the water heater, out of view of anyone who happened to open the door.

The last traces of sunlight had slipped behind the mountains when Josephine heard Michael's car enter the driveway. She ran out the front door and hurried up the steps. The car stopped, and Josie threw open the door, running to her mother.

Josephine lifted her daughter and pulled her to her chest. Her spicy smells, the tight grip of her arms around Josephine's neck, the spindly legs brushing Josephine's thighs were overwhelming. Josie was growing up too fast. She wished she hadn't left her at Aunt Ruth's so easily.

"You've grown in only four days!"

Josie squirmed to get down. "Mommy, somebody got kill-did in this big fire!" She stretched her arms out.

"I know," soothed Josephine. "Aunt Ruth was very upset. She told me. Who did you stay with when she went to the funeral?" Josephine had leaned down to talk to Josie, but she was watching Michael out of the corner of her eye.

"My new friend, Deel-yah," Josie was saying. "Aunt Ruth said I was a very brave girl." Josephine patted Josie on the head. Then she walked around the back of the car toward Michael.

"I've missed you," she said to him. She slid her hands up his forearms to put her arms around his neck, but Michael firmly grasped her arms and took a step back from her. "Me too," he answered, kissing her lightly on the lips.

"That is a totally unsatisfactory kiss," she said, shaking her finger at him, "and I want you to know you can't get away with it!"

He laughed, "Later. Lemme unload the car now, okay?"

She followed him to the back of the car without answering and grabbed some packages from the trunk. "I've cooked your favorite dinner, even strawberry pie."

"We ate at Hardee's. I was later than I expected. Josie was hungry." He threw a duffel bag over his shoulder and picked up his suit pack.

"Michael, you didn't." Josephine was shocked at his thoughtlessness. Surely he would know she would cook a nice meal for them. "I've been cooking all afternoon!"

"Sorry," he answered, shrugging as he headed down the stone stairs to the house. Josephine stared at his back with a sinking feeling. He might as well have hit her with his duffel bag. All her plans, all the efforts, had gone for nothing.

Later, when Josephine was settling Josie into her bedroom, she heard Michael in the kitchen.

"Some Chardonnay in the fridge," she called out to him.

"Think I'll stick with scotch," he answered back.

Josie was putting her doll on the bed. "This is your room, Pippi," she said. "You be a good girl, and tomorrow we'll have a tea party in the garden."

"I like that idea," Josephine smiled at her daughter, sliding a stack of clothes into the dresser. "You have a bath this morning?" Josie nodded. She had that "let's see if we can slip this one by Mommy" look, but Josephine let it go, thinking how nice it would be to have some time alone with Michael.

They found Josie's pajamas, and after she had put them on, Josie went into the living room to watch TV. In seconds she tiptoed back into the bedroom and motioned to her mom. "Sssh. Daddy's asleep!"

Josephine laughed softly. So much for tonight, she thought, reaching out to hug her daughter once again. At least her family was together again.

Josephine awoke the next morning to the smell of coffee brewing. She stumbled into the kitchen, where Michael was whipping up pancake batter. "Good grief!" she muttered, tousling her hair. "How did I sleep through all this?" The morning newspaper was on the counter, and he even had orange juice poured and waiting.

"Umm." Michael put down his mixing spoon and went to her, slipping his arms around her waist. "I love you in the morning when you're a mess."

"I was wondering when you'd notice me. Remember how we used to make a bee-line for the first place we could make love when we'd been separated?" She touched his face with the palm of her hand.

"B.J." he answered. "Before Josie."

He was kissing her when Josie padded into the room. She ran to them and threw her arms around their legs. "Me, too!" she cried.

Michael stooped down and picked her up. "Okay," he said. "On the count of three. Everybody hug. One, two, three." Lady, attracted by the noise, padded in the kitchen and began barking.

"Lady wants a hug," squealed Josie. She climbed down and threw her arms around Lady's neck and the two of them wandered into the living room. Michael and Josephine put the remains of breakfast together.

When they finished eating, Michael was reading his newspaper, and Josephine was having her last cup of coffee.

"Aries. Beware of a tall dark stranger." Michael loved to read Josephine's horoscope to her, especially when it fit.

"*Tall dark stranger*, umm," Josephine answered. "Can't be Angie. She's short and redheaded. Must be Lady. I've been hanging out with the two of them lately."

"Well, whoever he is, beware of him," Michael said, putting down the paper.

Josephine quickly changed the subject as if Michael might read her mind and see a tall stranger. "Want to go to Padgett State Park for a picnic today? I can make use of all that fried chicken we didn't eat last night."

"Sure." Michael called into the living room. "Josie, let's ride the boats at Padgett Park, okay?"

"Boat rides! Oh, boy," Josie was jumping up and down. "Pippi, you're gonna love this."

The day was full of promise, or so it seemed to Josephine. They hiked with Josie bouncing along on her father's shoulders. They locked Lady safely in the car and rented a boat. Afterward, they retrieved Lady and spread their blanket out in the sunshine and ate fried chicken and potato salad until they were warm and sleepy. And then they dozed in the sun.

Josephine was so relaxed and happy. If it could just go on forever.

That night, all together including Lady, they watched the sun go down and the stars come out. They ate a late dinner of homegrown tomato sandwiches slathered with mayonnaise on sourdough bread. The two of them polished off the bottle of Chardonnay.

When Josie had been tucked in, they crawled in their own bed and made love—long and slow and deep, so powerful that tears streamed down Josephine's face. She fell asleep against Michael, his arms wrapped around her, her head buried in the curve of his chest, his smells surrounding her and slipping into her dreams.

All night long the same theme played in her mind—over and over. *If it could just go on forever.*

The next morning the lavender edge of first morning light lulled her back to sleep, a sleep full of confused dreams. Sometime later, she awoke with Josie shaking her shoulder.

"Mommy, *please* wake up. Daddy's leaving!" Her daughter was close to tears.

When Josephine opened her eyes, the sun was already up and blaring through the shades. Josephine didn't like to sleep this late. It made her sluggish and irritable.

"What's going on?" she asked her daughter. "Why didn't you wake me?"

"Daddy said to let you sleep." Josie was whining. "Hurry, Mommy, he's going away."

Josephine grabbed a bathrobe. "Stay here, Josie," she said, pushing through the screen door and dashing barefoot up the steps. Michael was opening the trunk. She called to him, "Michael, what the samhill's going on?"

"I couldn't sleep last night. Tomorrow I start a special project for the Bank. Mergers and acquisitions. I've got tons of paper work to do before then." He shrugged his shoulders. "And the house. It's a mess."

She slumped against the car, breathless from the dash up the steps. Would they have to move, she thought with alarm? So often in the Bank, new projects meant moving to a new city. "What mergers and acquisitions?" A worrisome gnat burrowed into her hair and its buzzing echoed in her head.

Michael emerged from the trunk and walked passed Josephine to the front of the car. He said as he opened the door, "I've been asked to look into banks that might be merger or buy-out opportunities." Josephine's stomach tightened. Michael continued, "We want to be ready when statewide banking comes."

"By the way," he added, slamming the door, "it'll help out with the finances. I get a raise."

"And you're just now telling me this? Terrific," she said sarcastically. "I thought we'd have all day to talk and, well, be together." She folded her arms. "I mean, I'm glad about the project and the raise, but I was counting on today."

He came to her and picked up one of her hands as if he might say something, but after he examined it for a moment, he let it drop. Then he moved passed her and stuck his head in the passenger side of the car and began removing trash.

"I need to talk to you," Josephine said. She had rushed her words, and he pulled his head back out of the car when she was finished. "What?" he asked.

"Someone I know has bought the house next door. Aunt Ruth's nephew, Davis Williams. His grandfather owned that house, and Aunt Ruth's husband owned this one. Daddy bought ours from the estate after Uncle Jack died." He was staring at her with a puzzled look on his face. "He's not my cousin—it's the other side of the family—but we were thrown together growing up. But I never liked him."

Michael interjected impatiently, "So, what's the big deal?"

"He's been in a state insane asylum for the last sixteen years. Recently he was discharged, and he's bought that house! It is so ridiculous. He was supposed to be committed for life." She stopped short of telling about Davis's history.

"People do get cured, you know." Michael sounded condescending.

"Remember a long time ago when you asked me about the scar on my shoulder?" He nodded. "I told you somebody shot me." She tugged hurriedly at the collar of her pajama top, pulling back the neckline to reveal a small scar. "He was the one. I was only seven years old. Right here." She touched the mark on her shoulder blade. Michael ignored her display, and she let the collar fall back in place. "After he shot me," she continued, "he ran away. My aunt and the maid, Eula Mae, took me to the hospital. They removed the bullet, but I had to spend the night. I woke in the middle of the night. He was standing over me. I thought he was going to kill me, but he just started crying." She dropped her head. "He ended up in a school for emotional disturbed teenagers."

"Look. If you're concerned, just leave," Michael said evenly. "I never understood why you wanted to come up here anyway."

"Michael, you know this is important to me. I'm not going to allow Davis or anybody else to chase me away from my own house," she said angrily.

"Your house? What about our house in Matthews? You just walked off like you didn't have any responsibility."

"Michael, didn't you read all the stuff I left on the kitchen table? It lays out everything that happens in the house. I have lined up people to do *everything*! All you have to do is make the bed."

"I said I've been busy." His hair fell over his forehead.

She had turned around and resolutely pressed her back against the car. "Well, I've made up my mind to stay all summer. This is the right place for Josie and me at the moment."

He ran his finger over the stubble on his chin, making a grating sound. "You know the other night when I arrived? You were so complete. I didn't seem to belong. Maybe this is perfect for you, but there's nothing here for me."

Josephine felt a stab of fear. Their arguments always reached this point where Michael implied he would leave. Each time it panicked her. What would she do? How could she take care of Josie? She couldn't even take care of herself.

She lowered her voice. "You scare me when you talk like that. I don't know what you're thinking. We're here, Josie and I. We're your family."

"Then you're supposed to be with me. In our house. In Matthews."

She argued, "This house is ours, too. *All three of us.* Besides, I'm only talking about the summer. A vacation. That's all."

The screen door banged shut. "Mommy, I *need* you," Josie yelled from the front door stoop.

"Not now, Josie. I'm talking to Dad." Her voice flared with irritation.

Michael shook his head. "Go to her," he said. "This isn't going anywhere."

Josephine sighed, turning her head toward the mountain. She had vowed she wouldn't allow Davis to make her leave the mountain, but she knew before she spoke that if Michael insisted, she would acquiesce. "Michael, I don't want you unhappy because of me. I'll bring Josie home. I'll do anything you want."

"Mom-eee!" Josie cried.

"Josie, go in the house. I'll be there in a minute." Josephine suppressed an urge to scream at her daughter.

"Take care of her," Michael repeated. "I'll be back in two weeks. We'll talk then."

Josephine grabbed his arm. "Michael, you and Josie are what's important to me. You're everything to me."

He kissed her, then pulled away and climbed in the car. Josie jumped off the stoop and ran up the stairs toward the car.

"Daddy," she cried, about to run behind the car to reach him. Josephine grabbed her arm.

Michael stopped the car and stepped out to pick up his daughter. She dropped her head on his shoulder. "You forgot me," she whined.

"Punkin, I could never forget you," he answered. "I'll be back the Fourth of July. Be a good girl and mind your mommy."

"Okay, Daddy." He put her down and climbed back in the car. Josie returned to her mother's side.

They waved, watching the car take the hairpin turn. Standing there with her small daughter beside her, Josephine felt detached, as if she were two people. A green canopy of leaves shaded the deck from the sun. It felt cool and soft as velvet to her. A bird chirped overhead, a clear, crisp three-note trill. Through the trees, she heard the sounds of the Wilderness Falls splashing and coursing down the rocks to the Boone River below.

How could life hold such opposites? A man who made love to her as Michael had last night and this morning crush her with his veiled threats. Was one argument destined to be more right than another? Should she go home as Michael had said or was there a greater loss waiting there?

Her instincts told her that if she didn't stand her ground she would lose something priceless for herself, but also for Josie.

CHAPTER ELEVEN

The day was hot and murky. Early fog had burned off mid-day, but by three o'clock it reappeared in streamers and milky patches throughout the valley.

Blackie had left Davis to drive down to High Meadows to pick up his girl friend, Darlene, who was coming to work for them. Darlene was a nurse at High Meadows. Fortunately, she had agreed to cook and take care of Davis's medications, two things neither Davis nor Blackie has successfully managed in the brief week they had been in the house at Rocky Ridge.

As soon as Blackie left, Davis headed for the guest bedroom where boxes from his parents' house were stored. He wanted to unpack a box marked "Korean War Souvenirs." After his parents' funeral, when he and Eula Mae had gone through his parents' personal effects, he had found the box in the back of his old bedroom closet. He arranged to have it shipped to Rocky Ridge with the other the items he wanted.

Davis found his box without difficulty. It contained hand-carved puppets he had bought one Saturday when he and Celeste visited a Korean open-air market. Celeste has taken a fancy to the puppets and on a whim he bought them. Except for a few frayed strings and chipped paint, the puppets were in excellent condition. Their features were painted white, black and red in a striking, oriental style. Their costumes, although dusty, were brightly colored silks or satins and smartly sewn. Davis had always thought they looked more Tibetan than Korean.

As Davis pulled the puppets out of the box, he suspected he wanted to look at them because they had fascinated Celeste. She insisted she could write a puppet play for them. A parody, she had said, with singing in it. Strictly adult, but definitely comic.

As Davis examined them, he mulled over what he might do with them. Without Celeste he was hard pressed to think of any use for them. Still, he felt bound to have them cleaned and made operational.

At the bottom of the box, he found a package wrapped in white tissue paper. He pulled back the paper revealing one of the few belongings of Celeste that he had saved. A white cashmere sweater she had adored when he bought it for her.

The sight of the sweater overwhelmed him with longing. *Why had he kept it only to be reminded years later of how he loved her?* He buried his face in it as if he might find her lingering smell.

Instead the raw odors of the Korean market, which he and Celeste had explored twenty years before, came to him, and he remembered that afternoon.

They had bought the sweater one Saturday when they went shopping in an open-air market in Seoul. Celeste had nursed him when he received a serious battle injury. During his recuperation period, they began dating.

Because of the war, the market was makeshift. Items were displayed on jerrybuilt tables. Vegetables, such as bok choy, leeks, radishes and cabbages, were piled in wooden boxes and baskets. Live chickens, captured in wooden crates, pecked from inside their coops at the debris around them. Mounds of fresh fish, octopus and squid were laid out on buckets of cracked ice beside pigs' heads and feet. The ice had melted during the morning, and now it collected in rivulets in the middle of the alley and ran down the street.

Many of the vendors were cooking on woks, and as Davis and Celeste passed by the vendors bowed and nodded, urging them to buy their foods. The cooking odors, plus the smells of raw fish and vegetables, were not appetizing. They rushed by, laughing, with their faces covered to keep out the stench. They ran through street after street of food stalls trying to find their way out. *Would they ever leave this maze?* They wanted souvenirs! Not food!

At length, they turned down one aisle, and stumbled upon a clothing stall manned by a young Korean girl. To them, the stall looked like an oasis in the middle of a desert.

The girl wore the typical peasant dress of earth-toned trousers and matching blouse. Her hair was tied back into a thick, black switch. Between customers, she was sewing tiny seed pearls on a hand-embroidered sweater.

As they approached the booth, Davis could see that Celeste was drawn to the girl. She picked up one of the sweaters and ran her hand over the intricate embroidery.

"You sew?" she asked.

The girl looked up. Her long eyelashes fluttered. "Me sew," she said.

Naturally, Davis had bought the sweater for Celeste. But before they left, she reached across the table toward the girl, barely brushing her hand over the girl's cheek. "You so beautiful," she had said softly. The girl laughed, dropping her eyes shyly.

As they walked away, Celeste was quiet. "What's wrong?" Davis asked. She shrugged. "It gets me," she replied. "Imagine hand embroidering sweaters in the middle of a war. This whole market might be bombed by sundown. No matter. They'll just build it back tomorrow." She paused, then added, "Somebody ought to stop this damn war before we're all killed."

Just after that, they found the puppets. It also was the day

Davis knew he was going to marry her. At least if she'd have him.

Davis' memories were interrupted by Blackie's call from the front door, "We're here."

Hurriedly Davis rewrapped the sweater in its tissue paper and hid it in the bottom drawer of the dresser. Then he walked into the living room, where he greeted Blackie and was introduced to Darlene.

He couldn't help but draw comparisons between the "Celeste" of his memory and the mousy girl who stood in front of him. Celeste had golden, cascading hair. This girl had lumpy brown hair, which sat on her shoulders. Celeste, when on duty, wore a crisp nurses' uniform which rustled when she walked. Darlene wore faded blue jeans and a T-shirt with Elvis at Graceland on the front. Celeste had a musical voice. Darlene, a mountain twang.

He said some hollow, meaningless words to the girl, but he couldn't remember what. He was thinking how different things were at High Meadows. He was thinking of all the memories, all the events he and Doc Bostwick had examined in manageable pieces as if they were looking at them under a microscope. Now those memories were coming back to him in small bursts without any control. At his parents' house with Eula Mae, just now with the puppets and the sweater. Now this new girl—were all these things going to be vehicles to the past? Would he be a victim *again* of his own history?

It was too much for him. He knew he would never be truly free if he could not face down his past, no matter where it led him.

Several days later, when Davis and Blackie were taking their morning walk, they met a lady and her little girl going in the opposite direction. Davis and Blackie muttered an absent-minded "morning." The little girl, who was skipping and talking at the same time, grinned at them and spoke. The women hesitated a moment, as if she might stop, then added a quick "Hello" and moved on. During that brief pause, she had looked straight in Davis' face as if she knew him, or thought she knew him. The strangest thing about the incident was that Davis felt there was something familiar about the lady and her daughter. Whatever the thought, it was just beyond his reach, flickering on his brain like a spark on a damp log.

When they returned home, Davis called his realtor to see who lived in the house next door, where he judged the mother and child lived. "Michael Scarborough," the realtor answered. The name meant nothing to Davis.

Still the thoughts of the child and her mother persisted. The child's black hair swinging around her pixie face provoked some memory he could not quite grasp. Later that morning he was in the living room when his mind began putting together a picture. The eyes should be green, or hazel, not brown. He wasn't sure, but he thought the hair should be reddish-brown.

He ran to the living room windows, forgetting his vertigo for the moment, and pulled the curtains open. In his memory, he saw Josephine. She was tearing down the hill, *the hill in front of this house,* her wiry hair whipping about her face like the mane of a wild pony. She was spunky and tough but always last, behind him, Petey, Ellen and Laura, and they always had to wait for her to catch up.

But the face was the impish face of the little girl he had seen walking with her mother. The women and child he and Blackie had seen on the road must be Josephine and the young daughter he did not know she had. That meant that Josephine was the person who lived next door who had seen him cleaning his rifle.

The picture in his mind panned from the mountains to his house in Bishop, and the year was 1941, and Davis was fifteen years old.

Bishop, N.C.
July, 1941

It was late afternoon on a scorching July day. Uncle Jack's death two weeks before had left everyone in the family drained and confused. For Davis, the world he had known to that moment was collapsing, and he had no ability, or desire, to stop it. In addition, the headaches that plagued him were worse.

That afternoon he had pulled out his .22 rifle, "Belle." Somehow, in all the confusion of his uncle's death, "Belle" made him feel better. The cool touch of the metal barrel when he ran his hand down it. The bitter smell of burnt powder. The wood stock rubbed smooth by repeated use. Simply holding the weapon in his hands had flooded his mind with pictures of his uncle. If only for an instant, "Belle" had brought his uncle back.

But Eula Mae, mean to the core, as usual, had chased him out of the house. "I don't want no guns cleaned in this-here den. Now, out on the porch with you. Bad enough yore daddy keeping them guns in the cabinet," she had declared, literally shooing him out. He had obliged and moved his gun and cleaning paraphernalia, including shells, to the front porch.

He had just cleaned the barrel and reloaded the gun with a fresh round of shells when a car drove up the circular driveway. It was his Aunt Ruth in her "reliable" blue Oldsmobile, a car Davis regarded as boring.

Aunt Ruth was the last person he wanted to see. When Uncle Jack died, everybody in town, including Aunt Ruth, had turned against him. They all said Uncle Jack should have been in bed with Aunt Ruth instead of traipsing around the river helping Davis and his buddy, Mace, escape a raid by the Sheriff.

Doc Abernathy told Davis not to pay any attention to the gossip. Jack was going to die no matter where he was. People'd

get over it soon enough. They were just looking for somebody to blame, a scapegoat, the doctor had said. Otherwise,
they couldn't make sense of a thirty-nine year old man
dying.

So far Doc's theory hadn't proved right. Nobody had gotten over it, least of all Aunt Ruth.

Davis watched his aunt park her car beside a low, brick
retaining wall, which separated the lawn from the driveway
and house. She hadn't noticed him standing on the front
porch.

"You can play on the drive if you want." she said, speaking to somebody in the car. "I'll just stick this cake in the
door to Eula Mae."

A little girl stepped out of the car and began bouncing a
ball on the driveway.

Oh, no! Davis thought miserably. That's all he needed.
That brat made him mad just looking at her. He had first
seen her at the creek with Petey, then at Whitmire's swimming pool. The thud of her ball on the driveway was rever-
berating in his head. Coupled with the blaring rays of
sunlight penetrating his eyelids, he was feeling disoriented
and even a little sick. He couldn't take her, especially now
when he was having one of his awful headaches.

Annoyed, he called out, "What do you want, Aunt Ruth?"
He ignored the girl.

"Why, Davis," she called back. "I didn't see you up there.
I brought you a cake. Honestly, people have brought so much
food to the house we can't possibly use it all. I wanted to
share with you."

"I don't like cake. Anyway, we got all the food we need,
Aunt Ruth. People been bringing stuff here, too." He turned
his head away from her. "Uncle Jack *was* Daddy's brother."

"Why'd you say that? Of course people are just as concerned about your family as mine. I didn't mean anything."
She was standing on the top step from the driveway. "I'll
just take the cake in to Eula Mae. She can do what she wants
with it."

"Eula Mae's busy. I said we don't want your leftovers." Flushed with irritation, Davis started pacing across the front porch. He was rubbing his forehead with his left hand, and "Belle" was swinging casually in his right hand as if it were an extension of his arm.

Too many useless ideas were crowding his mind, he was thinking. They were getting confused with the throbbing in his head. One minute he thought Aunt Ruth and the little girl had no right to be on his property. The next minute this seemed the perfect time to straighten out a thing or two with Aunt Ruth, and he blurted out, "You blame me 'cause Uncle Jack died." She shook her head. But he went on. "Everybody in town does. Daddy's talking like I'm gonna be sent off somewhere. He says the Sheriff wants me to go to a hospital for tests. They think I'm nuts."

"Davis, I know you're not responsible for Jack's death. He had a bad heart. Doc Abernathy told me. Jack loved you, and he wouldn't want anything bad to happen to you any more than I would. If you want me to, I'll speak to your daddy."

Josephine stopped bouncing her ball. She tilted her head to the side, staring curiously in Davis' direction. Then she yelled with alarm at her aunt, pointing to Davis, "Aunt Ruth, he's got a gun!"

From Davis's perspective, her fear gave him a rush of pride. He liked the idea of scaring them. But Aunt Ruth seemed unmoved. Instead, she called out to the child, "That's just 'Belle', Jo." To Davis, she said sternly, "Put the gun away, Davis, before somebody gets hurt."

"Gets hurt! Somebody already got hurt, in case you didn't notice. Yeah, I'd say dead is pretty hurt."

"Davis, that's sacrilegious. You're not being fair." Aunt Ruth dropped the level of her voice.

"Fair! How 'bout Uncle Jack and Daddy selling our land to strangers? And the Sheriff putting me in some loony bin? And Uncle Jack's dying. Is all that fair?" In his right hand, he was brandishing the rifle around like a stick.

"*Please*, Aunt Ruth," Josephine pleaded. "He's gonna shoot us."

"He's not going to shoot us, Jo. You need help, Davis. We're all upset about Jack's death. Now put the gun down. In fact, I'm going for Eula Mae. I want to see her."

"Not on your life," Davis answered. "You better listen to the twerp. You better leave." He'd show them both, he was thinking. Then, with measured calm, he swung the rifle up to his shoulder and pointed it right over Aunt Ruth's head. He clicked the hammer back. The gun was ready to fire.

Aunt Ruth began backing up. "Davis, don't do anything stupid." A shot exploded over Aunt Ruth's head, and she scrambled for the car, yelling, "Get in the car, Jo. Quick!"

Davis reloaded the gun and aimed it at a large boulder in the front yard. The first bullet struck the rock and ricocheted, zinging through the air. The sound captured Davis's attention. He laughed momentarily, then reloaded and fired again repeatedly. Bullets were flying everywhere.

Davis saw Josephine running toward her side of the car. He watched, frozen, as she went down without a cry and did not move. One minute she was running, her short legs flying, her hair bouncing up and down. The next minute she was on the driveway motionless. For a second, he couldn't understand what happened. He expected her to jump up but she didn't.

He threw "Belle" down and ran toward the garage where his motor bike was parked. Aunt Ruth started to run after him, but stopped and shouted, "Help her, please Davis." And then she ran back to where Josephine had fallen.

Just then, Eula Mae, who had seen what happened, emerged out of the front door with towels in one hand and Davis's father's hunting rifle in the other. "You little piece of junk," she yelled after him. "You run off and I'll shoot your sorry ass." But he didn't stop. When he looked back Eula Mae was running after him, but she gave up and headed to where Aunt Ruth was bending over Josephine.

Davis reached the motorbike, pushed up the kickstand and jumped on. As soon as the engine fired, he gunned it and sped down the driveway. He looked back to see the two women kneeling beside the child.

He entered the highway that ran in front of his house. He had no destination in mind, only to get away. He pressed down the gas pedal, urging the bike to go as fast as possible. His head was pounding. Still he maintained his speed. The dirty roads, teetering mailboxes, gravel driveways, wilted clumps of flowers that whizzed passed him seemed to mock him as if to say he didn't belong there. He was only passing through. Wasn't that really his problem? He didn't belong anywhere. But it was more than that. He didn't belong because everything he touched died. His uncle had died in his arms. Whether he caused it didn't matter. He had walked with his uncle to the door to eternity. He had been turned back while his uncle walked through.

Now it could happen again. The little girl could die, and this time he caused it, and he knew it.

He found himself at the top of the footpath that led down to the creek where he had first seen Josephine and Petey. He steered his bike onto the dusty path and followed it to the creek. He was thinking he had to put a stop to everything right now. The headaches, the angry feelings, the guilt for always doing things wrong. He had to take matters in his own hands.

He parked his bike beside the creek, and for a time he just sat there listening to the noises in the woods. The stream gurgled. Leaves rustled. Birds chirped. There was no need to hurry he was thinking. He was in control.

He unfastened his watch. His fingers lingered lovingly over it. Uncle Jack had given it to him. He slipped it on the handlebars. Then he noticed dust on his bike. He took his shirt off and wiped down his bike, shook out his shirt and put it back on. Having performed those tasks, an urgency overtook him. He began to hurry again as he scrambled down the bank where Petey and Josephine had run away from the snake.

By now, his breath was coming in short gasps, and he had

begun to cry. When he reached the creek, he stepped in. The cool water seeped into his boots. It was refreshing, even comforting, and for an instant, he felt renewed.

Why hadn't he helped Petey and Josephine that day when he first saw them? Was he really mean? Or was he crazy like everybody kept saying?

Once his boots were soaked, he ran faster. The water was splashing to the side as his feet pounded the rocks. The going was tougher than he imagined, and he momentarily appreciated the difficulty Petey and Josephine had faced when they ran down the stream.

When he reached the swimming hole, he walked into the water until the bottom slipped away from him, and then he swam. The water grabbed at his clothes, surging over his trousers legs and rising to his waist.

When he reached the middle, he spread his arms like a preacher who was about to baptize the chosen. And then he let the water accept him, his heavy boots pulling him down, the way God accepted sinners.

Before the water reached his lips and nose, he took one last deep breath and then went under. The water felt cool to his hot face. Bubbles began rising from his nose. He relaxed, his muscles yielding, and drifted to the bottom.

The water was murky. He could feel it stir across his face, feel it swirl around his body, lifting his clothes away, caressing his skin like a lover. His hair was swaying above his head.

His lungs began pressing now. All he had to do was take one deep breath, and the thundering thoughts in his head would go away. He pulled his arms around himself as if he were cradling a child. He was still holding his breath.

When his uncle died, he had held him in his arms just like he was holding himself. *"Take care of the kids,"* Uncle Jack had said. Those words had pierced Davis's heart at the time. Now they reverberated with him with sudden clarity. His uncle was counting on Davis. Uncle Jack was gone but he was still here. His uncle expected him to help the children he was leaving behind. Davis couldn't die! He had promised his uncle. He'd be letting Uncle Jack down!

Having changed his mind, Davis began to fear he was too late. Surely his lungs would explode before he reached the top! But his sense of direction was skewed. In the muddy water, he wasn't sure where the surface was. It had to be the thin layer of light he saw above him. That's what he should swim for. He scissor-kicked and pulled his hands through the water.

When he burst through the surface, his lungs gasped at the air. He was near exhaustion, and tears were streaming down his face. With all the strength he could muster, he drug his arms through the water sideways and splashed it toward the snake holes.

"Come out," he cried, arms flailing. "Come out, you sons of evil and meet your brother."

Later that night, Davis slipped into Josephine's hospital room.

When she woke up and saw him sitting by her bed, she said to him, "You gonna shoot me again?"

He dropped his head in his hands and started crying. "I didn't mean it. You have to believe me. I'm going to make it right if it takes me the rest of my life."

His memory of the incident was so real. What would it be like living beside her almost thirty years after he shot her? His feelings toward her were completely one-way. After the shooting, he had wanted to take care of her. She, on the other hand, had always been scared of him. Long after they had grown up, he continued to try to keep in touch with her, but she discouraged it. He made her nervous, he knew. He couldn't blame her.

Would he finally be able to change her opinion of him? Was this summer going to be his chance to make things right with her? There was a possibility.

CHAPTER TWELVE

After Seoul, the plan was to advance north of the 38th parallel. Wonsan was the target. The 101st marched back to Inchon, boarded LSTs, and sailed around the southeastern tip of Korea up to Wonsan. When they reached Wonsan harbor, the North Koreans had seeded the harbor with Russian mines.

For five days the troops, pitching in a rolling sea, were stuck on carriers while demolition teams detonated the mines. Well, you know Marines. They'll bet on anything. They started betting on when another mine would go off. The deal was the explosion sent a geyser into the air. The things shot up 35 feet in the air, or more. It was something to see.

Marines'll bet on anything, but it was still scary.

July, 1970

Ezekiel Highfill, otherwise known as Stoop, Pigman, Dummy, Mountain Man, or the preferred Easy, had been preparing for today, the Fourth of July, for months. Easy was a carver of children's toys, and last night he had packed 350 of his best paddle toys, including hens 'n chicks, buck dancers and mountaineer-chasing-bear, plus wooden pull toys and trucks. If he could sell enough toys at the Fourth of

July parade, he would earn fifty per cent of his yearly income before nightfall.

Since Easy's mama died five or so years ago, life had been hard. He had been by her side since his second grade teacher sent him home with a note saying, "Ezekiel can't learn anymore. Let him stay home with you."

Leaving school had been a disappointment he never forgot. But today he was full of expectation, and he took special care to look his best. He had begun getting ready yesterday when he had filled the old cast-iron tub with steaming water and wrestled his hunched, twisted body into the tub to soak away the accumulation of dirt. He had scrubbed painfully with Lifebouy until he was sure a layer of skin had sloughed off. He had washed his long salt and pepper gray hair and beard and trimmed both to his shoulders. Also his mustache, which now resembled an awning over his upper lip. He was confident he could pass even Mama's inspection, including the ears, if she were still alive.

This morning he had selected a red and white checked long-sleeve shirt and his newest bib overalls, fresh washed and board stiff. Of course, he added the most important piece to his outfit, a red bandana handkerchief dangling from his back pocket.

By seven a.m. he had his pickup truck packed, and he was ready to begin the drive from his hut beside Wilderness Creek, up the steep incline of Wilderness Trail and into Rocky Ridge. He would spread his toys just where he always did, to the right of the parade viewing stand, on the stone wall, that surrounded Rocky Ridge Park.

Angie Dennison woke early on the Fourth of July. For the tenth year, she was in charge of the majorettes for the Rocky Ridge High School Marching Band. She was a natural choice for the job since she had served on the squad for three years, two, as drum majorette.

But this morning, the day of the parade, Angie had a

nasty headache. She was thinking each year was harder than the one before, but she couldn't quite fathom why. The girls were prettier than ever, their skin as smooth as peach ice cream, and Angie would kill over their figures—firm, perky breasts and legs like alabaster statues. But when they danced, *oh, my*, Angie shuddered, they jerked and bumped from one song to the next as if they had never heard of rhythm.

"Count!" she had yelled last April when she started rehearsals. "Starting on your right foot, now, six, seven, eight and two, three, four." But despite all her attempts, one girl, Maylynn Eberhardt, simply could not count and toss a baton at the same time.

"Maylynn, it's your feet that keep the beat," Angie had insisted. "Listen to the drum. Bum-bum-bum-bum-now-throw-the-baton."

"Well, if I do that, Miz. Dennison," Maylynn had answered, "I have to stop marching." Finally, in desperation and fear that Maylynn's baton would conk somebody on the head, Angie had told her "Concentrate on marching. Let the others toss their batons."

That day Maylynn had looked at Angie like she had slapped her.

This morning, with her head pounding like a base drum, Angie could not get the picture of Maylynn's wounded face out of her mind. She reached for the aspirin bottle and downed a couple with her orange juice. Maybe she could get Tara, the girl who marched beside Maylynn, to coach her when to catch the baton. Anything to get that pathetic look to go away.

At eight o'clock Angie called Josephine. "Michael get in?" Josephine answered "yes."

"Can I join you guys for the parade?" "Yes" again.

"I'll meet you on the right of the viewing stand, just in front of the stone wall to the park," Angie told her. "By the way, if something happens and I don't get there, watch out for the majorette marching on your side. If she throws a baton, duck."

The Fourth of July Family Parade was a time-honored tradition, which began in the twenties and had been held each year with one exception. During World War II, large gatherings were discouraged. It was rumored that the President and chiefs-of-staff of the armed forces would be hidden in the Appalachian Mountains in case of an attack on Washington. The Rocky Ridge city fathers, somewhat inflated with self-importance, agreed it was best not to hold the parade.

After the war, the event was brought back with new fanfare, and now everyone who was in Rocky Ridge on the Fourth, including tourists, renters and mountain residents, attended the parade and the fireworks which were set-off later that evening at Doodle's Theme Park.

The morning of the Fourth, the Scarboroughs had an early breakfast. After hearing from Angie, Michael dropped Josephine and Josie off on Main Street around ten o'clock so they could stake out the "spot" where they had agreed to meet Angie. Michael was going to take the car back home to leave it and walk back to the park with Lady. It was only a mile and a half but still too far for Josie to manage.

Crowds were already gathering on both sides of the street. The air was cool, and Josephine zipped up Josie's jacket, then her own, thinking how good it felt now versus how hot it would be in the afternoon. By then Michael and Josie would pass their jackets off for her to carry.

Josie could not contain herself. She bounced beside her mother, chattering, "Where's the parade, Mommy?"

"It's not time yet. But if you're real quiet, I think you can hear the band warming up."

"I don't see a band," Josie insisted.

"Remember I told you Angie was helping with the band?" her mother replied. "The people in the parade are down on the highway with her. That's where they line up."

Josie dropped her mother's hand and turned to look around. "Psst," she heard. "Over y'ere, girlie." An old man motioned to her. "Wanna see a toy?" The old man was holding a paddle toy for her to see. He pulled the strings, which protruded from the bottom, and a carved hen and biddies began to peck on top. Josie moved closer to see. "I ain't gonna hurt cha.' Here you'uns try." He extended the paddle toward her.

Josie looked back at her mother for permission, but she was looking in the other direction. Josie took that as a sign it was okay to move closer to the funny old man. She accepted the paddle, turning it over to look at the strings on the bottom. The man said, "Pull on them strings and see whut hoppens." Josie followed his instructions, and the chicks' heads bent down and pecked on the wooden paddle. Josie laughed.

When Josie laughed, Josephine turned and called her back. Josie handed the paddle to the man and returned to her mother's side. "Don't talk to strangers," Josephine warned. Michael and Lady arrived, and the mountain man began demonstrating the paddle toy to a lady and her son. Josephine encouraged Josie to concentrate on looking for Angie.

The fun of the Fourth of July Parade was that anybody could march. All that was necessary was to pay the entry fee and decorate "something or somebody, including animals" in patriotic colors. It ended up being a melange of people representative of the mountains and their family pets, plus visitors in area. There were Scottish dancers in kilts with make-shift American colors around their waists; Englishmen in tomato red hunting jackets, with a touch of blue added; hippies wearing peace necklaces and tossing flowers; and ordinary people decked out in any combination of red, white and blue. They were walking, riding, or marching to the music of the local band.

Dignitaries, mostly politicians, sat on the backs of convertibles. Firemen waved from the sides of the oldest and newest fire trucks in town. And, of course, the Rocky Ridge High School Marching Band played and marched all the way down the four blocks of Main Street to the Big Dollar parking lot, where all the participants turned around and paraded back up the street. For a special fee, spectators could watch from a viewing stand, which was located to the left of the Park.

At eleven sharp the fire siren sounded, announcing that the parade was about to reach the corner of Main and Highway 221, its official beginning. The crowds pressed out into the street eagerly waving and encouraging the parade participants to hurry. Those lucky enough to be in front could see movement down the street.

Excitement rose. Then, the county's newest fire truck, leading the way in glinting sunlight, broke into view. Firemen and some children were perched on steps and nooks in the side and rear of the truck. They were tossing handfuls of peppermint candy out to onlookers. As the twirling candy tumbled through the firemen's hands, children scrambled high and low to snatch the candy from the air. The mayor waved from the backseat of a light green 1956 Olds convertible. The crowd cheered him as if they adored him, calling him by his first name.

Local politicians followed in assorted old and new cars, their brightly painted automobile hoods gleamed in the sun and blinded those in the wrong spot. The Veterans of Foreign Wars came next, led by five soldiers carrying a royal blue banner announcing their post number. Servicemen wore every type of military uniform from Marine dress blues to Navy bell-bottom trousers, from Army fatigues to Green berets, and even a few military high school uniforms. Following were the old-timers, soldiers from World War I who were too old to march. They rode in a jeep, their uniforms reeking of mothballs.

Michael lifted Josie on his shoulders so she could see everything. The children came next, some pulling reluctant dogs after them. One had a goat. A few rode ponies or horses, streamers plaited in their manes. Parents carried children or pulled them in wagons. One family marched with four generations. They carried a sign that read, "America Rocks. From Rocking Cradle to Rocking Chair."

The Scarborough's spot by the park was perfect. All the participants straightened up before they came to the viewing stands, and the band stopped to perform right in front of them. Josie squealed with delight when the music started. The majorettes were so close they could see sweat glistening on their smooth bodies.

The oldest fire truck in the county was last. The parade marched into the Big Dollar parking lot, where they took a brief break. After the break, they would turn around and march back down the street.

Michael lowered Josie to the ground, and he took Lady's leash back from Josephine. Angie still had not arrived.

The crowd of people surged and pushed, intent on getting something to eat or drink during the break. Before Josephine knew what was happening, she was separated from Michael and Josie. She craned her neck to see them, but all she could make out was a sea of strangers. They had become completely separated, but the area was small, and the spirit of the crowd was friendly. She was not alarmed. Still, she struggled against the swell of people to return to their spot. When she reached the curbside, Michael was standing there, a perplexed look on his face.

"Where's Josie?" she asked.

"I thought she was with you. All of a sudden you both were gone. Lady and I were standing here by ourselves."

Fear flushed across Michael's face. He pushed passed Josephine and began frantically searching near the viewing stands, calling Josie's name. Josephine turned toward the mountain man. "Did you see my daughter?" she asked him, and when he shook his head, her concern grew. She scrambled for a park bench and managed to climb on top, where she could see.

"Josie! Josie," Josephine, teetering on the park bench, screamed above the crowd. She could see Michael over by the viewing stand, parting people as he dragged Lady behind him. When he looked her way, she could see his mouth moving, but she couldn't hear him. Down the street, in the direction of the Big Dollar Store, the fire siren blared out again, signaling that the parade was about to come back down the Main Street. Once the parade started again, it would be that much harder to find her. Josephine began to panic.

Michael made his way back to her. "I don't see her! The parade's starting up again," she yelled to him. "Stay where you are," he yelled back. "Just keep looking and calling."

A flash of bright colors caught Josephine's attention. It was Josie, wearing her brightly-colored blouse. Her daughter's tiny figure was weaving in and out on the fringe of the crowd, at least a block and a half away in the direction of the Big Dollar Store. She could see her head bobbing back and forth, her dark hair flashing in the sunshine.

How did Josie get way down there so fast—at least a block away? Josephine noticed a man was beside her. Was he holding her hand! What was going on? Who was the man? Then she saw in the sunlight the scraggly hair and the slump of his shoulders. Was he familiar? Was that the man next door who was cleaning his gun in his yard? Could that possibly be Davis?

"Michael," Josephine cried over the crowd. "Down there!" She jumped from the bench and bolted through the crowd, pushing people out of her way. Angie appeared at her side. "What's wrong?"

"Josie!" Josephine cried. "Somebody's got her!" She had begun to cry. Angie fell in behind Josephine, and the two of them struck off down the block, running, jumping over obstacles and pushing passed people.

Josephine reached them first. The man's back was to her. She grabbed his arm and wheeled him around. At the same time she jerked Josie's hand from him and pulled her daughter to her side. Angie was beside her and Michael was approaching.

"Don't you dare touch her! I know who you are. What are you doing with her?" Josephine yelled in the man's face.

"I..."

"Mommy, it's the man next door. He found me."

"Stay behind me, Josie."

Michael was beside them now. "What's going on?"

Michael asked. "What were you doing with our daughter?"

Josie began to whimper. She pushed her face into Josephine's legs.

"It's Davis, Michael," Josephine said. "The man who moved in beside us. He had...Josie...by the hand...they were a block from us!"

"I...found...your daughter...wandering around, lost. The crowd was pushing this way. We were looking for you. I meant no harm to her. Surely you don't think..." Davis's eyes darted from Josephine to Michael.

"I don't want you anywhere near her, do you hear me?" Josephine was shaking her finger in his face. "Do you think I've forgotten you? It's me, Josephine. I know you better than you know yourself. And there's no way I believe you were trying to find us. *No way in God's green earth.*"

Josie began to cry. "Mommy," she said, "we were looking for you and Daddy! That's what we were doing. We were looking everywhere but I couldn't see you. I couldn't see you anywhere."

"Oh, Baby, don't cry." Josephine picked Josie up. "Daddy and I aren't mad at you. We'll talk about it later. Okay? But right now, Daddy and I need to take care of this. You be a good girl." Josie pressed her face into her mother's shoulder and stuck her thumb in her mouth.

"Listen, mister," Michael said. "My wife says she had trouble with you when she was young. We don't want you around our daughter. You got that?" Michael clinched his fist at his side. Josephine could see the veins bulging, and she was afraid he was about to take a swing at Davis.

Angie, a puzzled look on her face, was looking from one person to the other.

"I'm a different person now," Davis insisted. A man and woman approached the group.

"Anything wrong?" the man asked.

"Darlene, Blackie!" Davis exclaimed with relief as he greeted the people. "Thank God you're here. This little girl... was wondering around. I was trying to help her find her parents."

"Where'd you know her?" Darlene asked, concern clouding her face.

"Blackie and I passed them on the road the other day. They live beside us."

"You didn't mention that," Darlene said. Davis shrugged.

Angie interrupted. "Josie, you want to come with me to watch the rest of the parade?" She looked at Josephine to see if it was okay, and Josephine returned a look of gratitude and mouthed silently, "Thank you." Josie pulled away from her mother's shoulder and nodded, stretching her arms out to Angie. Angie took the child, crooning to her, "Yeah, baby. Let's split this joint."

The man stepped toward Michael and extended his hand. "I'm Blackie Statton and this is Darlene Adams. We live with Davis. He's an out-patient from a nearby hospital."

"High Meadows Mental Institution, right?" Michael said, refusing the man's offer of his hand. The man ignored Michael's rude gesture and continued talking, "High Meadows has started an experiment for qualified patients. They're allowed to integrate into a community and live in a private home. Davis qualified. Of course, proper supervision is required."

"Frankly, Mister, I'd have to question your 'proper supervision.' Why did you leave him?"

"We stepped away only for a moment. Sir, Davis is reliable. He would not hurt anyone. Let me assure you of that."

Davis turned to Josephine, "I *was* looking for you, Josephine. You have to believe me."

Josephine sighed. Unconsciously her hand found the back of her neck and began massaging a sensitive spot. Her head felt heavy, and she was tired. Had she just witnessed a rite of passage? Had she, a mother, unknowingly handed off a legacy of danger from herself to her own child, just as one runner might pass off a baton to another runner? Further, did she have the ability to protect her own daughter when Josephine's mother could not? She sighed again, understanding she had no answer. But she was going to try. As long as she had breath, she would try.

She was standing in front of Davis. Out of the corner of her eye, she was watching her small daughter, cradled in Angie's arm, as they merged into the crowd.

"Davis, stay away from my family," she said. "Will you do that for me?"

He nodded and quickly disappeared into the crowd.

Angie and Josie had found a spot near Easy. Did Josie want to get down, Angie asked, and Josie shook her head.

Word had passed through the crowd that a mountain man was selling hand carved toys for only ten bucks. Everywhere children could be spotted pulling on strings that made carved figures peck on a paddle. One women was so entranced she bought two gross for a chain of minute markets she owned in eastern North Carolina.

Easy was thinking how proud Mama would have been of him and how wrong his second grade teacher, whose name he couldn't remember, had been. He could teach her a thing or two, he was thinking, like how to carve the best darn paddle toys on the entire mountain.

A block and a half away, Maylynn Eberhardt was approaching the viewing stand when she was seized with a blast of courage, and she tossed her baton high into the air. Beside her, Tara, who was stunned, tensed as she watched the baton whirl end over end through the air. When the baton had fallen to within three feet of Maylynn's head, Tara hissed to her neighbor, "Now!" Maylynn thrust her arm into the air and snatched the baton. Boom, boom, boom, boom, she heard the bass drum! She actually heard the beat! And her white booted-yellow-tasseled feet marched in perfect time. Maylynn threw back her shoulders, and a huge smile spread across her face as she strutted passed the viewing stand.

"I got it," she was screaming in her mind. "I feel the beat!" And she marched tall and proud to the corner of Main and Highway 221.

CHAPTER THIRTEEN

July, 1970

Sister Agnes of an Irish order of nuns began her day at 5
a.m. She rose in her dark room and allowed her toes to
search the space on the cool floor where she left her slippers
the night before. Once she found them, she slid her feet into
their luxurious fuzziness and sighed with pleasure.

She dispensed with the light, preferring to permit her
eyes to adjust slowly to the austerity of her surroundings
while she contemplated the business of the day before her. In
the dark she collected her personal belongings and headed
for the bathroom, which she shared with all the sisters.
Privacy, however, was not an issue as few of the sisters were
up at this early hour.

She went about her daily bathroom routine without
thought, except for a cursory glance in the mirror that ran the
length of the wall above the lavatories.

She was always surprised by what she saw. The blush of
youth was gone, but the face was a strong, pleasant Irish face
that was holding up well with age. The eyes, her best feature,
still sparkled. William, her older brother, used to say, "Those
eyes have a bit of the devil in them." Of course he was kidding, for even as a child she wanted to be a nun. But this

morning she thought of William and missed the closeness they had shared. She wondered what he would say if he knew she had been appointed head of nursing for Our Lady of the Hills Nursing Home in Rocky Ridge.

Back in her room, she hurried with her underclothes and stockings and stiff white nurse's uniform. She brushed her sparse hair and dropped her head to receive her chasuble, a shortened version for ease in nursing. She made a quick decision to go for comfort that day and selected the bone Hush Puppy shoes, saving the stiff, white oxfords for the day "Doctor" made his weekly rounds to attend to the medical needs of the patients. She grabbed her wool shawl and gave her room one last glance before picking up her bible and closing the door.

Morning light, a slim, pink cast beyond the mountains, was approaching. Sister Agnes hardly noticed. She was focused on her day. She wanted to check in with the night shift before Morning Prayer. And she mustn't forget to call that attractive young woman whose mother used to be a resident. Scarborough was her name. She wanted to involve Josephine in "Adopt-a-Grandparent Day."

As she ticked off her plans for the day, she quickened her pace and prayed silently: *"Please, dear Heavenly Father, if it be thy will, let the patients survive the travails of the night."*

It was a wonder Josephine was home that July morning when Sister Agnes called. Usually, while Josie attended day camp at Padgett State Park, Josephine went horseback riding at Padgett Stable. But on this particular morning she had skipped riding to clean house and run errands. Both chores had reached the desperation point, and Josephine was tackling the house first.

When she picked up the phone, the voice on the line said, "Josephine, this is Sister Agnes from Our Lady of the Hills Nursing Home. How are you, dear?"

"Oh, Sister, I'm glad to hear your voice." She reached down to turn off the vacuum cleaner and dropped into the chair by the telephone table. "I've been meaning to bring Josie by to see you and Momma's friends. But I've been so tied up." Before her death, her mother had been a resident at Our Lady of the Hills for ten years.

"As we say in Ireland, child, it's never too late," the Sister responded. "And that's precisely why I called. I have an idea for you. Could you come this afternoon with the precious child and discuss it?" The lilt of the nun's Irish brogue was like music.

"Of course," Josephine replied, relieved to do anything to ease the guilt she felt upon hearing the Sister's voice.

"Good then," Sister Agnes replied. "Three o'clock. And Josephine—I've missed you, dear."

"I've missed you too, Sister." Josephine replaced the phone in its cradle, her hand lingering over the black headpiece. She slumped against the telephone chair, abandoning the vacuum cleaner.

A wave of nostalgia and sadness swept over her. Of course, she had put off seeing the Sister. The memories they shared were too painful. Sister Agnes had stood by Josephine when her mother died. By happenstance, Josephine was having lunch at the nursing home that day when her mother choked. Emergency measures failed to revive her, and Sister Agnes called for an ambulance to take Josephine's mother to the hospital.

"You ride with me," Sister Agnes had told Josephine. "We're going to need each other."

Josephine jumped in the Sister's car, and they sped down the highway after the ambulance that carried Momma. Sister Agnes drove like a woman possessed. Her slender hands worked over the steering wheel like a baker working dough, kneading in time to her chanted prayer, *"Hail, Mary, full of grace, pray for us sinners in our time of need. Pray for our sister, Emma, that she may be delivered from pain."*

Josephine, sitting on the seat beside Sister Agnes, prayed, too. But she knew she was praying for herself, and not her mother, because Momma had left her long ago.

When they reached the hospital, Momma was stretched out on an examining table. The doctor's coat gleamed as white as lightening and the chrome instruments in the room flashed like burning metal. He carefully inserted the forceps into Momma's throat, withdrew a piece of meat, and dropped the instruments and meat into a chrome dish. The clatter echoed through the room.

"Give me the electric paddles," he instructed the nurse.

Josephine swallowed the lump in her throat. "Not the paddles," she said stiffly. "We have a living will." Her words hung in the room. Sister Agnes nodded to the doctor.

"We have to do everything in our power," the doctor protested.

"She's in God's power now," Sister Agnes replied as she folded her slight arms around Josephine and pulled her to her.

The three of them watched to see if Momma would breathe on her own, but her chest didn't rise. Josephine pulled away from the sister and bent to kiss her mother. She felt no whisper, no warm stirring on her lips. The doctor, standing at Momma's side, cleared his throat and gently moved Josephine away. Then he withdrew a stethoscope from his coat pocket and pressed it to Momma's heart. After a time, he removed the scope and began drawing a sheet over her.

Over Emma, Josephine's beautiful mother, whose eyes danced like hot chestnuts and hair circled her head like cotton candy, who in death, at least for Josephine, became every age she had lived. She was the precocious child with tousled, curly black hair Josephine had seen in a gold-framed picture in Aunt Ruth's living room. And the striking young woman in the black and white photograph, who was tucking her smart bob into a bathing cap as she stood on a high diving tower. When Josephine had looked at that particular picture as a child, she had felt such a strong pull toward her mother. How daring she was to dive from that height into the water below. Anything could go wrong. A swimmer could get in the way. She could have flipped over too far or hit the platform.

But Josephine's favorite image of Emma was not portrayed in a photograph. It was in her mind. Her mother was wearing a flowered dress with a pinafore apron over it. She had on her favorite shoes, wedges. She was in the kitchen, and she moved as she prepared supper with the grace of a ballerina from the sink, over to the refrigerator, across to the stove and back again.

That day in the hospital when Momma died, as Josephine looked down at the woman her mother had become and remembered what she had been, Sister Agnes stood beside her. The sheet was almost over Momma when Josephine whispered to the doctor, "Wait. Look how peaceful she is," she said, turning to Sister Agnes. "She looks like she's forty years old. All the pain is gone."

Coming out of her reveries as she fingered the telephone receiver, Josephine whispered to herself, "Why did you get sick, Momma? Was it going to California and loosing your baby boy? Most of all, why did you end up in a nursing home?"

Momma's eyes were wide and perfectly set in her oval face. In sufficient light, flecks of gold shone in them, but in the evening they were quiet as lavender, her favorite color.

When Josephine was thirteen, her father invited her mother to accompany him to California on a business trip. Momma was thrilled at the opportunity of seeing her three brothers, who lived on the West Coast. But after Josephine's parents arrived in California, her mother became ill. Her father described the problems as female, and they had to delay their return. Josephine had to remain in Piedmont with Mrs. Saffrit, the baby sitter.

When her parents returned from California, her eyes were wistful, a look that seemed to say she needed more from the family than they were giving her. Most of the responsibility fell to Josephine because Laura was away in college. She responded by trying to be better, more cheerful, more helpful, smarter in school. Her father, for his part, bought her mother flowers and small gifts. But also he kissed her and gave her lengthy hugs and told her over and over what a wonderful mother and wife she was. No one ever told Josephine exactly what happened in California. If indeed her mother had an illness, it went unnamed, and nobody spoke of it aloud. Still, this sadness which could not be named hung over their house.

Josephine recalled those days with guilt. There were long stretches, especially when Josephine was in college, when she was so centered on her own life she didn't realize her mother was withdrawing. She seemed reasonably happy, managed the house, worked in the flowerbeds and attended her club meetings.

But as time went on, she began having spells. There were falls and slight strokes. Prescriptions from the doctor became too important to her daily routine. As her need for personal care increased, it became harder to provide. Dad decided they would move to Rocky Ridge where she could live at Our Lady of the Hills, a Catholic nursing home noted for its excellent care. He would be close by to check on her every day.

Everything worked smoothly for a while. In January the weather was bitter and Daddy caught the flu. By March he still wasn't well, and the doctor decided to hospitalize him. Tests showed his kidneys weren't functioning properly. The doctors suggested that Laura and Josephine prepare their mother for the worst. He died quickly, and their mother hardly had time to adjust to his being in the hospital before they had to tell her he was dead.

Laura and Josephine weren't sure she understood. Her only reaction was to turn away from them toward her window, which overlooked a courtyard, barren with winter. Did she want to go to the funeral, they asked? She shook her head.

After the funeral, Laura and Josephine drove back to Rocky Ridge to be with her. They took some of the flowers and one of the programs and told her everything they could remember, but she didn't seem to take it in.

After that, they both visited her as much as possible. One day about two weeks after Dad died, she looked straight at Josephine and said, "Daddy's gone." She said it as a statement but in her eyes was the question as if she were begging Josephine to say it wasn't true.

Josephine wanted to lie, wanted to say anything but those awful words. She went to her mother and put her arms around her and rocked her. "Yes, Momma. Daddy's gone," she said softly.

Josephine felt her mother turn cold. She gasped as if struggling to refute what Josephine had said, but her only response was to shake her head. And Josephine knew the only way her mother could stand the awful news she had just heard was to travel to a place in her mind she could never leave. No matter how hard Josephine struggled to hold on, her mother was going to leave her. And it was happening right before her.

On the way to pick up Josie from camp, Josephine began to wonder if it was a good idea to take her daughter to the nursing home. Old people could be frightening, especially to a child. They smelled bad and said crazy things. Sometimes they had cumbersome medical paraphernalia hanging off of them.

By the time Josephine had reached the camp, she was still vacillating about the visit she had set up with Sister Agnes. When Josie got in the car, Josephine blurted out, "Do you remember Sister Agnes?"

Josie nodded brightly, "The flying nun!"

"No, no," Josephine laughed. "She's the nun who runs the nursing home where Grandma Emma lived. She wants us to come see her this afternoon."

"Oh, boy," Josie answered, squirming into her seat.

Allowing her reservations to slip away for the moment, Josephine answered, "We'll go after your nap."

While Josie was napping, Josephine decided to check out the letters she had found in her mother's document box. She retrieved the box from the closet and took it to the living room. First, she checked to make sure the birth certificate was still in the bottom of the box. Leaving it there, she went on to the stack of war letters, which were tied together. The first letter she picked up was from Bruce, her mother's oldest brother, who was in the Seabees during World War II. The letter was to his mother, Josephine's grandmother. He reported that he was on a South Pacific jungle island..."of no-name because it would never pass the censor." The letter went on to say he was returning a letter from Emma, which their mother had mailed to him, as was the family custom. "I'm returning the letter from Emma because it describes so well what she's doing for the war-effort. I thought you should put it in your WWII scrapbook."

Josephine unfolded the letter and began to read.

September 17, 1943

Dearest Mama:

Well, what did I tell you? I said you'd look up some day and one of your sailor boys would be standing in the door. I got a letter from Tom, and he said he had about 12 hours with you. If 12 hours is all the leave the Navy allows, they could never have made it to the East Coast. Know you are glad you

*went to California to be close to your boys. We miss
you more than I can say, but I know you did the
right thing, Mama.*

*Nate said he told you this once, but we both
want you to know again—if you get in a tight spot,
just call on us! We are never flush, but the service
department and body shop of the car agency are
doing pretty well. Counting used cars Nate runs
down from Pennsylvania, we make out. We can
always scare up enough to get you home!*

*I have been working at the U.S.O. It's lots of fun
because the soldiers seem to appreciate what we do
for them. Different societies and clubs around town
send in sandwiches, cakes, tea or punch. I'm a senior
hostess and in charge! Besides me, we have five or
six cute girls in every afternoon to dance and play
ping-pong with the boys. Of course, I don't dance or
anything like that. Naturally, Laura is just dying to
come down but she's way too young (and getting
very pretty by the way). We have a jukebox, card
tables, reading tables, comfy chairs. We have over
1,000 soldiers a week! Imagine in a small town like
Piedmont.*

*I have been working with pears today. Made
apple-pear preserves. I have put up over 200 jars of
jellies, fruits and vegetables from Nate's victory garden. I'm very proud because it has been quite an
effort to get them done between our usual three hots
a day.*

*Thank heaven Jo is no longer terrified of air raid
drills. She used to cry every time we had one. Laura
has helped immensely! We sing until the all-clear
sounds.*

*I finally mailed Tom his lightless cigarette lighter
for his birthday. I am starting scrapbooks for all the
boys. Send me any pictures of their West Coast
friends and three real good ones of you.*

*Don't get discouraged. This war will be over
some day, and your boys will be home, safe and
sound. Write to me. I think of you everyday and
pray for you each night.*

*Lovingly,
Emma*

As Josephine read the letter, she walked into the living
room and sat down. Air raid drills. Her mother had been
right. She had forgotten how they terrified her.

One night when the siren went off, Josephine had begged
to stay upstairs. "Please, Momma, don't make me go to the
basement. I'll hide under the bed. I won't turn on a light for
anything!" Heartlessly, her mother had replied, "Jo, do you
think the U.S. government can make an exception for you?
It's just a drill. We could be in England where it's real."

"Momma, there're rats in the basement!"

"Dad caught the rat. You can sit on my lap. Now come
on. Nate, you go down first. Laura, get the blanket off the
linen closet shelf. Jo, pick up the box of candles and flashlights as you go down. They're at the end of the kitchen
counter."

They descended the steep, wooden steps into the musty
basement. At the end of the steps were floor-to-ceiling
shelves, where Momma's canned goods were stored. The furnace rumbled from the middle of the room, where the last of
the day's supply of coal was burning. Yellow embers glowed
around the iron door of the furnace. It was enough light to
cast oblique shadows across the floor, but not enough heat to
warm the damp basement.

Daddy worked his way between the pipes and around
the water heater to two small windows, which hung like eyelids at the top edge of the back wall. Momma, with Jo on her
lap and Laura beside her, waited on a crude bench while

...pped the blackout curtains over the wind...

...ejoined them, they huddled togeth...

...n had stopped, but the furnace c...

...nging a weak rendering of "Over...

...w bars when Laura jumped up, "Hey,...

...Sisters. *'Boogie Woogie Bugle Boy.'*

...elody. Mom and I'll harmonize. Dad'll...

...e words," Josephine whined.

...a argued. "I've heard you sing 'em...

Reluctantly Jo rose with her mother, and the three of them started singing *"Boogie Woogie Bugle Boy from Company B."* By the time they moved into *"Three Little Fishes and a Momma Fish Too"* swimming all over the dam, they were laughing and Daddy was clapping.

A tap on one of the windows interrupted them. Frightened, Jo dashed for her father's lap.

"Mr. Broughton, it's Mrs. Richards from across the street. Mr. Richards sent me to get you." Mr. Richards, a policeman, was the air raid warden.

"What's the matter, Mrs. Richards?" Dad lifted Jo off of his lap and stepped away from her.

"Miss Minnie fell down her basement steps. We think her arm's broken. Mr. Richards wants you to drive her to the hospital." Miss Minnie lived two doors down the street.

"Take a flashlight, Nate," Momma said.

"Will you all be all right?" he whispered back to Emma.

"Of course. We'll wait right here until the all clear."

"Mrs. Richards," Dad called out. "I'll be right there."

A puddle of light surrounded Daddy as he walked up the basement steps. But when he stepped into the kitchen, he clicked off his flashlight and disappeared in the darkness.

Josie padded down the hall from her bedroom and into the living room, startling her mother and bringing her out of her revelry. "Josie, I wish you had known Grandma Emma when she was young. Her eyes had flecks of gold in them in the daytime, but at night they were quiet as lavender."

"What's lavender, Mommy?"

"You know the color of the sky just after all the sun had fallen behind the mountain?"

Josie nodded.

"The color that's left is lavender, Grandma Emma's favorite color."

Josephine and Josie found Sister Agnes on B Hall of Our Lady of the Hills Nursing Home.

"I've been waiting for you," Sister Agnes said, embracing Josephine and bending down to greet Josie. "Child, you've grown," she crooned. "I've arranged for tea in the Activity Room. Will that be all right?"

"Thank you," Josephine nodded, and Sister led the way down the hall into a sunny room, which was used as a gathering place for the residents.

The room was furnished with wicker furniture with flowered cushions, giving it a light, airy feeling. Residents, many of whom were in wheel chairs, and their visitors were seated at tables placed throughout the room. Everyone nodded, or smiled at Sister Agnes, and some recognized Josephine and greeted her, too.

Sister Agnes, Josephine and Josie settled in at a table, and one of the servers emerged from the kitchen with a tray of tea and a plate of cookies. "Would'cha be caring for a spot of tea, Josie dear?" Sister Agnes asked Josie.

"Yes, m'am," Josie replied, glancing at her mother for approval. "Lots of milk please."

After the tea was served, Sister Agnes turned to Josephine. "Tell me about yourself. How're you getting by these days?"

"It's been hard, Sister," Josephine began, looking down at her hands. "Losing all my family members so close to each other was a blow. I seem to be very teary these days. I'm spending the summer in Rocky Ridge with Josie, trying to get my feet back under me."

"Perfectly normal, child," the nun was saying. "And Michael, how's the dear man?" She took a sip of tea.

"He's fine, thank you. He's taken a different job at the Bank. Traveling, actually. It's worked out fine for me to be up here. He's on the road all week. Comes up on the weekends." Inwardly she flinched, knowing Michael did not feel it was fine for her to be in Rocky Ridge with Josie. Also saying Michael came on weekends was a "little white lie." He had been twice.

The nun turned to Josie. "Would you like a cookie, dear?"

Josie said, "Yes please," and added a "thank you." Josephine noted with pride that her young daughter was doing everything just right, and she made a mental note to praise her when they left.

"You said you had an idea, Sister?"

"Aah, yes," she began. "Here at the home we have a day where people from the community are invited to visit the residents. We call it 'Adopt-a-Grandparent' Day. It will be held on August 15th. I'd like you to help me with the festivities. Josie, too. Sometimes volunteers put on a short program for the residents."

Josephine was about to say "yes" when Sister Agnes added, "In fact, I'm thinking of asking a neighbor of yours to help out with the program."

"Who would that be?" Josephine asked.

"I believe his name is Williams. Davis Williams."

Josephine could hardly believe her ears. The Sister might as well have poured ice water down her back. She stiffened noticeably. "Why, Sister…" struggling to control her shaky voice. "I don't like to say anything about a person, but ar..ah.. you aware of Davis's history? He's been in a mental institution for the last sixteen years. He's a distant relative of mine, and frankly, we have a very bad history with each other."

The nun leaned over and patted Josephine on the hand, nodding. "I've spoken to his psychiatrist, a Dr. Bostwick, who assures me that Davis is quite safe. In fact the doctor contacted us and asked if Davis might volunteer here as part of his out-patient program."

Josephine began unconsciously tapping on the table with her thumb. "Sister, let me caution you about having him around the patients. He simply is not reliable."

"Josephine, his doctor gave quite a different picture. He said Davis has made great progress at High Meadows. He feels confidant that Davis, as well as the patients, can benefit from his volunteering here."

"Of course, you have to make your own judgment. But I do not want Josie around him. We have already had one incident at the Fourth of July Parade that could have been most unfortunate. I'm very concerned about his living so close to us. And well...frankly, I want nothing to do with him, Sister."

The sister stiffened her back. "Why, Josephine, that's not like you." Josie was nibbling on the edge of her cookie as she looked back and forth from her mother to the nun.

"Believe me, Sister. My feelings come from years of experience."

"Perhaps, child," the nun replied, "it's time to forget. After all, he is one of God's creatures and as such worthy of our forgiveness."

Josie had wandered away from the table. Josephine heard a woman close by speak to her. The woman was saying, "What's your name, little girl?" When Josie answered, the woman replied, "Mine's Daisy."

"That's a flower," Josie answered.

"I'm a flower," the woman said, raising her hands. "You know how to dance?"

Josie nodded, "I take ballet."

The lady grinned and said. "Imagine that. Do a dance for me."

"Well," Josie twisted her body back and forth shyly. "I could do the fluffy yellow duck. We learned it in four-year-olds."

"That would be lovely!" Daisy clapped her hands.

Josie tucked her hands under her arms and flapped them like wings. Then she danced to the left, spun around and danced to the right and made a little leap. The lady cheered and clapped. The other residents in the activity room began clapping, too. Josie curtsied.

"Now you dance," she said to Daisy.

"I can't dance. I'm tied to this chair," the woman spread her arms out, further this time, revealing a belt holding her in the wheel chair.

Josie took hold of Daisy's hands and swayed from one side to the other in a makeshift dance. Then she twirled under one of Daisy's arms and curtsied again. Everyone loved her dance and clapped again. Josie ran back to her mother and Sister Agnes and buried her head in her mother's lap.

"That was wonderful, dear," Sister Agnes said. "You'll have to dance for Grandparents Day."

"Sister Agnes," Josephine urged, "please respect my feelings about this. The child doesn't understand. I do not want to be around Davis."

"If you insist," the nun replied, stiffly.

"Thank you for the tea, Sister. I'm sorry about our difference of opinion."

They said their goodbyes. As they reached the front door, Josie looked up at her mother. "What don't I understand, Mommy?"

"I have to protect you."

"But what don't I understand?"

"That you can't wonder off like you did at the parade. You scared Daddy and me to death!"

"But the man next door helped me find you."

Josephine leaned down and grabbed Josie's arm. "Josie,

you must not talk to strangers. Do you understand me?"
Josie began to whine. Josephine added sternly, "It's very
important. How would you know if someone is nice or not?"
Josie began to cry.

When they reached the car, Josie climbed into the passenger seat, huddling near the door. She put her thumb in her
mouth and stuck out her lip and stared out the window, not
looking at her mother.

CHAPTER FOURTEEN

Daily skirmishes kept the outfit busy. Each new encounter with the enemy found Davis acting with heightened valor. Routinely, he was the first to volunteer for dangerous missions. The first to jump from cover. The first to run into battle.

One day his commanding officer, Capt. Russett, approached Sgt. Wilbur, who had returned from the hospital. "I've been watching Williams, Sgt. Wilbur. Anything strange about him?"

"What do you mean strange, sir?" Wilbur replied. "He's a hellava soldier. Just wish I had a squad like him."

"I find it unsettling when I run across a soldier who's always first in battle. Doesn't seem natural. He get along okay with the troops?"

"Far as I know," Wilbur answered. "They're in awe of him, if that's what you mean. He's a leader, but a loner. But I'll tell you this, he saved the squad when we lost Fuller, his best friend. He's still struggling with that, sir."

"Keep an eye on him, Wilbur," the Captain replied. "I'm always more comfortable when a soldier's scared shitless."

"Yes, sir," Wilbur saluted. The Captain turned away and their conversation was over.

Davis Williams judged the time to be 5 a.m., the usual time he woke. It would be several hours before the sun rose from behind his house, but for the moment a gray glow rimmed the horizon and cast a warm shadow across his room.

Davis still relished early mornings before anyone stirred. Today he was listening to dewdrops fall on the bushes outside his window. He imagined them collecting one by one in treetops high above him, collecting until each leaf was so weighted it tipped like a pitcher, pouring water below. Of course, in the process the dewdrop-rain fell anywhere it could. On downed logs and forest vegetation. On spider webs, sending a doused spider scurrying to restore its complicated home. Or on the heads of roosting birds, startling them into chirping, which in turn woke other critters.

But those sounds were muted and distant. Just down the hall more pressing sounds rose from the bedrooms where Blackie and Darlene still slept.

Blackie was snoring. Perhaps snort was a better word because in Davis's opinion what went on in Blackie's nostrils was certainly not normal. Darlene, on the other hand, made dainty puffs as if she were gently blowing out a candle. They reminded him of Celeste.

This morning, despite the birds and the noises down the hall, Davis was thinking about his mental condition. To be specific, how was he going to get well. Listening to his two caregivers in their bedrooms, he had difficulty believing they could help him.

To Blackie's credit, he had put Davis on a physical fitness program, and he literally forced Davis to walk, and in some cases run, to town every day. Furthermore, Blackie insisted that Davis do pushups and crunches, reminiscent of what he had done in the Marine Corps. While he hated Blackie's regime, he felt reassured by it. Blackie was making him follow a routine that was leading somewhere.

Darlene, on the other hand, had made no requests or demands on him, and he couldn't figure out why. He felt a tension between them as if they were on a seesaw. When she was up, he was down and vice-versa. Surely Doc Bostwick had instructed her as to how she should act around him. Just yesterday Davis and Darlene almost collided in the down-stairs hall as he came out of his bedroom. She was carrying a stack of lingerie from the bathroom into her bedroom.

"More undies, Darlene?" he asked, trying to joke with her.

"My underwear bothers you?" she retorted, clutching the clothing to her chest.

"I am a man," he answered. Her eyebrows had flared in astonishment. He continued, "Please have the decency to keep your bathroom door closed when you're drying those lovely dainties."

"If I close the door, my dainties as you call them, won't dry," she answered sharply.

He had walked past her and started up the stairs, but he knew she was still staring at his back. He called back over his shoulder, "Don't worry. I prefer older women."

Darlene had no sense of humor, he thought, remembering yesterday's incident and recalling another more troubling episode, the Fourth of July Parade. There was nothing funny about that awful day. After his encounter with the Scarboroughs, he, Blackie and Darlene had left the parade. When they reached their car, Darlene had lit into him. "Where were you going with that little girl?" she asked.

Davis had replied, "I told you. I was trying to find her mother."

Darlene flew back at him. "How did you know her? What were you going with her?"

Angrily, he had jerked open the car door and climbed into the back seat, settling in the corner. "Her mother's my cousin. The little girl is my cousin, for God's sake. I thought I saw her parents near the bandstand."

Darlene had seemed unimpressed with his answer that day, and she opened the front door and stuck her head in. "It doesn't matter if she is your cousin. That woman looked at you like she'd seen the devil."

"Really, Darlene," he said, changing the subject, "what do you know about the devil?"

Darlene, now in the passenger's seat, hunched down and

lowered her voice. "I know all right," she replied. "When I was growing up, he lived beside my parents."

Trying to get the gist of Darlene's shocking remark, Davis asked, "Did somebody molest you, Darlene?"

"That's none of your business."

"If so, I'm very, very sorry. That's a horrible thing. Horrible! But you have to know I wanted to protect that little girl the way somebody wanted to protect you when you were little."

"Don't you get it?" she answered. "That's the whole point. Nobody did."

He wanted to say something to her, to comfort her. He knew what it was to hurt so deeply that survival meant sealing the pain up like a tomb where the mind couldn't grab it and write it over and over in your brain. Those were the kinds of pain that made you crazy. Those were the pains nobody could cure.

To be honest, Davis didn't believe he could be cured of his pains. In fact, he wasn't sure what a "cure" would look like. Would he feel different? Be different? And the most important question of all: how could a world he didn't fit into as a child, one that had rebuked him as a young man, punished him as an adult, welcome him back like a prodigal son?

As he lay in bed waiting for the household to awaken, he thought back to his life at High Meadows. The patients grasped any weak hope of being cured and leaving. He had marveled how they crowded around the television set in the activity room every Sunday to watch TV evangelist and healer, Ernest Paisley, cure one after another the believers who came before him in a steady stream. The circle of patients in the activity room held their breath as Rev. Paisley pressed his hands, which some called sacred, to the temples of the believers and spoke the powerful prayer, *"Heal! In the name of Jesus, heal!"* The people on TV attending the service and those in the activity room at High Meadows collectively sang out *"oohs"* and *"aahs"* of adoration as they listened to the newly-cured raise their voices, lifting their arms skyward, shouting, *"Praise the Lord."* The patients themselves hoped against hope that one day their names, sent in by a generous relative, would be called out on the TV land prayline so that they too could be cured of the diseases that took their minds.

No, there would be no miracle cure for Davis. Whatever occurred, he sensed, would occur on this mountain, under this stretch of sky, in this house. And even though he knew he could not throw open the living room curtain and look into the face of the mountain, he knew it was embracing him. It was there, waiting to pull him to its breast like a wounded dove.

One day he would be ready.

When Blackie and Davis ran to the park that day, Easy, the old mountain man, was selling his paddle toys. As the two men passed by, Easy was showing a mother and child how the toys worked. "Hang on, Blackie," Davis motioned to his companion. "Let's look at these toys."

Davis stopped and picked up one of the paddles and examined the strings, which made the wooden figures move up and down. "These toys work like my Korean puppet. The strings cause a chain reaction." Blackie glanced at the toys and mumbled something inaudible, then said, "Hey, man, I'm gonna run on. Pick you up later." Davis nodded.

The woman purchased the toy, and her child began swirling the paddle around. The movement of the ball, which hung by strings from the bottom of the paddle, caused the figures to bob up and down.

Davis turned over the toy he was holding. The strings were threaded through a small hole in the paddle and attached to carved, wooden figures. On the bottom, the strings were connected to a wooden ball.

Davis approached the man and spoke to get his attention, "Excuse me. How did you learn to make these toys?"

"This yere toy's been 'round these mountains a long time. Reckon I lernt then."

Davis touched the ball and the figures began moving.

"They're really interesting. Similar to puppets I bought during the Korean War."

The man ignored that information, saying, "You gwine buy one 'er 'em?"

Davis nodded, digging into his pocket for money. "How much?"

"Reckon ten bucks'll do."

Davis handed the man a ten-dollar bill and asked, "Would you be willing to come look at my puppets? I think you'd find them interesting."

The man scratched his head. "Where you live at?"

"Valley View Trail. I'm the first of three houses before Lover's Leap."

"Wall, I reckon ah could. 'At's on my way home."

"Good," Davis replied. "What time?"

"'Fore sundown. Gotta get my cow up to the barn."

Davis nodded, wondering what he was getting into. "I'll see you before sundown."

The man nodded and turned away to look for another prospect.

An hour later Davis was in the kitchen fixing a cheese sandwich when the telephone rang. The voice on the line said, "This is Sister Agnes of Our Lady of the Hills. Is this Davis Williams?"

"Yes, Sister." Just before Davis's parents died, he had mentioned his interest in puppets to Dr. Bostwick. They were discussing the importance of Davis's volunteering in a community project after he left High Meadows. The doctor had suggested Sister Agnes might be an excellent contact for him. Still Davis had expected to contact her, not the other way around, and he was startled to hear from her.

"Davis, I'm glad I reached you," the nun was saying. "Dr. Bostwick suggested I call you. He told me you are interested in puppets. I'm looking for a show, something to appeal to children and grandparents alike, to be given during our 'Adopt a Grandparent Day.' The event is an opportunity for the community to visit with our residents. As you can imagine, we like to keep things light and festive. A puppet show is just what the day needs."

Davis felt a swell of nervousness overtake him. "Sister, Dr. Bostwich mentioned he was calling you. I'm afraid he misled you. I don't have a show ready. My puppets have been stored for twenty years and they need to be restored."

"The event isn't for a month. I'm sure that will be plenty of time. Besides, the Lord has his ways, Davis, mysterious though they may be." The Sister sounded determined.

Davis hedged. He couldn't think of anything to say. Clearly he could not pull together a show in one month. He didn't have a theater, or a script, and the puppets were far from working. "Sister, I'm feeling my way with this…"

"Davis, it needn't be elaborate. Just bring the puppets and show the residents how they work. They'll love you no matter what. Sometimes I think that's why I'm a nun. Everybody appreciates the effort."

Against his better judgment, Davis found himself agreeing to the Sister's proposal. After saying goodbye, he abandoned his cheese sandwich and raced to the back bedroom where the puppets were stored. He pulled out the box and began lifting out the puppets.

He had really done it now, he thought miserably. The paint was chipping off the puppets' heads. Their strings were frayed, and their costumes were stained and dingy. To say nothing of the fact that he had no script or theater. The project was immense, he thought with dismay. And he had just agreed to do a show in one month!

Eula Mae, he thought. If she would agree to dress the puppets and the Mountain Man could restring and restore them, Davis thought he could put together a script. That left the theater. Maybe Blackie would help him with that. As for Darlene, he'd ask her to pitch in any way she liked.

That afternoon, after he placed a call to Eula Mae, Davis packed up his scant belongs and moved from the basement to the upstairs bedroom, where the puppets were stored.

CHAPTER FIFTEEN

A relentless fog had settled on the mountain. It pressed against the windowpanes of Josephine's house and would have seeped under the doors if they had not been tightly closed. Lady had taken a quick relief-walk around the front garden and returned with water beading up over her coat. When she came inside, she immediately plopped down between Josie and Josephine, who were in front of the fire.

"Yikes," Josie squealed at the dog. "You're getting my PJs wet!"

Josephine ran for a towel, and when everyone was dry and reorganized, they huddled again in front of the fire. They were fighting off the chill by drinking mugs of steaming hot chocolate with plump, white marshmallows floating on top.

Michael had called earlier to say he was not coming to the mountains that weekend. He was in the eastern part of the state, and it would take him eight hours or more to drive up. He added he had important things to do in Matthews. Chores, no doubt, that Josephine would have covered had she been at home.

"We can meet you in Matthews," Josephine offered. No, he replied. He'd see them the following weekend.

Josephine's heart sank when she realized they weren't going to be together for another ten days. How could he give up their time together so easily? She hadn't realized how lonely she would be without him, and she knew Josie felt the same way. Yet Michael had only managed to come to the mountains twice, and both times they had argued about Josie and her staying in the mountains for the summer.

Certainly she was willing to meet Michael anywhere—not just this weekend, any weekend—but she was not ready to leave the mountains for good. In fact, it felt more important than ever that she stand her ground.

Facing a dull weekend without Michael, she made a quick decision. She picked up the phone and called Aunt Ruth. "I just heard the weatherman," she said to her aunt. "Believe it or not, the sun's going to shine on Saturday. Why don't you come for a visit?"

It was decided. Aunt Ruth would arrive on Saturday around noon.

By afternoon the fog was as thick as ever. Josephine and Josie summoned the energy to dress in warm sweat clothes, and together they grilled cheese sandwiches for lunch. Then they collapsed again by the fire, Josephine with a paperback, and Josie with stickers and coloring books.

The phone rang again. This time it was Dutton. "Whole mountain's socked in," he reported. "Too dangerous to drive."

"Don't worry. Josie and I aren't leaving this house," Josephine replied.

"Need anything?"

"No, we're fine. But while I have you, let me ask you something that's been on my mind. Remember that glove Lady found on the catwalk?" Lady perked up at the sound of her name. "Did you ever find out whose it was?"

"Not exactly."

"What does that mean?"

"Well," Dutton went on, "there's some new folks moved on the ridge below you. Some of 'em's pretty rough, so I hear."

"You think one of them was on the catwalk? What about Davis? Could it have been him?"

"Ain't likely. Don't seem like the type. Been doing some work for him. Seems like a decent sort."

Dutton's defense of Davis was as irritating as Sister Agnes's. Josephine knew better than either one of them what Davis was like. "He may be a terrific person, but can he get on the catwalk from his place?"

"Now that, I can't rightly say," he said and changed the subject. "Didn't you go square dancing at Tammy and Tom's the night before Lady found that glove? Maybe somebody followed you home."

The thought had never occurred to Josephine. "Dutton, you're scaring me."

"They ain't been back, have they?"

"You'd have been the first to know, if they had," Josephine responded.

"Well, that's good to know," Dutton said, adding, "Uh-oh, the missus's calling. Best run see what she's after. You know how that is."

Josephine knew when she'd been brushed off. Dutton was holding something back.

On Saturday morning, Josephine woke early. The fog was finally gone, and Josie was due for her first "real" horseback riding lesson. It was scheduled at nine o'clock to allow plenty of time before Aunt Ruth arrived.

After a hurried breakfast, Josephine and Josie headed for the barn. As soon as the car stopped, Josie bounded out of the car and ran inside. Josephine gave her daughter time to find her riding instructor, and then she followed.

The barn was dim and musty. Despite the early hour, activity inside was lively. The horses had been watered and fed, but they were still jittery, probably from being penned up for two days, and they snorted and paced in their stalls.

When Josephine's eyes adjusted to the dark barn, she saw that Josie was talking to T.J. Butts.

"I have two ponies," Josie bragged.

"I see you two are getting acquainted," Josephine interrupted, walking toward her daughter and T.J. They were standing beside a saddled pony. "I'm surprised to see you, T.J. Several people around the barn said you worked here, but I never saw you."

T.J. chuckled. "I've been on the road showing horses and looking at a couple of mares." He changed the subject. "I'm going to give Josie her lesson."

"Good," Josephine replied, folding her arms in front of her chest.

"We'll work inside first."

Josephine nodded, then stepped aside and found a seat on a nearby bench.

T.J. skillfully steered Josie through several basics of horseback riding, including mounting on the left side, never walking behind—or under—a horse, keeping a calm, steady voice, giving consistent commands and respecting the animal—especially its size. Next he showed her how to grasp a lead rope close to the pony's neck while holding the loose end in her other hand. Then he taught her to cluck to the horse to get it to go and say "whoa" for stop. After Josie was comfortable with those commands, he lifted her into the saddle and led her down the hall, praising her horsemanship the entire time.

Josephine, who had moved to the entrance of the barn, observed Josie's calm manner with pride. She could see that T.J. was doing an excellent job of building Josie's trust.

At length, they progressed to the outside ring where T.J. advanced Josie to collecting her reins and steering the pony. Then, walking close beside her, T.J. let loose of her, and she was riding by herself.

At the end of the lesson, they turned the pony loose in one of the pastures. Josephine bought Josie a Coke, and her daughter went out to watch her new animal friend romping in the pasture.

Josephine tracked T.J. down in the tack room, where he was putting away the saddle. "T.J. you were wonderful with Josie. In fact, masterful." He turned around to face her, and she casually dropped her hand on his forearm and squeezed. "Thank you for getting her off to a good start," she said.

She meant the touch on T.J.'s arm to be a gesture of gratitude, but before she could think, he grabbed her arm and pulled her to him, kissing her full on the mouth. It was a soft, tender kiss. Harmless really. The kiss of young lovers or the first kiss of a high school romance.

"Wait a minute," she said, stepping back. "That was a surprise." The back of her hand had flown up to her lips.

"I've wanted to do that since the first time I laid eyes on you," T.J. said.

"I don't know how I feel about this. You know my situation…"

He was staring at her, not moving a muscle. Later she recalled that his face looked so guileless she believed she was seeing everything about him written on his face.

Still later she remembered the gentle touch of his lips, the slight pressure of his hands on her shoulders. And that he had shaved that morning and tasted faintly of yesterday's beer and tobacco and today's sweat.

But when she picked up Josie and drove away with her that day, all she could remember was guilt. Josie could have walked into the tack room at any minute. If she had, she would have seen her mother kissing the man who had just given her a riding lesson, her first.

Back home, Josephine took a long, hot shower. She lathered her body—arms, legs, torso, even the bottoms of her feet—with soap. She doused her hair twice with strong-smelling shampoo. Between each new application, she smeared fresh soap on a washrag and wiped her lips. Still the feel of T.J.'s kiss remained.

By the time she got to the kitchen, she was at least able to concentrate enough to put lunch together. She was adding fresh strawberries to their plates of chicken salad when she heard Aunt Ruth's car pull into the driveway. Josephine, Josie and Lady all met at the front door and ran together up the steps to greet her.

Aunt Ruth emerged from her car, prattling on about how good the house looked, how good it was to be there, and how wonderful it was to be with Josephine and Josie. They carried her bags inside and led her to her bedroom. Josie carried her great-aunt a glass of water to drink while she was unpacking.

When they sat down to lunch, Aunt Ruth looked refreshed and happy. She began doling out small gifts to Josie and her mother. Body lotion for Josephine and a new book on horses for Josie.

In the middle of lunch, Aunt Ruth blurted out, "I almost forgot. Eula Mae asked us for Sunday lunch."

"Eula Mae?" Josephine asked, holding a spoonful of tomato soup in front of her mouth, a puzzled look on her face.

"Oh, heavens, you remember her. She worked for Davis's parents for ages. As I recall she held you that time you were shot while I drove us to the hospital. Anyway, she needed a ride up, and I invited her to come with me. She's going to help Davis with some project or other. Puppets, I think."

"You...you.. dropped her next door?" Josephine stammered, incredulous at what her aunt was saying. "I told you Davis lives right next door and how awful that is for us and you still went over there?"

"Well, I didn't go in," Aunt Ruth defended, "but I was with Davis quite a lot after his parents were killed in the fire. Eula Mae and I talked about it all the way up here. We both agree he has changed."

Josephine's appetite vanished. She put her spoon down and glared at her aunt. So Sister Agnes had invited Davis to do the puppet show despite Josephine's warning! Trying to gain her composure, Josephine muttered to her aunt, "He's doing a puppet show for activity day at Our Lady of the Hills where Momma was."

"Well, anyway," Aunt Ruth continued, not appearing to notice Josephine's despair. "Long as I can remember Eula Mae has cooked this wonderful Sunday lunch. A real feast. She's going to do it up here tomorrow, and she's invited us. It'll be lots of fun."

"Aunt Ruth, you know I can't do that," Josephine said, still reeling. "What's the matter with you? You just finished saying Eula Mae held me after Davis shot me!"

"Josephine, to be honest with you, if that poor man can get any happiness out of this life, he deserves it."

Josephine sat up straight in her chair, "Frankly, Aunt Ruth, his happiness is not my concern. But Josie's and my safety is. Davis is unreliable. You know that. He always has been and he always will be."

Josie was looking from her great-aunt to her mother as the conversation changed. "I'm safe, Mommy," she said.

"Yes, baby," her mother replied, trying to signal Aunt Ruth to quit talking about Davis in front of Josie. "Aunt Ruth, please go on and enjoy yourself. But Josie and I will decline."

They fell silent, and the chink of eating utensils against china filled the space in the dining room.

In the middle of the afternoon, the telephone rang.

"Josephine, this is Davis Williams," the voice said. Josephine didn't answer, and Davis continued, "Eula Mae tells me she's invited you, Aunt Ruth and Josie for lunch tomorrow. I wanted you to know I think it's a great idea— can't think of anything I'd like better. But I was afraid you might hesitate to come. Look, I know this is awkward. I need to explain where I've been for the last twenty years, but I did want to make one thing clear immediately. I would never hurt your little girl. When I found her at the parade, I was trying to get her back to you. I'd seen you earlier by the reviewing stand. When I realized she had strayed away from you, I thought I knew where you were. I wanted to return her to you. I meant no harm in the least, and I am sorry for any distress the incident caused you or your husband."

Josephine remained silent, and Davis continued with a sigh, "If you can't accept that I was trying to help her, then it's pointless for you to come to lunch."

"Yes, it is," Josephine answered.

Davis cleared his throat. "Where do we go from here? Are you at least willing to give me a chance to explain myself?"

"What good would it do?"

"A lot of good. I hope you'll understand that I'm not the person you think I am."

"Davis, I'll be honest with you. I don't think there's much chance of that."

"I'd like to try. Just give me five minutes."

"How…when…under what circumstances?"

"Well, as for 'how,' I can come to your house one evening after Josie is asleep. 'When,' I'd like to do it as soon as possible. As for the 'circumstances,' you can ask one of your friends to be with us if that would make you more comfortable."

"All right. You can come Tuesday. And yes, I will have someone here to put Josie to bed and read to her."

"Thank you, Josephine. You won't be sorry." He hesitated momentarily as if he might add something, and then said, "Goodbye."

"Yes, well, goodbye," she signed off. The line went dead, and Josephine dropped the phone in its cradle with a thud.

"What was that all about?" Aunt Ruth asked.

"I'm going to talk to Davis on Tuesday."

"I'm so glad you're doing that, Josephine."

"Aunt Ruth, it isn't going to change a thing."

Chapter Sixteen

Eula Mae and Darlene giggled as they rounded the corner of the dining room and headed down the hall toward Davis's bedroom. He heard them from inside his room and wondered what they were doing. As soon as Eula Mae had arrived, she and Darlene seemed to have an instant understanding of each other. The whole thing made Davis nervous, as if the two were conspiring against him. He jerked open the door and found them outside his door.

"What are you two up to?" he asked the two women.

"Puppet business!" Darlene spoke up, stumbling into Eula Mae, who had stopped abruptly at the door.

"Yeah," Eula Mae said, adding, "We needs money. We're going to Kmart for material to dress them puppets of yours. And we're stopping for lunch, too."

Davis dug into his pocket, withdrew two twenties, and handed them to Eula Mae.

"Thanks," she said. "See you later," she added, stuffing the bills in her pocketbook.

"Yeah, see you later," Darlene repeated, giggling and waving her fingers in a goodbye.

What had he created, Davis wondered, following the women down the hall. He was surprised Eula Mae had agreed to come to the mountains. Was it possible he and Eula

Mae were more attached than they cared to admit? Whatever Eula Mae's reasons, she was an important figure in his puppet crew. She could run the house and keep everybody in line at the same time.

By luck or accident, Davis had managed to assemble a competent crew to launch his puppet theater. Blackie turned out to be an amateur carpenter. As soon as Davis told him what was needed, he designed a portable theater large enough to conceal adult puppeteers. In a few days, he drew a plan, bought supplies, picked up his tools from his mother's house and launched into ripping the boards to his specifications.

Although Easy could not read or write, he was a woodworking savant, particularly how moving parts work. The first time he picked up the puppets, he described how he could restring and paint them. "'Tween sticks and strings," he told Davis, looking him in the eye, "I kin make 'em do most anything you want, even dance a jig."

Eula Mae and Darlene had agreed to dress the puppets. When they returned from Kmart that morning, they staked a claim to the dining table. They set up Eula Mae's sewing machine on one end and stacked their material on the other. There were silks and brocades, snippets of fur, gleaming buttons, colored feathers and dime-sized fish scales. The fish scales, they declared, were for a dragon, which a puppet show with Korean puppets would surely have.

When Davis walked through the room after they returned and saw the table stacked with sewing supplies, he asked forlornly, "Where're we going to eat?"

Eula Mae looked at him with disdain. She said, "You want food or you want puppets. Take your pick." Davis shook his head.

The job of writing the play was left to him. He had something in mind—something tricky but effective. An oriental theme combined with a children's fairy tale. It must be humorous but also have appeal to both children and adults. And, yes, it would have a dragon.

Tuesday evening at 8 p.m. Davis left his house to keep his appointment with Josephine. He headed up the stone walk where abandoned flowerbeds spread out on either side. The borders had been recently planted with plugs of ivy and red geraniums, a testament to Eula Mae's tenacity. They looked like an oasis in a desert of stalks and weeds.

Davis could care less about the flowerbeds—living or the dead. Fine for Eula Mae to struggle against all obstacles for a few flowers. She was welcomed to attempt to restore the gardens. He had other worries. He had asked Josephine if he could come to see her. Now that the moment had arrived, he was full of dread.

As he left the stone walk and headed toward his parking deck, he looked down at his outfit. Khaki pants and white cotton shirt. As dull and lifeless as the old flower gardens, he thought miserably. Why hadn't he worn something with spark in it? He *had* to buy some new clothes.

At the parking deck located between his and Josephine's houses, he looked down on her gray rooftop. He could see the catwalk that ran from his kitchen door to her parking area. It stopped there, then picked up below her house and continued to her back door and on to Lover's Leap. As children, he and his cousins, including Josephine, had used the walk to run between the three houses on this end of the ridge. Now his end was overgrown with briars and rose bushes, and he made a mental note to ask Dutton to trim them back.

He paused to remove a stone, that had lodged in his shoe. It was only a small pebble, but it had managed to work its way into his sock and was stuck there. He picked it out. When he straightened up, he felt a sharp pain shoot up the nape of his neck into his hairline. He traced the discomfort with his fingertips until he touched his shoulder muscle. Pain resonated down his back and arms.

Considering the flash of pain in his neck, the slower burn of his muscles, the annoying ache on the bottom of his foot, he instantly thought about returning home. Something was warning him. Clearly he should call and postpone their meeting. But that idea brought a torturous picture of Eula Mae laughing her head off if he said he wanted to cancel because of a sore neck and a pebble in his shoe.

Eula Mae with her burdensome sense of family. Her digging around in dead gardens. Her cooking like crazy on Sundays. She had been the reason he was standing on his parking deck, trying to get up his nerve to walk down the driveway to Josephine's house. Eula Mae had practically forced him to call his cousin last Saturday. Not that Davis wouldn't have come to it himself at one time or other. He preferred to wait until he felt fully ready to see Josephine.

Now it was too late to turn back. His neck hurt. He couldn't remember any of the things he had rehearsed to say to her. The sentences were going to come out wrong. He couldn't explain why he hurt everybody he loved. But despite his fears and misgivings, he continued walking toward her driveway. By the time he reached her house, he had talked himself out of some of his uncertainty. And as he knocked on her door, he was prepared to do his best to convince her of his sincerity and ask for her forgiveness.

When Josephine opened the door, she was wearing blue jeans and a flannel shirt. With the late sun behind her, her hair looked darker than at the parade. For a moment, she reminded him of a picture in his college Greek myth book of Medusa, only Medusa's hair was black. Any minute, he thought, that hair, whatever the color, might turn into snakes. He managed to compose himself, and he stumbled out, "Hello," as he stepped through the door she had opened.

"You can have a seat there," she said coolly.

Josie poked her head around the doorway to the hall. Maylynn Eberhart was with her. "Do you live next door?" Josie asked Davis. He nodded. "You found me at the parade," she stated, coming into the living room.

"Jo—see," her mother warned. "This is Maylynn Eberhart. She's going to read Josie a story—in her *bedroom*— while we talk."

"Pleez'd to meet cha," Maylynn muttered.

"Wanna see me twirl a baton?" Josie asked Davis. "Maylynn taught me."

"Come on, Josie." Maylynn guided the child toward the door. "I'll read you about Mulberry Street."

"Oh, boy! See ya." The child and her baby sitter disappeared down the hall.

"Sorry about that," Josephine said.

"No," Davis stammered. "That's fine."

Actually Davis was relieved at the brief reprieve Josie had provided him. He took a seat in the chair Josephine had indicated for him. It was across from the unlit fireplace where Lady was lying. The dog looked up as Davis settled in his chair, licked her chops, and then dropped her head back on the floor. Josephine looked surprised. "She usually isn't that friendly."

"I'm afraid she's a regular at our house. We give her selected scraps. I hope it's okay."

Josephine shook her head. "Actually, I'd rather you didn't. Dogs don't digest bones and scraps." She continued, "I'm going to have coffee. Maybe some brandy, too. Would you like some?"

"That sounds fine," he agreed. "Would you mind if I stepped out on your porch and looked at your view?"

She shrugged. "Sure," she said, walking toward the kitchen.

He rose from his chair and walked through the living room onto the porch, where a view similar to his unfolded in front of him. The sun, still glaring against a vivid blue sky, was ready to slip behind the mountains. Down below, the small valley town of Globe was a speck nestled on the banks of the Boone River. To the right was Grandfather Mountain. To the extreme left were miniature-sized houses on the outskirts of High Meadows.

Surprisingly, Josephine's view did not frighten Davis as his own did. The house sat lower on the property, allowing the trees that lined the edges to softened the otherwise steep landscape.

When he returned to the living room, Josephine was coming from the kitchen with a tray of coffee, which she set on a table at the end of the sofa.

"Your view is almost the same as mine," he said to her. "But not nearly so startling."

"Something like our lives, you might say," she responded curtly.

"If you say so," he chuckled. "So life has been good to you."

"It has its moments," she answered. "I'm trying to get over the death of Mom and Dad and Laura."

"I'm sorry. I didn't realize you lost them all." He had remembered her as spunky and full of humor.

"I know you lost your parents, too. Josie was visiting Aunt Ruth when it happened. It must have been a horrible shock." Changing the subject, she asked, "Brandy in your coffee?"

"A big slug," he said, nodding and returning to the previous subject. "I left High Meadows when my parents died."

"You hadn't planned to leave?"

"Well, my mother was set on it. I was against it. It's hard to imagine, but I felt safe at the hospital. Now I have a lot of catching up to do. It's hard."

"Davis, why are you here?" Josephine asked. She had taken a seat on the sofa as far away from him as she could and still remain in the room.

Her question was so blunt it took him back. His words caught in his throat, but he managed to answer, "It never dawned on me that you lived here."

"Did you ask?

"Well, I had no reason to think…"

"My father owned the house for years," she stated. "You had every reason to think I would inherit it."

He moved up to the edge of his seat and placed his hands

on his knees. "I lived in a different world, Josephine. I survived on an hour by hour basis. Regardless, it does come back around to us, doesn't it." He wanted to remain calm and controlled. Instead his words were rushing out. "I want to say so much to you but I don't know where to start. I do know this with all my heart—I would never hurt Josie or you. I never wanted to hurt anyone." He wished he hadn't said "heart." It was sappy and emotional. Josephine had started talking.

"—That's the way you always were. You never wanted to hurt anyone but you always did." Her cup rattled against the saucer. "I wasn't the only one."

"That's true," he sighed, wondering how much she knew. "And I've paid all my life for it. But, Josephine, I can't erase that. I did shoot you, and I know it was because of my anger. My willfulness. I've spent sixteen years in a mental institute trying to accept that people are capable of hurting people they love. Forgive me! Give me the chance to make it up to you. Whatever you say I need to do, I will do. Just give me the opportunity." He dropped back in his chair. He heard a door close off the kitchen and supposed Josie was asleep.

Josephine had turned away and was looking out the window at the view. The sun was disappearing, leaving scarlet brushes across the horizon. "'Hurting people you loved,'" she repeated slowly. "Funny way of saying it." She turned back toward him. "You certainly never loved me. Far from it. You seemed to hate me. I was just a kid. Two years older than my own daughter! Yet you tried to drown me. And you did shoot me!"

"Josephine, I don't remember it that way at all. I was fifteen years old! Horsing around the pool. Jealous of you. Afraid you were getting all the attention because you were so cute." He leaned forward again with his elbows on his knees and lowered his head to his hands. "I'm willing to take responsibility for the things I did, but try to drown you? Absolutely not."

"Admit it! You held me under the water at Whitmire's

swimming pool until my lungs almost exploded. I've had nightmares all my life about it."

He stood up again, frustration and anger spreading across his face. "Josephine, I tried to watch out for you. Don't you remember the time I saved you from those hoodlums? They had their hands all over you. It could have gotten very bad if I hadn't been there. Don't you think that should count for something?"

Josephine's demeanor changed. By the time he stood up, she was staring at him with a blank look on her face. "I don't know what you're talking about. You're making that up." He was watching her closely. A small shadow rippled across her right eye. It was so quick he couldn't be sure he had seen it. She shook her head. "You're trying to change the subject."

Clearly, she wanted to forget the incident, he told himself, but he remembered. Six or seven boys about her age had surrounded her at a public swimming pool at Bishop. They held her hands behind her back and took turns feeling her. Davis had seen it happen and rushed to her aid. He ended up smashing the gang leader and getting thrown of the pool for it.

"Okay, so you don't remember the boys at the pool. Forget it. I never realized how things were for you."

"There was no incident with hoodlums. Don't you think I'd remember if there were? And you don't know—certainly not twenty years later—how anything was, or is, for me." She reached for the bottle of brandy and poured more into her coffee and returned the bottle to the table.

He continued, "I tried my best to be there for you. Maybe behind the scenes, but there. And, yes, I was a stupid, rebellious kid, but you have to believe me. I did not—ever—mean to hurt you."

"Hurt! Are you kidding? You're trying to tell me it didn't hurt when you shot me? The scar never left, you know." She pulled back her shirt revealing her bra strap and left shoulder. "See—?" She leaned toward him. He could see a purplish red, irregular scar about the size of a quarter. The mark was about an inch below her shoulder. It looked like a cancer.

Pulling her blouse back in place, she went on. "You followed me everywhere like I was some dumb kid who had to be looked after? You call that being there for me?" She swiped a wisp of hair off her forehead.

"I felt responsible for you. I wanted to make it up to you," he answered. He was shaking. For a moment neither of them spoke. Davis broke the silence. "I understand why you let me come tonight. You don't want to forgive me the way I thought. You want to punish me. 'An eye for an eye.' Right?" He was watching her, wanting to be reassured. She looked away.

"I'm going," he said abruptly. He moved toward the door, Lady following. As he pushed open the screen door, the dog and Davis stepped onto the porch, and the screen slammed shut.

Josephine scrambled up from her seat and rushed after him. He was already by the steps. She yelled, "You can't leave. We're not finished!"

He turned and looked back at her. "You're never going to forgive me the way I'd hoped," he said. "No matter what I do, you'll never forget." He continued up the steps, Lady trailing behind him.

She yelled after him, "You asked what I want you to do. Here it is. Leave Josie and me alone. You know why? Because you just might decide you 'love' us. And people *you* love get hurt. In fact, they get so hurt they die!"

He stopped on the steps and looked back at her. He spoke slowly. "You don't have to worry about that, Josephine. You'll never have to look at me again." Then he reached down and patted Lady. "Go home, Lady," he said. "Your mistress doesn't want you associating with the likes of me."

Josephine stormed back into the house, slamming the door so hard the glass panes rattled. Everything about Davis infuriated her, especially the fact that he had walked out. Even Lady, who had returned to the stoop and was barking again, was a target of her anger.

"Shut up, Lady," Josephine snapped from behind the closed door. She was headed—reeling—for the bathroom. The brandy, warmed by the coffee, had gone straight to her head. The floor was a wavy obstacle course. Once she reached the bathroom, she wrung out a wash rag with cool water, wiped her face and laid the rag on the back of her neck. Then she dropped to the floor in front of the john and rested her head against the cold porcelain.

Lady barked again. "Please don't bark, Lady," she whispered. "*Please* don't wake Josie." Even whispering, the sound of her own voice resounded in her head. Another series of *ruffs* came from outside. Josephine struggled up from the floor to let in the dog.

"Mommy," Josie whined from her bedroom. "Lady's barking."

Josephine's stomach was pitching. "Just a minute, Josie. I'm letting her in." By the time Josephine managed to walk back to Josie's room her daughter had fallen back asleep.

Gingerly, Josephine returned to the living room to lock the doors and turn off the lights. Then she stumbled into her bedroom, found her nightgown and fell across the bed.

The room was tilting slowly. She felt around in the dark until she located her pillow and carefully slid it under her head. Then she rummaged around the bed until she hit the washcloth, waved it in the air to recool it, and plastered it against her forehead. The relief was immediate. *So cool.* She inched one of her legs over the edge of the bed until her foot touched the floor. Mercifully the bed stopped spinning. In minutes she was asleep.

Once Davis was in his house, he passed without a word the three people watching TV in the living room. He knew Darlene and Blackie would want an explanation. He hoped Eula Mae would stop them. He had to be alone. Surely they all would realize how his evening had gone.

He entered his room and shut the door.

The puppets were stretched across his bed. He wanted to destroy them—throw them away—get them out of his sight. How had he imagined he could turn a bunch of rag-tag, ne'er-do-wells into a puppet troupe? The project was a huge undertaking for a person with all his faculties. He was a misfit who couldn't outlive his past. It was impossible.

Josephine would never get over what happened when they were children. Once he saw the ugly scar on her shoulder, her pain resonated with him. He remembered his war injury and the difficult recovery that followed, the lengthy physical therapy, the emotional stress of believing his injury would end his military career.

It was all so stupid. His mother had actually convinced him he could have a future like real people. Of course, that wasn't true. Josephine had been right—everyone he loved died—Uncle Jack, Mace, his parents, Celeste. He tainted them all. All except Josephine. She had managed to survive.

He piled the puppets on top of the dresser. At least he had maintained enough self-control not to destroy them. He turned out the light and fell across the bed. His confusing evening had exhausted him. He drifted off to sleep where he dreamed he was a puppet tied by strings. But the puppeteer was hidden. All that could be seen was a hand manipulating the strings that controlled him.

The snap of a twig. The rustle of dead leaves, and Josephine was awake. She bolted up in her bed, listening. The clock on the table said 2:30 p.m.

Was the sound by the back door? In the front garden? By the side of the house?

Dark leaf shadows from outside her window moved across her umber window shades. She waited breathlessly to hear the sound again, but nothing came. Inside her house, the usual night sounds created an undercurrent. Lady snored on the floor beside her. From the kitchen the refrigerator whirred. In the bedroom next to her Josie sighed.

A raccoon had caused the noise, Josephine guessed, and she slipped quietly out of bed to check the back stoop where the garbage can was. When she walked passed her mother's old bedroom, she glanced out of the window. A flicker caught her eye. A small dot floated in the dark. Concerned yet curious, she moved closer to the windows. The glow intensified. Someone was outside smoking a cigarette and apparently when they dragged on it, the ash burned brightly. Someone was watching her. The same person, no doubt, who had left the cigarettes in the glove Lady had found in June.

What if that person could see her now? Horrified, she dropped to the floor, huddling under the window, trying to decide what to do. She had on a thin nightgown and no robe. Her teeth were beginning to chatter. Who was out there? What should she do?

Her head was splitting. If she tried to get an Alka-Seltzer from the bathroom, the cabinet light would come on. Maybe she should bundle up Josie and dash for the car. But where would she go? Angie was her only friend, and she couldn't wake her up.

It had to be Davis. He was so mad about last night's encounter he had come back to spy on her. It was a terrifying thought to have a man who had recently left a mental institution outside her house, watching her. Still, she reasoned, he hadn't really acted irrationally last night. Hard as it was for her to admit, she had been as out of control—maybe more—than he. Their arguments were over the past. Logically, they both should want to keep them there.

What if it weren't Davis? What if Dutton had been right, and someone who lived below her house was watching her? She crawled on her hands and knees through the kitchen into the front hall where she could reach the telephone. She had to call Michael or the police. But which? She decided on Michael, and ticked off in her mind the places he had recently been. Kinston over the weekend examining books of a bank they were considering buying. Monday driving back to Matthews. Tuesday working in the main office. Tonight he should be at home.

She dialed their number. Four agonizing rings and Michael's voice came through. "Hello," he mumbled gruffly.

"Michael, it's Josephine," she whispered.

"What's the matter? Why're you whispering?"

Even grouchy, the sound of his voice was such a relief that she almost cried. When she had regained her composure, she whispered into the phone, "Michael, somebody's outside the house. I don't know what to do."

"Josephine, you have a huge imagination. I'm sure nobody's out there."

"That's unfair, Michael. Somebody is outside. I can see their cigarette burning."

"Maybe it's those mountain lights—Brown Mountain, I think they're called."

"Don't make fun of me! I'm serious. Somebody's out there! What do I have to do to convince you that I'm telling the truth?" Michael didn't reply. Josephine added, "I'm thinking of picking Josie up and running for the car."

"No, God! That would be stupid."

His annoyed manner, his word choices, his condescending tone. The hairs on the back of her neck bristled. When she spoke again, she did not whisper. "If you call me stupid, I'm hanging up this phone, and you won't know what happened to your wife and daughter."

"Josephine, I did not call you stupid. I said *that* would be stupid. Do not run to the car with Josie! Do you hear me? Just do exactly what I tell you."

"You're doing it, Michael. You're putting me down," she sputtered into the phone. Now he was making her mad.

"Look, you called for help. Now do what I say. Load the gun. It's in the front closet, shells in the box beside it. Get two shells. It's a double barrel."

"I don't know how to load a gun."

"It's simple. Open the breech and drop in the shells. Snap

the barrel back in place. Just keep the safety on. Put the gun where you can get it quickly. Now, do that."

"This is not a good time to teach me to load a gun. Even if I could load it, I wouldn't have any idea how to shoot it. I'm going to hang up now and call the police. I'll call you after they leave."

"Wait, Josephine—"

The activity in the hall had awakened Josie. "Mommy," she called.

"It's okay, honey," Josephine replied. "I'm just talking to daddy." She didn't tell her daughter she had just pressed down the plunger on the telephone and broken the connection.

Josie didn't reply, and Josephine guessed she had fallen back asleep.

When Josephine called the police, the dispatcher who answered the call told her what to do. "Until we can get there," he said, "turn off every light—inside and out. Under no circumstances should you leave your house. We'll be there as fast as possible."

Josephine paced back and forth in the darkened living room, waiting for the police to arrive. Every time she heard a car start or a noise she couldn't place, she rushed to the window. Finally the police arrived. They investigated the catwalk and reported back to Josephine.

"Somebody was there alright," the officer said. "Found half a dozen cigarettes on the ground near your catwalk. Know anybody smokes Winstons?"

"I have no idea," Josephine replied, looking at the plastic bag which held the evidence. There were six crushed cigarettes with tan filters on the end, the same kind Lady found last June in the glove.

When the police left, Josephine called Michael back. He answered in the same gruff, sleepy voice.

"I thought you might be worried about us," Josephine said. "I see it didn't bother you enough to keep you awake!"

"I just dozed off. What happened?" he replied.

"Somebody was here, but we're okay now. Josie slept right through it all."

"That's a relief. Josephine, I'm sorry about earlier. You know how I am with emergencies."

"Michael, we have to talk. There're things you need to know about me. Things I've realized while I've been up here this summer. Come this weekend and I'll tell you all about it."

"Look, I'm up to my eyeballs at work—"

"Michael, get out from behind those damn bank books and get up here! Your wife and daughter need you. I've had an awful night and I'm exhausted. I don't mean to be rude, but I have to go to bed."

They said hurried good nights and hung up.

Josephine turned out the lights and made certain the windows and doors were locked. Then she checked on Josie.

Josephine collapsed on the edge of Josie's bed. Her daughter's chest was rising and falling with the precision of a machine. If she could only sleep with such peace. No doubt the key was innocence. Her young daughter was shielded from everything vicious and mean in the world. But how long could she protect her? When would the day come when her innocence would be lost?

Sitting on her daughter's bed, thinking over the events of the night, several thoughts gnawed at her. Why had it been so difficult to convince Michael that she and Josie were in danger? Didn't he hear the panic in her voice? She would have thought his reaction would be immediate concern.

On the other hand, why had Davis repeated several times during their talk that he felt responsible for her when they were kids? Was there something she was overlooking?

A picture she had pushed out of her mind long ago began to fall in place, bit by bit and piece by piece.

She was eleven, and she was wearing her brand new two-pieced red plaid swimsuit, the one Momma couldn't afford but bought anyway because Josephine adored it with all her heart. Everybody thought it was so-oo cute. They were at the swimming pool in Bishop. Some of her girl friends, their hair tied back in bunchy curls, their faces red from the sun, were slathering each other with baby oil with iodine in it, preparing to stretch out on their beach towels and sunbathe until their bodies were pink as babies' butts.

Other girl friends, including Josephine, were playing tag. In and out of the water, splashing and laughing with anyone who wanted to join. As she recalled, quite suddenly, the scene changed. A menacing cloud drifted over them. When she looked around, she couldn't locate any of her friends. They seem to have vanished, and she was surrounded by a group of boys. One boy—blond, blue-eyed, bristly crew cut, fresh pimples emerging across his cheeks, scrawny around the chest with ribs like sticks trying to poke through the skin—this boy grabbed her arms and pulled them behind her. "Go on," he said to the others. "I got her."

The others advanced on her, the circle tightening, and she screamed. The sounds—her screams—fell like drops of water in the pool and floated away. The lifeguard would look her way, she thought, but he didn't notice anything. One boy was feeling her breasts. "Shit, she ain't got nothing," he said. "Her cherries ain't ripe yet." Some of them laughed. Several went under water. Suddenly she felt a hand pushing aside the bottom of her bathing suit. She screamed again, kicking and twisting with all her might. She managed to get her mouth around somebody's arm and clamped down as hard as she could. He yelled.

That boy's cries, fresh in her ears, layered with fingers touching her private parts, searching in the folds of her vagina where she had never touched. Too many feelings. Hands were everywhere like bugs on her. Here she twisted, there she kicked. Down below, squashing the feelings that came from places she did not know. Everything in her body was screaming. And then it all stopped. She closed out the screams, the splashing water, the feelings in her body, the foreign hands touching her. She closed it all down.

The memory, too, clinching her fists and clamping her eyes shut, she tried to push away the images, but the traces of the flashback were still there. How had it ended? She couldn't quite remember. Somebody broke it up. Somebody called her mother.

The disturbing memory along with the emotional magnitude of her meeting with Davis, the sweet brandy and coffee, the intruder and the police—all of it erupted. She ran from Josie's room into the bathroom and lost it all.

Later she curled up in her bed, exhausted and spent, and wondered if there would ever be a morning to this long, long night.

CHAPTER SEVENTEEN

When the telephone rang, Josephine was on her way out of the house to drive Josie to day camp.

It had been a wretched start to the day. They had overslept, and she had to give Josie a Pop-Tart for breakfast and throw a sandwich together for her lunch. She grabbed a Coke for herself in the hope it would settle her stomach. It was eight forty-five in the morning.

The voice on the phone said, "This here's Eula Mae from next door."

"What's the matter?" Josephine asked, catching the concern in Eula Mae's voice. She motioned Josie to sit down while she took the call. Her daughter thrust her hands on her hips, and Josephine shook her finger at her.

"We can't get Davis outta his room," Eula Mae said. "He ain't said nothing to nobody since he was up to your house last night. What happened?"

"I'll tell you what happened," Josephine snapped, last night's anger rising again. "Davis had some stupid idea he'd sail in here, ask me to forgive him, and I'd forget everything he did to me. Even shooting me."

"Honey" Eula Mae replied, slowly, "sometimes the past's just gotta be the past."

Her back stiffened at Eula Mae's remark. "Not for me, Eula Mae. Davis and I are oil and water."

"If we can't get him out his room, Blackie's gonna call Doc Bostwick at High Meadows. They's likely to make him go back."

"Eula Mae, in my opinion Davis is better off in an institution."

Eula Mae's voice rose. "That's a mean thing to say, hard as that man's trying. Listen, we's all God's children, and we gits out the bed the same way every morning."

Josie, who had been watching her mother, grimaced and plopped in the chair by the door.

"Eula Mae, I swear I don't even know how to answer that. Last night we didn't resolve a thing. He ended up storming out. I hate that man."

"Hate! You don't know the meaning of the word. Besides, he ain't the same person he used to be." There was a long pause. "Can you come talk to him?" Eula Mae sounded tired.

"I can't, Eula Mae," Josephine answered with an unexplained stab of guilt. "I have some important business I have to take care of this morning."

"Well, after you do that 'important business,' maybe you'll have second thoughts. After all, you is his cousin."

"Why does everybody keep saying that? I'm *not* related to him! My aunt married his uncle. I don't even think that counts. Look, I'll call you later. I have to get Josie to day camp or she's going to be late." Josephine was shaking her head.

Eula Mae sighed. "Well, everywhere you go this morning, you just keep thinking 'bout it. See if somethin' don't change yo' mind."

Josephine was about to sign off when she remembered the cigarettes the police found. "Does Davis smoke?" she asked Eula Mae.

"I guess. Sometimes. Why?"

"What kind?"

"I dunno."

"Never mind. Just wondered," Josephine replied. She said goodbye and gathered her things to leave.

Josie had grabbed her lunch bag and headed out the door. "Finally," she said with a sigh.

"Don't give me a hard time, miss," Josephine replied as she locked the door behind them. Her brain was swirling.

Josephine's business was more than "important." Before last night's encounter with Davis—long before the prowler and Michael's disappointing response, she had made up her mind to set the record straight with T.J. She had decided to end any association with him.

It had been an easy conclusion to reach. After Josie's riding lesson, Josephine had told Angie about the kiss. Angie was furious. "Michael's the best thing that ever happened to you, Jo," she had said to Josephine. "You're determined to mess it up with a sleazy nobody like T.J."

Angie's needling had helped put the arguments in place, but it was not the reason Josephine had already cast aside any thoughts of T.J. Neither was loyalty to Michael, although it certainly played a part. In fact, Michael's insensitivity last night over the phone might have worked in T.J.'s favor.

The real reasons were more complicated, Josephine reflected as she drove toward the barn. It had something to do with her reconnection with her mother and the importance of family. Reading letters written by her mother and other family members, holding belongings her mother had treasured, renewing her own childhood memories had stirred her moral fiber. Josephine's mother would have been appalled at the idea of another man kissing her daughter. For now, that was reason enough.

Josephine found T.J. at the barn in the manager's office, sitting behind the desk. He was talking on the phone. When Josephine walked in, he grinned widely and motioned for her to sit down. "Zeke," he said into the phone, "I'll check on the mare tomorrow. Something just came up. Gotta run."

The office was a window-less cubbyhole with a desk and chair, faced by two straight-back captains' chairs. A small circle of light from an outdated lamp fell across the desk, revealing scattered papers and ledgers. Around the walls were countless black and white photographs of people mounted on show horses. Different colored prize ribbons were clipped to the frames.

Josephine slipped into the chair closest to the wall. T.J. dropped the receiver in place and turned to her, "Well, hello, pretty lady." He was grinning, his most appealing look, and she felt her resolve weakening. He rose and came around the desk, pulling up the chair beside Josephine.

He said, "I was about to think you were a figment of my imagination."

"I need to talk to you," Josephine said, shaking off her momentary indecision and trying to sound businesslike. He faced her, his arms extending over the chair. His hands were so close to her arm they almost touched.

"The kiss was a mistake," she said, looking down. "I'm very sorry it happened. I should have made it more clear that I'm not available. I don't want to mislead you."

T.J. continued to stare at his hands. "What do you mean, mistake? That was no mistake."

Sounds from the barn rose around them. The horses shuffled and snorted. Jeeter, the stable boy, was singing in a high reedy voice, which hung in the air. Outside, a couple of blue jays argued. Time seemed insignificant.

Josephine didn't reply. He lifted his head to look at her. His gray green eyes were like two fresh drops of ocean water, drawing her to them like a swimmer caught in an undertow.

When he spoke again, his voice was soothing. "You're too late. A woman doesn't have to tell me when she's interested. Men know. That kiss wasn't a mistake. It was an invitation."

She swallowed hard. His cowboy boots scraped across the floor, crunching into the dirt and hay that littered the floor.

The sound was raw and grating, unlike T.J.'s gentle voice. She shook her head, unsure of her mixed feelings.

"But that's the reality of it, T.J.," she said, not totally convinced. "It meant nothing." She had planned to avoid using his name. It had such a disarming ring.

Abruptly he stood up, surprising her, but the tone of his voice was as patient as before. "Look, Josephine," he was saying, "You can't turn me on, then walk away. It doesn't work that way." She scrambled out of her chair, facing him.

What was he really saying to her? That she shouldn't have led him on? "I was honest with you from the beginning. I was flattered. That's all," she defended.

While she spoke, he was shaking his head. His demeanor was shifting. His lips pursed in a tight, unfamiliar way, and his gentle look was changing into a threatening scowl. He grabbed for her, but she jerked away. Instinctively, she shoved the chair he had been sitting in against his legs. She pushed harder than she intended, pinning him against the desk. His arms flew up, and he winced with pain. Taking advantage of catching him off guard, Josephine ducked out of the office and ran down the main hall of the barn.

Somewhere in the dark hallway, she heard Jeeter cleaning stalls. She heard the metal fork chink against the wheelbarrow as horse droppings were tossed, and she smelled the steamy rawness rising from the clumps of manure.

Jeeter was still singing. She hurried toward him, knowing T.J. wouldn't dare grab her around Jeeter. But when she glanced back toward the office, T.J. was still running after her.

When she reached Jeeter, she greeted him with relief, and slowed down. Near the entrance to the barn, she glimpsed an object hanging from a nail. It was a tan glove like the one Lady found on the catwalk earlier in the summer. Hastily, she glanced down the hall. T.J. was still following.

"This glove yours?" she called back to Jeeter, knowing as she asked that Jeeter had no reason to be in her yard.

"Naw," he replied.

"I think it might be my husband's," she answered. "May I take it home to check?"

Jeeter nodded. Josephine jammed the glove in her pocket and dashed for her car. T.J. was running down the hall after her.

When she reached her car, she climbed in and locked her door. T.J. stopped at the entrance and leaned against the barn door, watching her.

Safely in the car, she turned the key and pulled out of her parking space. As she drove away, she glanced back. Dust billowed from the rear of her car. Through it, she made out T.J., leaning against the barn door. As the dust cleared, she saw him pull a pack of cigarettes out of his breast pocket and withdraw a cigarette. Then he tossed the empty pack on the ground. As the crumpled ball of paper tumbled through the air, it flashed Winston red.

Impossible thoughts clashed in her mind as she patted the tan glove in her pocket. The intruder had returned last night to watch her. She had just found a tan glove at the barn, which could be a mate to the one Lady found on the catwalk. T.J. had tossed away a red cigarette pack. Coincidences, or did they all lead in the same direction? Josephine shuddered.

She had seen an aggressive side of T.J. Angie had warned her. She should have paid attention to her.

Josephine pulled off the highway into the first Seven-Eleven she reached. She steered the car to the phone booth, gathered up her pocketbook and car key, and headed for the phone.

"Rocky Ridge Realty?" she asked when she had dialed the number. "Angie Dickinson, please."

After a few seconds, Angie came on the phone.

"Angie," Josephine's voice was shaking. "I told him. T.J., I mean."

"Josephine, is that you?"

"Yes, I told T.J. to leave me alone."

"You're kidding."

"No, I really did it." Josephine blurted out what had happened, even how ugly things became. "I'm a wreck," she concluded to Angie. "I'm shaking all over. Can you meet me?"

"Oh, I can't! I have to show a guy some property in Tennessee. But I'll call you soon as I get back this evening. I am so proud of you, Josephine. It was the right thing."

Josephine replied, "I'm counting on it."

Josephine returned to the car and collapsed against the seat. Somehow when she was talking to Angie, everything had seemed right. Now the reality of what she had done was sinking in. T.J. could come after her. He could threaten her, and worse, Josie. Why had she been so stupid as to get herself in this mess?

She drove back to town and headed for Lonnie's Grill, thinking a cup of coffee might help. She glanced at her watch, noting she had two hours before picking up Josie. When she reached Main Street, empty parking spaces were available up and down the street. She pulled into one near Lonnie's and quickly walked the short distance to the diner.

Lonnie's was a spartan, fifties-type diner with a light green counter lined with chrome barstools. Large plate glass windows on either side of the front door overlooked Main Street. Muslin café curtains covered the lower edge of the windows, and philodendron, planted in terra cotta pots, twined up the wall, running around the windowsills and over the top of the windows. Booths lined the far wall. Early morning sunlight filled the room.

The breakfast crowd was thinning out, and Josephine took a seat on one of the barstools. She had intended ordering a coffee and nothing else, but the smells coming from the kitchen made her feel unsettled. Oddly, they reminded her of her mother and their early morning breakfasts.

"Breakfast special, please," Josephine heard herself saying to Lonnie, who was behind the counter.

Lonnie swiped his hands on his butcher's apron and yelled into the kitchen pass-through, "Sam, one special."

"That last booth okay?" Josephine asked.

"Sit where you like," Lonnie shrugged, pouring a cup of coffee for Josephine. "Won't be long," he added.

Josephine took her cup to the booth next to the window where the sun was streaming in. She crawled into the far corner and huddled over her coffee. The sun spilling over her was warm and comforting, but her mind kept returning to her encounter with T.J. She hadn't heard the last of him, she knew. Whatever she did, or wherever she went, she would have to be extremely careful. If Michael suspected, he might never forgive her. Angie had been right. She had been foolish.

In the middle of breakfast she noticed a pay phone and remembered Davis and Eula Mae. She left her food and phoned Eula Mae. When she answered, Josephine said, "It's Josephine, Eula Mae. Did he come out?" The reply was no. "Okay, I'm coming down. But I can't promise anything."

She signed off, placed an order with Lonnie for half dozen ham biscuits and waited for her order to be prepared. Her breakfast was abandoned in the booth. Her appetite had suddenly vanished.

When her take-out order was ready, Josephine headed for the ledge where she and Davis lived. As she negotiated the hairpin curves and turns of the road, she reminded herself she had meant to stay away from Davis. Now she was driving toward his house where another confrontation awaited her, this time with Davis. Would this one end like the other? Or had Davis changed the way everybody said. Was he a harmless cousin with mental problems he had overcome, or was he still dangerous?

Her mind shifted to Michael. What would he think? He seemed far away, not just in miles, but also in emotions. Certainly he wouldn't understand about T.J., but he would be afraid for her to get involved with Davis, too. She might get hurt, he would say.

Josephine reached the part of the road called the "wilderness." Davis's house was just beyond. Whatever awaited her, she had accepted the consequences when she told Eula Mae she'd come by. There was no turning back now.

She drove into Davis' parking deck, checked the rearview mirror to see if she still had on lipstick and picked up the bag of ham biscuits. Then she made her way down the stone steps to Davis's house.

Eula Mae answered the kitchen door.

"Good morning," Josephine said, smiling. She had a sudden urge to hug Eula Mae but resisted.

"He still ain't out," Eula Mae answered without a greeting.

"Has he talked to you?" Josephine asked.

"Oh, he talks," she said, shaking her head. "He jest don't come out."

"Did you tell him I was coming?" Josephine questioned.

"Naw. We thought we'd leave that to you," she answered with a sly grin.

Josephine nodded as she pulled three ham biscuits and coffees from her sack. "From Lonnie's. For you, Darlene and Blackie. These are for Davis." She glanced through the doorway leading to the rest of the house. "Where's his bedroom?"

"This way." Eula Mae led the way through the dining room into the hall. She was comfortably dressed, and her customary apron was tied around her waist. At the doorway she pointed down a hallway. "That's his room on the right."

"Wish me luck," Josephine said, passing Eula Mae, who rolled her eyes toward the ceiling.

"You gonna need it."

Once Josephine was positioned in front of Davis' door, she took a deep breath and knocked. "Davis, it is Josephine. I've brought you breakfast."

"Go away."

"It's country ham biscuits from Lonnie's. Best in the south." She tried to sound pleasant.

"Don't want any breakfast. Besides, you're the last person I want to see."

"I'm going to ignore that remark, Davis," she laughed but felt the sting of irritation. "Come on. Open the door."

"No."

Josephine knocked sharply on the door. "You open this door right now or I'm going to open it."

"Don't you dare. I'm not dressed."

Despite Josephine's resolve to remain calm, she found herself getting angry. "Well, get dressed this minute because I'm coming in. I've taken the time and trouble to come down here, and you're coming out. Eula Mae," she called loudly enough for Davis to hear. "Bring me a small screw driver. I'm going to open the door." She could hear Davis scrambling around inside the room. She leaned down to peer into the keyhole. There was a key in it.

Eula Mae was coming down the hall with a screwdriver. Josephine walked to meet her and whispered, "I can see a key in the keyhole."

Eula Mae whispered back. "Push it out with the screw driver."

"I need a piece of cardboard to catch it."

"Pull it under the door with the screwdriver."

Josephine nodded and inserted the screwdriver in the lock. She heard the key fall to the floor.

"Well, aren't you the clever one," Davis said from the other side of the door. "You were going to try to pull the key under the door!"

She peeked into the keyhole again. Davis was leaning over to pick up the key. Then, to her surprise, he stuck the key in and turned the lock.

As the doorknob turned, Eula Mae began backing down the hall. "Where are you going?" Josephine asked.

Eula Mae threw up her hands. "This ain't my mess."

Davis opened the door and stood blocking the opening. Josephine was standing in the hall alone, holding her take-out bag. Davis still had on his pajama top with a pair of tan khakis. His hair was tousled and his eyelids, inflamed.

She shoved him aside. "I thought you'd never get that thing open," she said. "These are for you." She held up the sack of biscuits and coffee. "Where can we talk?"

Davis stood by as she pushed open the door and entered his room. "Just like that?" he said. "`Where can we talk?' We talked last night."

"Seems we didn't finish." She headed toward two slipper chairs with a small table between, where she dropped her pocketbook and the sack. The chairs were located in front of a plate glass window. She added, turning to look at him, "What are you doing in this dark room, for heavens sake?"

Davis had taken a place on the bed and was watching every move she made.

"This is ridiculous." She stepped around the chairs and headed for the windows, rummaging through the drapes for the pulls. "It's too dark in here."

Davis jumped up from the bed and ran to grab the drapes out of her hands. "Oh, no you don't," he said. "The sun hurts my eyes."

"Davis, we face west. We get the afternoon sun," she argued.

He shook his head. "It's still too bright."

She abandoned the drapes and returned to the table, where she pulled the biscuits and coffee from the sack. "I brought you two biscuits," she said, taking the top off her coffee and sipping.

He turned away.

"You're acting like a spoiled child," she said. He didn't answer and she settled back in the chair. "Okay, maybe I did overreact last night," she said. "But you really made me mad. All of a sudden you just got up and left. What happened?"

He went to the table beside her and picked up his coffee, pulled the top off and returned to the bed.

The bed was in shambles. "Why did you show me your scar?" he snapped. "Can't you imagine how that made me feel? You're still bearing a grudge after all these years, and you're never going to forgive me."

"You *did* do it to me," she insisted sternly.

"Okay, so I had no right to *ask* for your forgiveness." He shook his head, then looked back at her. "It's something between us that'll never go away. Besides, it's not just you. It's everybody. Like you said, people I care about get hurt! You're just lucky you didn't die like the rest."

"What are you talking about?" she asked in surprise.

"You said it last night. People I love get hurt."

"I shouldn't have said that. It was mean and I'm sorry."

He was silent for a time, and she suspected he was trying to decide what to say. When he did speak, his cross tone was gone, and his voice, soft. "When I was little," he began, "I stayed in the woods all the time. One day I caught a baby rabbit and took it home. My father said the bunny was going to die because it had my smell on it. Other rabbits in the burrow, even the mother, would chase it away because it had a human smell on it. I wanted to make a pet of that bunny and take care of it. But daddy told me it was going to die because of me. That's the first time I knew I could hurt something I loved."

Josephine rose and walked toward him, but as she crossed the distance between them she felt awkward and uncomfortable. Once beside him, she didn't know what to do. She dropped her hand on his shoulder and patted him sympathetically, but he didn't respond. Her fingertips were resting on his shoulder, where warmth and sweat began spreading to her hand.

She had spent the better part of her life collecting bad deeds to hold against him. Now he seemed as vulnerable as a child, and her instinct was to put her arms around him the way she might comfort Josie. Stunned by her own response, she sat down on the bed beside him.

"Davis," she said, shaking her head, "that is so sad. Your father shouldn't have said such things to a child. Particularly not a sensitive one."

Davis left the bed and walked to the picture window. She watched as he pulled back the drapes and faced the mountain, looking at the range of Blue Ridge Mountains before him.

"I grew up," he said, "in the shadow of the Blue Ridge Mountains. I measured the seasons of my life by them. I watched them through wire mesh windows at High Meadows. Now I can't even look at the view for more than a few minutes."

Josephine held her breath as she watched him, unsure of what he would do next. A quiver run down his neck, and he lifted his face to the sun. Then he breathed deeply and began to speak.

Josephine listened, sitting on the end of the bed he had just left, hearing the words fall around her with a soft cadence. He said everybody blamed him for Uncle Jack's death. His uncle had driven out to the River to pick up Mace and him, and he had ended up dying in Davis' arms, begging him to take care of his children, Ellen and Petey. A promise he was powerless to keep.

Then there was Mace. He had promised Mace's mother he would protect him, but he died in a foxhole in Korea, laying next to Davis.

"There's one part of my life I can't talk about. It's both too beautiful and too ugly at the same time. How can that be?" he asked.

First as he spoke and then as he fell silent, Josephine could feel his weariness settle over her like a heavy cloak.

CHAPTER EIGHTEEN

Waiting was worse than fighting. Their platoon had been camped in a field near Wonsan for days, waiting to advance into the area of the Chosin Reservoir.

The men were ready to fight anything. Even Chinese, if they had too. They didn't care. They'd fight Russians to get home.

One evening about sunset, Russett called in Sgt. Wilbur to brief him on the nightly patrol for his squad. Russett told Wilbur that outposts had reported sighting an enemy tank. The tank surfaced at night and disappeared during the day. Nobody could figure out where it was hiding during daylight. Russett said he was sending the whole platoon out. "Let's nail the bastard's ass to the ground," he said.

The platoon left the secure main road about 5 miles out from camp. They were traveling northwest of Wonsan on a dirt road. Their speed was at a good clip because the road had been swept for enemy mines. They were traveling toward the mountains, which were in the distance about 15 miles away.

There was no cover to speak off. Not like marines think of it. Only waist-high saw grass and stubby Korean pines, which couldn't hide a dog, as Wilbur said.

They traveled about 8 from the base, and the terrain was getting hilly. Undulations and ravines. And they were approaching where the tank was sighted. By now, it was dark as pitch and the scouts put on their night vision goggles.

They were coming up on one of the ravines when Williams hit a trip wire. He must have struck it across his combat boots. For a second, he froze stock still, trying to figure if the trip wire was set to ignite on contact or release. It was impossible to know. The wire must have stretched over 50 yards. Flares went off all along the wire. Davis lit up like a Christmas tree. He looked iridescent. His arms, fatigues, legs. Sgt. Wilbur shouted, "Hit the dirt, Williams!" He fell to the ground but the turret on the tank was already sighting him. You could hear its motor grinding. Everybody stood there watching while the gun swung around toward Davis and fired. Davis was knocked back two feet. Davis screamed out, "Sarge, I'm hit." Bullets were ricocheting everywhere.

"Stay down, Williams! We'll get you." Sgt. Wilbur yelled. "Scully, Kenny, get the god damn bazookas going! What the hell you waiting for? Get the bastard! Corpsman, on the double. Get up there and help Williams!"

The tank, still firing, started backing out of the ravine. Bazookas were going now, their rockets blasting into the sides of the tank, but the damn thing didn't stop. Scully and Kenny, who were operating the bazookas, took chase; and once the tank had gained some distance, the hatch opened and two North Korean soldiers scrambled out and made a run for it. Scully and Kenny were right there on top of them.

Sgt. Wilbur was running toward them, shouting, "The tank may be booby-trapped! Get the fuck out of there!" He reached the two marines, who had thrown the Koreans on the ground and drawn their weapons on them. The three marines grabbed the Koreans by the scruff of the neck and drug 'em back to their line. They barely reached the rest of the squad when the tank exploded. The explosion was so powerful about half the men were knocked to the ground. Everybody stood there in amazement watching the tank burn to the ground.

The corpsman had rushed to Davis. He was semi-conscious and

losing blood fast. He was loaded on a stretcher and airlifted by helicopter to the hospital in Seoul. The corpsman went right on to Seoul with Davis, tending him every minute.

That corpsman saved Williams life, that's for sure.

Davis's story unfolded in the evenings that followed. He spoke in a low, steady voice, Josephine listening, seeing the characters come forward in sepia tones like old photographs, Josie asleep close by in her bedroom.

The terrain of Rocky Ridge, he said, especially in lower elevations, reminded him of Korea, where he had met his wife, Celeste. He did not mention she was constantly on his mind. He had spent years trying to forget her, but since he left High Meadows, his memories of her had returned. Every woman he saw made him think of her. Whenever he came upon a dark corner, or took an unexpected turn into an unfamiliar spot, he imagined her there singing. When he closed his eyes, her perfume spread over him like the smell of the lemons she liked to warm in her hands. At night he dreamed her fingers were skimming his body, and when she leaned to kiss him, he could smell her hair before it touched his body.

Davis told Josephine he was wounded in the Korean War. He was taken to a hospital in Seoul, and Celeste had been his nurse. His left shoulder wound required surgery. She was assigned to his case. At first, he thought he might have imagined her in the drug-induced sleep that followed his operation. But when his head cleared, he knew she was real.

One morning she entered his room singing. "So we have finally decided to join the living!" she said, smiling.

Her left hand was resting casually on the railing of his bed. He reached up with his good hand, the right one, and grasped her wrist.

When he spoke, his voice was hoarse. "Marry me," he whispered.

"No," she laughed, tilting her head back. "But don't think

you're the first bedside proposal I've had. I will go out with you, though. After all, I've seen what's under the covers."

He blushed.

"Don't worry, soldier. I've seen it all, and I never tell. Your shoulder's doing fine by the way. The doctor'll be in later to tell you about it. In the meantime, I'm leaving you in the hands of Kim Young-he, my nurse's aid. She'll take care of you. I'll check in on you before I leave for the day."

Leave for the day, he thought wildly. She was his life blood and she was talking about leaving. He couldn't live through the day without her.

"She always sing?" he asked Young-he when Celeste had gone.

"Celeste? She sing plenty, plenty. Sing with band in bar downtown Seoul. Soldiers love. Ve'ly pretty."

Very pretty indeed. That hardly covered it, he thought. She was the most beautiful woman he had ever seen. She was saving his life and he was going to marry her.

Later Celeste returned with the doctor.

"I'm Dr. Bradley, Pfc. Williams. I performed the surgery on your left shoulder. You had a pretty serious wound there. We normally transport injuries like yours to Japan. But when you came in, you had already lost a lot of blood. It looked like you caught an M-30 on the top part of your shoulder. That sound like what happened?"

"The bullet came out of the side of a tank." He was trying to focus on what the doctor was saying, but he could not take his eyes off Celeste.

"Well, in that case, you're doubly lucky," the doctor continued. "The bullet must have entered here." He traced the route of the bullet on his own shoulder blade. "And traveled down, exiting here." He turned his shoulder and indicated a spot about an inch and a half down his back. "Lot of muscle, tissue and bone between those two points. Anyway, you're doing fine but you do have a nasty wound, and it's going to require intensive therapy. I'm going to let you stay here in Seoul until the wound heals. Then I'll transfer you stateside where you can get the rehab you need. Your days in Korea are over, soldier. How you feel about that?"

"Not too good, Doc. I don't want to leave my fiancée."

"You have a fiancée here?"

"Yes sir. Your nurse, Celeste."

"Oh, Celeste." The doctor laughed. "We always assign Celeste to the hard ones. She pulls 'em through."

The doctor turned to leave, and Celeste fell in behind him. But she turned as she left and mouthed to Davis a silent, "I'll be back." Then she pursed her lips into two quick kisses and was gone.

He lay captured by the dimensions of the hospital bed, waiting for her to return. Moving was an impossible feat. His left arm was bound to his chest like a mummy. The hospital sheet was tucked tightly across his chest and legs. His right arm was free, but the angle was wrong to reach the glass of water on the bedside table. He dozed and dreamed of the tank sighting him, and woke in a sweat. Kim Young-he came to check on him and found him thrashing about the bed in frustration and despair.

"Arm hurt bad. Get nurse." She darted back through the doorway and returned with a nurse. The nurse swabbed his right arm with alcohol, pinched the skin and plunged the needle into his muscle. Kim Young-he sat down to stay with him until he relaxed.

Celeste returned around six-thirty. She was wearing a burgundy dress with bouquets of pink and yellow flowers splashed over it. The dress was loose, and it skimmed across the curves of her body in all the right places, leaving just enough to the imagination. The light from the hall behind her played through her hair and turned it golden.

"I'm going off duty now. Thought I'd say goodbye. You doing okay?" Celeste asked.

Davis nodded. "I'm all right now that you're here," he said, adding, "Where do you go at night?"

"I sing in a bar in Seoul."

"The dress. It's beautiful. That what you wear?"

"This ol' thing? Heck no. I have a costume."

"What's it look like? I want to know."

"You'll have to come down when you're better."

"What do you sing?"

"Anything the soldiers want to hear. Long as I know it. Popular songs, jazz, show tunes, old favorites. Whatever."

"You have a nice voice." Celeste raised her eyebrows and Davis continued. "I heard you moving around the bed and singing after my surgery. I thought I was dreaming. Guess I was doped-up."

"Yeah," she shrugged. "I don't even realize I'm singing. Hope it doesn't bother anybody. Anyway, I've never had any complaints."

"I'm glad you were here. I haven't said thank you for taking care of me."

"Listen, that's my job, but I'm real glad you're better. Probably take you a couple of days to feel like anything, but you *will* get better. I promise."

"I will if you keep coming to see me."

"That's a deal!" She leaned over the rail and kissed him lightly on the check, then turned and walked toward the door. As she moved into the doorway, she turned back and waved.

He listened to the echo of her high heels in the empty hallway. He wondered if she treated all her patients this way. He didn't know Dr. Bradley had taken her off his case as soon as he regained consciousness.

His recovery was slow. He was not allowed out of bed until any chance of infection was gone. When he was finally permitted to get up, Celeste began taking her lunch break with him—at least when there wasn't an emergency. Sometimes she wheeled him into a makeshift solarium. Once, on her day off, she brought a picnic of Korean wine, rice cakes, fried pork and Korean apples. They piled the rice cakes high with pork and apple slices. It looked strange, but it tasted delicious to Davis.

When he was strong enough to leave the hospital for an outing, he and several other patients went down to hear Celeste sing. The bar, called Silver Moon, was located in one of the few hotels in Seoul to survive the air strikes. The bar was considered classy and had a good reputation. Both Republic of Korea soldiers, called ROKs, and U.S. servicemen, many of who were high-ranking military personnel who stayed in the hotel, frequented it.

The decor of the Silver Moon was a blend of Asian and American styles. It was advertised as "glitzy." A long ebony bar stretched down the right wall, beginning near the entrance. The bar was backed with counter-to-ceiling mirrors. Across from the bar was a dance floor. Cocktail tables covered with embroidered red cloths rimmed the dance floor. Glittering crescent moons, interspersed with painted glass rectangles, dangled from the ceiling. They twirled and swayed in the air, sending reflections across the room.

Davis was unprepared for the reception Celeste received when she stepped onto the stage. Since most of the soldiers in the bar were officers, he expected polite clapping. Instead the men exploded to their feet, whistling and applauding, and calling her by name. Clearly, most of them had been to see her before.

She was dressed in a long black velvet dress with thin, rhinestone straps. She wore black, high-heeled shoes and her hair, gleaming in the bright lights, tumbled freely across her shoulders. He had adored the way she looked in her starched uniform. Her hair held back behind her ears by barrettes, a stiff white nurse's cap perched on top of her head, crisp apron over her uniform, white-laced shoes that made a muffled sound when she walked. Everything clean and fresh and efficient. But when she stepped through the stage curtains, he gasped. She was as exquisite as a movie star.

She bowed a sweeping bow from the waist and said, "Tonight I'd like to welcome each and every person here, especially our fighting men from the Republic of Korea Army and the United Nations military forces." *Loud bursts of applause.* "I'd like to say a special thank you to those men who have been wounded in battle and are now recovering at the U.S. Naval Hospital in Seoul." *More outbursts of clapping.* "If you've been to hear me before, you know my theme song is always my first song of the evening. And now I dedicate to that one special soldier, my theme song, 'Tenderly.'"

She stepped back several feet and dropped her head. The curtains behind her opened revealing a small band on stage. The band struck the opening measures, and she drew the microphone up to her mouth and sang, "...*The evening breeze caressed the trees....*" Everybody in the place jumped up and clapped. Celeste continued singing, and the men settled back in their chairs and listened, spellbound.

Davis was mesmerized. Had she meant him? Did he dare hope he was that "one special soldier" or was that a play to the heart of every man in the room? He could only hope she meant him. Still, he was disturbed by the attention she was receiving. Clearly she thrived on it, fed on it, came alive with it. He had no right to feel jealous, but he did. He did not want to share her. He wanted all that beauty and energy directed at him.

While Davis struggled with his emotions, Celeste moved from song to song with ease, giving in to the music more and more. When she reached the rock songs, her hips gyrated to the beat of the music, and the men were on their feet again, dancing themselves and clapping. Quickly she pulled them back down by slowing the tempo until she ended with the romantic Nat King Cole song, "A Blossom Fell."

After her show, she came out to greet his table.

"Well, how're my patients getting along? Having fun?"

She dropped her arm over Davis's right shoulder. All the men rose to greet her. When Davis got up, her hand slipped down his back before it fell to her side. The casual brush across his back sent waves tingling down his spine. It was the sexiest feeling imaginable to him. But before he could react with a touch or a look, she had turned to someone else. The men surged around her, congratulating her.

"Can you dance?" Davis whispered to her when he could get close, yearning to feel her electricity again.

She shook her head. "Policy of the establishment. Another time, but not here, okay?" And then she was gone, moving on to another table greeting other people, leaving Davis to wonder where he stood with her.

In four weeks time he was transferred to Naval Hospital, Bethesda, Md. She had told him she was due to transfer stateside, and he begged her to follow him as soon as possible.

"Please ask for Bethesda," he pleaded. "How will we ever know if we're meant to be?"

"Whatever happens is what's meant to be," she answered. "I can't promise anything. I'll think about it, but there's one thing you have to understand. *Nothing stands in the way of my music!* I'm not sure you understand."

"You let me worry about that. I love you enough to handle your music. If that's what's important to you, I'll make it work."

He must have convinced her because she followed him to Bethesda. It was harder to convince himself because his gut was on fire each time she performed.

Davis stopped his story abruptly.

"Go on," Josephine urged, "this is getting good." She was sitting on her feet in the big chair by the front door.

"That's all," he replied, his shoulders slumping forward. "She died in an accident." He rose and grabbed his jacket from the chair by the front door. The jacket grazed Josephine's head as he pulled it away. "I have to go." He moved swiftly to the front stoop. Josephine followed.

"Hey, we don't have to talk anymore," she said.

"There's nothing more to say."

He crossed the distance to the steps. A patch of bright light from the back bedroom spilled over the lawn and played across the stone steps. They reminded him of a white stretch of beach he and Celeste had walked one night long ago.

Quickly he reached the driveway. The blacktop looked midnight blue, as blue as the ocean they had skipped through that night.

He kept walking around the hairpin turn and up the hill passed the boulder at the top of Josephine's driveway. At length, he stepped under the only streetlight. He was on the dirt road at Lover's Leap, a favorite parking spot for young lovers. The toe of his shoe caught on a half-buried beer can, making him wonder what remnants of love he might find scattered across the ground.

He couldn't go home. He couldn't face Eula Mae and the rest of his household. He trudged up the hill.

Lover's Leap was a huge granite outcrop located at the summit. The rock was shaped like an anvil with its point protruding over the cliff. The back half of the rock was flat, and Davis climbed there and sat down.

The wind was strong so he raised the collar of his jacket and crossed his arms across his chest for warmth. The valley below him was dark but he could make out the shapes and forms of the Blue Ridge mountains. Tiny lights dotted the terrain. Bishop was on the left and High Meadows on the right. The two places where he had spent so much of his life. But they were not what colored his life or what defined who he was. That was in another place and another time.

Chapter Nineteen

Fort Bragg and Camp Lejeune
North Carolina Coast, 1952

Celeste and Davis were married in May at Ft. Bragg in Fayetteville, N.C., where her father had mustered out of the army. The small chapel was jammed with guests, mostly friends of Celeste and her parents. Davis and his buddies from the outfit, wearing dress whites, were the hit of the wedding. Sgt. Wilbur, also in whites, was his best man.

The wedding reception was at the NCO Club. Her band, the one she sang with in high school, played. Everybody danced, and they toasted Celeste and Davis, and she sang "Because," but she wouldn't sing anything else. Davis's father drew him aside and said he was going to set up a fund to give them some monthly income. After all, a *PFC* in the Marine Corps didn't make much money!

Finally he was alone with her in a private reception room in the NCO Club. He wanted to ravage her and adore her and be everything to her that she was to him. But she said they couldn't *"do it"* now because everybody was waiting for her to throw the bouquet. So he guarded the door while she slipped off her wedding clothes and put on a sexy navy blue suit with a pale blue blouse and a little navy hat with next to nothing to it except two navy bands and a veil. Then she kicked off her satin wedding shoes and put on navy and white sling-back high heels.

Later they drove to the beach and took a hotel room. When they registered, rice spilled out of their clothes and the desk clerk grinned knowingly, but they could care less and Davis ordered cold champagne in a bucket of ice and two champagne glasses.

In the room she slipped into a long white gown with a V-neckline decorated with creamy lace, and they lay on the bed laughing and remembering the toasts everybody made. Her friends questioning what secret weapons Davis had used to catch her, and Vince and Scully and the guys from the outfit all declaring he planned the whole thing, taking it in the shoulder 'cause he knew he'd land in the hospital, and she'd nurse him back to health. *Oh, the romance of the thing.*

He pulled her to him and ran the back of his hand across her face. "You are so beautiful."

"You aren't so bad yourself, soldier," she whispered.

"I adore you."

"Adore me," she answered.

He slid his hands beneath her gown, easing it up to reveal her creamy body, then slipping the gown over her head and brushing it aside. His left arm was still stiff, and it got in the way, and finally he had to lie flat on his back while she slipped his T-shirt over his arms and head, her red nails flashing as her hands moved across his chest. She kissed him on his lips, then his neck, reaching down his chest to his nipples, and then up to the scars of his wounds. He followed her lead, first her mouth, exploring, then her breast, cupping them one at a time with his hands until he kissed her nipples, first one and then the other. Then their hands moved between their legs, and he entered her, and they made love, and he thought, *Oh, the beauty, the sweetness.*

When they had rested, they decided to walk on the beach. They dressed in jeans and loose sweaters and grabbed a blanket off the bed and slipped out into the night through the sliding glass door that opened onto the beach. They walked south along the shoreline, letting the waves splash over their feet but the water was so cold they couldn't stand it. So they snuggled close together with the blanket thrown over their shoulders.

The beach was deserted. They walked, and as they walked they talked about the past and present, and they both agreed they knew enough about each other. Love was the important thing. The rest would fall in place. And when they were tired, they stretched the blanket on the sand and made love again to the sound of waves slapping on the beach with the moon and stars as witnesses.

He would never get enough of her, he was sure of it. Never.

They had timed their wedding to coincide with the end of Celeste's tour of duty in the nurse corps. Davis's outfit, including Davis, was assigned to Camp Lejeune, but his doctor had not released him for full duty. In fact, he had told Davis his arm might not fully recover no matter how hard he worked at rehabilitating it. Davis had been thinking more and more about a career in the Marine Corps, but if he could not regain full range of motion, he would be rejected.

They rented a small house, a *dump* really, near the base, which they nicknamed "Roach Villa #1." When anyone asked where they lived, Celeste answered by singing: *"Roach Vil-la Num-ber One."* Their landlord (*they nicknamed him "Slicky-Dicky"*) acted as if the apartment were some beautifully finished home in the best part of town. Celeste and Davis found this hysterically funny. The only items in the place when they signed the lease were a chrome and gray marbleized formica kitchen table and three chairs (*Slicky-Dicky claimed somebody made off with the fourth*) and a souvenir white satin wall hanging with gold tassels sewed on the lower edge. The wall hanging featured a midnight blue screen-printed picture of

Harry S. Truman, President, with Washington, D.C. in red ink beneath.

They bought a double bed and good mattress, two cheap easy chairs and a second-hand coffee table from an Army-Navy Surplus Store.

The Naval Hospital was so short of nurses that they hired Celeste as a civilian. The work was routine and frankly, boring since she was a surgical nurse. But it was Navy pay and more than Davis made even with his promotion to corporal.

When summer came, Celeste got out her guitar and started buying new sheet music. All her material was *"old,"* she claimed, and she needed to learn new hits, especially rock-a-billy, which was hot at the beaches along the Carolina coast.

Davis was finally released for active duty, including driving, and was given a supply billet, which *"stunk"* in his opinion. Every afternoon he worked out either at the base gym or ran the obstacle course. Gradually his strength was coming back.

None of it mattered. They were in love. All Davis could think about was making love to her. No matter how he tried to concentrate on his work, she would slip into his mind. Suddenly, she would appear on the beach, on the floor of Roach-Villa #1, on the bed. Her skin like velvet, her wisdom ancient, the mysteries of life were being revealed to him.

One afternoon at work, he received a call from her. She was so excited she hardly made sense.

"I've got a gig!" she squealed into the phone. "Dorsey called and said Doc wants me to sing with the band tonight down at Carolina Beach. I can't believe it! This is my chance to get back to singing. Oh, God, I hope I'm ready."

"Hey, slow down! Who're Dorsey and Doc?"

"From the wedding! You remember. Dorsey's my girl friend. She goes with Doc. He leads the band I sang with before I joined the nurse corps."

"I guess I thought you'd given up on singing again."

"Honey, where have you been? I practice all the time! You *know* I want to sing. I will always want to sing! We talked about this." Her voice rose with each sentence.

"Hey, it's okay. I know you've been practicing. You just hadn't mentioned singing in bars for a while. Look, it's no problem," he insisted, changing the subject, "Are you scheduled to work at the hospital tomorrow?"

"Yeah, I'll sleep on the way home. Listen, I'll leave the name of the place on the kitchen table. It's only about seventy miles. Come on down when you get off work. Show'll start around eight-thirty or nine."

"Can't. Probably be nine before I could get away. We're expecting a huge shipment and we have to inventory it."

"Well, come if you can. Otherwise I'll see you around one."

"Hey, good luck, gal. Knock 'em dead!"

She was gone. He had hoped she was losing interest in performing. Now the old jealously of having other men watch her on stage was coming back to haunt him.

Celeste and Doc's Rock Rockers were part of the swell in popularity of the Carolina beaches. Young people from high schools and colleges in both states flocked to the coast. By day, slathered with baby oil, they walked the beach, or spread out their towels to sleep in the sun. By night they jammed into beer joints, who booked live bands like Doc's Rockers. There the young people shagged and drank with equal dedication until closing.

Doc's band had so many bookings that Celeste quit her job at the hospital and devoted all her time to practicing and performing. When Davis could leave early, he drove her to her gigs.

One night they were coming home from Myrtle Beach, where the band had performed at the Bowery, when she said bluntly, "You don't like it do you."

"I told you I'd handle it, but no, I'm not crazy about other men ogling my beautiful wife."

"Ooo-gling me? That's what they're doing, ooogling me? How about enjoying my singing."

"You know what I mean. Listen, you've got a terrific voice. I'm not going to ask you not to sing. I promised you. I meant it then and I mean it now."

"Don't ever ask me not to sing, baby, 'cause that's who I am."

"I told you, I won't. Not ever. Now can we just drop it?"

They traveled in the dark, neither of them speaking. He was beginning to get a headache. Recently his headaches had returned, and he had been forced to go to the hospital for a prescription for painkillers.

After miles in silence, he said to her, "Come over here next to me, woman." She slid over, and he put his arm around her, pulling her so close she rested against his side. She reeked of beer and cigarette smoke. It didn't matter, he told himself. He had her all to himself and soon they would be home.

One day Davis was coming out of the PX when he ran into Sgt. Wilbur, who had been promoted to staff sergeant.

"Hey, Marine. How the hell are you? I haven't seen you in ages," Wilbur said, shaking Davis's hand. "Come on with me over to the NCO Club. Let's have a beer and catch up with each other."

"You think they'll let a lowly corporal in the NCO Club?" Enlisted men were not allowed in the Non-Commissioned Officers Club.

"Corporal? Listen to you! No stopping you now. Course they'll let you in, if you're with me! Club manager is one of my buds," Wilbur laughed. He steered Davis toward his car, which was parked in front of the PX.

They settled into the car, an olive green military vehicle, and Wilbur pulled out of the lot onto the main road at

Camp Lejeune. They headed out toward the ocean at Courthouse Bay, where the NCO and Officers Clubs were located. Wilbur pulled into the parking lot of an attractive building, landscaped with shrubs and flowers. Unlike the typical tall, stark white operations buildings of the base, this building was stained a natural color and looked like a small country club. Here, non-commissioned officers and their families came to relax. There were dining rooms, bar facilities, pool tables, outdoor swimming pools, plus a sandy strip of beach with a lifeguard. A similar facility for officers was next door.

"So," Wilbur drew Davis's attention, "how're the honeymooners?"

"Old married folks by now. We're fine. Celeste's back singing. Going great guns doing gigs all over the coast."

"That girl's born to sing, yessir." Wilbur signaled the bartender for two beers. "And you?" Wilbur leaned toward Davis. His arms were resting on the table and his hands were clasped, a familiar gesture to Davis.

On an impulse Davis wanted to level with Wilbur, tell him his fears. "I'm worried," he said abruptly.

"'Bout what?"

"Shoulder for one thing. Doctor won't say it's going to heal completely. I plan on applying to Officers' Candidate School, but I can't if I don't totally rehab my shoulder."

"You working on it, ain't cha?"

"My-ass-off. Every god damn day!"

"How?"

"Weights and obstacle course."

"That'll do it. Just takes time. It'll happen."

"If it don't, how the hell can I support Celeste? She'd hate Bishop. It's a smug southern town with nothing but barbecue huts and beer joints. No places like the coast. 'Sides, people in Bishop would never approve of her. She sings in bars."

"To hell with 'em. Man's gotta do what he's gotta do. You and her'll work that out. You love each other!"

"There's something else. It tears my guts out when I watch her perform. I can't stand the thought of other men wanting to put their hands on her! It drives me nuts!"

"Son," the older man reached out and rested his hand on Davis's arm. "You gotta know the battles you can win and the ones you gonna lose. This one's a loser." Wilbur was divorced.

"That's not all," Davis continued, shaking his head. "She drinks. Mostly when she performs but I've watched it coming. She'll start out light when she's getting ready to perform. Just beer. But by the time she's done two shows, she's into hard stuff. The scene, singing in bars I mean, looks to me like that's where it's headed."

"Drugs?" Wilbur questioned.

"I'm not sure," Davis answered. "She says she needs something to get her in the mood. Claims that's all there is to it."

"Don't sound good, I agree. You talked to her about this?" Davis nodded. "You go with her most of the time?" Davis nodded again. "Tell you what. Why don't you take the heat off. Let her alone with it for a while. She can ride with somebody else, can't she? Give it a rest. Tell you what. Scully, Vince, me and a couple other guys from our old outfit have a regular poker game. Why don't you join us? Give you something else to do for a while."

"Okay," Davis agreed and Wilbur gave him the time and place of the next game.

Several days later Davis noticed some pills were missing from his bottle of painkillers.

Vince folded his cards and tossed them in the center of the table.

"Well, that cleans me out." He pressed his hands over his dark hair as if he were smoothing back his old ducktail hairdo the Marine Corps had buzz-cut. Vince had never forgiven the Corps for removing his thick sweep of hair, and the habit of replacing strands no longer there was Vince's way of expressing his discontent.

No doubt about it, Vince was a lady-killer. Broad chest, narrow hips, about five-ten, Italian coloring. He had a way of flexing his shoulders that women loved, but Davis thought it was phony. He may be a lady's man, but Davis had always found him lacking in battle, and he had made certain Vince never covered his backside.

"I ain't coming next week," Vince was saying, standing. The rest of the men pushed back their chairs and stood.

"Well, we'll get a sub. Your turn to have us, Scully," Wilbur was saying. "You got a hot date, Vince?"

"Working on it," Vince answered.

The poker group rotated locations. Last week they had been at Davis's. Celeste's gig that night had been canceled so she made spaghetti for them, and they had all made a night of it.

This is the way married life is supposed to be, Davis had thought at the time. Celeste cooking for them and checking to see when someone wanted a beer. He had been so proud of her.

The next week they met at Scully's. Nobody got a sub for Vince and the game was lopsided. Around nine-thirty they decided to call it a night.

Davis drove home and pulled into the driveway. A car was parked across the street by an empty lot. *That's odd,* Davis thought. He couldn't recall ever seeing a car there. Celeste was scheduled to go to Wrightsville Beach with the band, but lately their bookings had been slim. Sometimes they were canceled at the last minute. Soon the beach bars would close until spring.

Maybe that's what happened tonight. The car, Davis supposed, belonged to Doc or Dorsey, but why hadn't they parked in the driveway?

Davis turned off his motor and got out of the car. *Something didn't feel right.* He hurried to the front door. He could hear music but it didn't sound like Doc's music. He turned the knob. *Locked.* He rummaged through his pocket for his key. *Why didn't she come to the door?* They weren't rehearsing. He slid the key in the lock, turned it, and opened the door.

"Celeste?" he called. "I'm home." Rustling noises came from the bedroom. "Celeste!" he called again. Worried now, he ran across the living room to the bedroom. The door was closed. *They never closed the bedroom door!*

He threw open the door. To his astonishment, there were Celeste and Vince tumbling around on the bed. Vince scrambled out first, grabbing for his clothes, jamming his legs into his trousers, snatching up articles of clothing. Celeste was wrapping the top sheet around her body. She slid toward the far side of the bed, then pushed aside a whiskey bottle and a couple of glasses to reach the radio. She turned it off and stood up.

"What the fuck?" Davis cried. "Vince! My God, Celeste! Vince? You and Vince? Jesus, I can't believe this. I can't believe my eyes!"

Vince was still fumbling around near the bedroom door.

"Listen, Davis," he said, covering himself. "Don't do nothing crazy. I swear. This wasn't nothing."

"Nothing? You're screwing my wife and it's nothing? You better run your ass off, Vince, 'cause if I get my hands around your neck, you're dead meat. Get the fuck out of here, quick!"

Vince turned and ran, slamming the front door behind him.

"Look, Davis," Celeste was saying, "it just happened. I don't know why. It just happened. It's the only time. Honest."

"You let that scum-bag put his hands on you? You kissed him? Oh, Jesus, I can't even think." Everything was collapsing in on him, their nights of making love, her beauty, her singing, his dreams for their future. All of it was crowding his mind. His head was pounding as hard as his chest.

"It's like you want too much from me," she was explaining. "More than I can give." The sheet was slipping and she pulled it back over her. "Maybe we shouldn't have gotten married."

"Don't say that. God, don't say that. I love you more than I love breathing."

"That's it, Davis!" She snapped her fingers and pointed at him. "Nobody can be the life and breath for another person!"

She was off the bed now, and she took several steps toward him, still clutching the sheet. Her bare feet reached the scatter rug beside the bed. It was bunching up under her feet. He raised his right hand up by his shoulder and then came down across her cheek, back-handing her. Her head whipped to one side with an audible snap. He hadn't thought, reacting from instinct, but the force of the blow was too strong. He could see that. The way her head jerked away from the blow. The quick snap he heard. The way her feet were still slipping. He could see it all, as if in slow motion. Her bare feet, the tops bronzed by the sun, her toes flecked with red polish, couldn't regain a footing. The rug was tripping her. Her arms were up, fighting the air. He reached out to catch her, but she was falling away, not toward him. Her head hit the edge of the dresser with a "whack" and she crumpled to the floor like a rag doll.

"Celeste! Oh, God, no! Celeste!" He kneeled down and bent over her. A trickle of blood was coming from the back of her head. "Celeste, baby!" he cried. "I didn't mean it." She was still alive. He *knew* she was still alive. He ran across the room to the phone, rummaging through the phone book until he came up with an emergency number for the base hospital.

As soon as he got an answer, he yelled into the phone, "My wife's hurt. Send an ambulance, quick! 703 Green Street. Straight out the base to the highway...turn left. Three blocks, go right. I said right! Third house on the left. Yes, my wife. She fell and hit her head. I don't know how bad! Bad! Jesus, just hurry. Her head's bleeding. M.P.s? We don't need M.P.s!

It was an accident. We need an ambulance, for God's sake! Williams. I'm Cpl. Davis Emerson Williams."

He pressed down the phone plunger, released it, and then called Sgt. Wilbur.

The ambulance arrived first, followed by the M.P.s. Davis was sitting on the floor beside the dresser, cradling Celeste in his arms. The sheet was still around her body, and he had wrapped her head in a towel.

He had heard them knock and call his name, but he had not moved. After a brief pause, they opened the door and spoke louder, "Cpl. Williams? M.P.s and medics here. We come in?"

"I told you I don't need M.P.s. You're too late anyway," Davis answered as they entered the room. "She's dead," he said. He was still holding her.

"That your wife, Corporal?" Only one of the M.P.s was talking. Davis nodded. "Okay if the medic checks her out?"

"She's dead, I said."

"I understand, Corporal, but the medics have to verify that. Could you step away, please?"

Davis didn't move. "I don't want anybody touching her."

"Corporal, we need to examine her. Step aside now." The M.P. has shifted his hand to the pistol on his hip.

Davis withdrew his arms from around her and gently eased her to the floor, resting her head, still wrapped in the towel, on the floor. Then he rose and stood beside her.

"In the living room please, Corporal." One M.P. and the medic remained in the bedroom. The other M.P. led Davis into the living room. When they reached the living room, the M.P. turned and asked, "What happened here, Corporal?"

"It was an accident. We were having a disagreement, and she slipped on that scatter rug by the bed." Davis was shaking. "Her feet flew out from under her. I was trying to grab her to...to stop her from slipping but I couldn't reach her...she was falling away from me...and her head...came down on the edge of the dresser with a loud crack. " Davis demonstrated each move with his hands as if he were reliving the event, detail by detail.

"I noticed a red mark on her cheek. Any idea how that got there?" the M.P. asked.

"Yes, I hit her, but I didn't mean to. God, I didn't mean to."

Just then, the front door opened, and Sgt. Wilbur stepped through. The M.P. looked up as Davis rushed to greet his friend. They hugged and Davis mumbled, "God, am I glad you came."

"What happened?" Wilbur asked.

"Celeste's dead," Davis said, tears filling his eyes. "It was an accident."

"I'm Sgt. Wilbur." Wilbur had turned to the M.P. "I was with Davis earlier tonight. He called me a little bit ago and asked me to come over. Could I speak to my friend alone, Cpl. Oakes?"

The M.P. was wearing a nametag. He nodded and mumbled, "Yes, sir."

Wilbur led Davis into the small, darkened kitchen. Davis flipped on the light, and the two men sat down at the kitchen table, pulling their chairs close so the M.P. wouldn't hear them.

"What happened?" Wilbur asked, whispering.

"When I got home, Vince was here. I can't even believe it but Vince and Celeste were...in the bed...getting it on." He shook his head slowly. "Anyway, I told Vince to get the hell out of my house or I'd kill him...HE was the one I wanted to kill...not Celeste!" He banged his fist down on the table, and Sgt. Wilbur quickly covered Davis's fist to muffle the sound.

"Sshh," he indicated, glancing through the kitchen door to see if the M.P. had heard.

"Anyway," Davis went on, still whispering, "Celeste and I started arguing. She stood up. Had the bed sheet wrapped around her. Sarge, they were naked...in the bed...fucking!

Anyway, I backhanded her...I swear I didn't think I hit her hard. But she...was standing on a scatter rug and her feet just few out from under her. I tried to catch her but her head hit the dresser. And...and she died. I didn't mean it...Oh, Jesus, Celeste, I didn't mean it." He pushed away from the table and dropped his head in his hands and cried.

Abruptly, he looked up at Wilbur. "What do I tell them about Vince? I don't want anybody to know she was with him."

"Lemme think a minute." Wilbur had pushed back from the table, too, and he was slumped forward with his arms resting on his legs. Finally he spoke, "Keep Vince out of it. He sure as hell ain't gonna tell nobody. Just say it's an accident. This could get sticky. Say you hit her once. You didn't mean to hit her hard. Was she already falling when you hit her?" Davis nodded. "Maybe she would have fallen into the dresser anyway. Tell it like that. That's what happened, ain't it?" Davis nodded. "Leave the other out." The older man put his hand on Davis's knee. "Listen, don't dare change a word of it. You were arguing about anything else...not Vince...her singing...nothing important...whatever you decide...but once you decide, don't you dare change a word of it. You hear me?" He shook Davis's knee. Davis nodded. "Now, you get me your mama and daddy's phone number. I'm gonna call 'em."

"Please, Sgt. Wilbur. I don't get along that good with my father."

"They gotta know. I'll tell 'em you're okay. They don't need to come. Now go back in there with the M.P. and remember what I said...everything!"

Davis stood up. He added, "Would you call Celeste's parents, too?" Wilbur nodded, frowning. Davis found a pad on the kitchen counter and wrote down both numbers. As he passed the slip of paper to Wilbur, he grabbed his friend's shoulder and squeezed. "Thanks, Wilbur, thanks."

And then he walked back into the living room to be interviewed by Cpl. Oates, the M.P.

Around three o'clock, the ambulance left with Celeste's body. Wilbur had stayed and literally held Davis up while Celeste's body was being strapped to the gurney and rolled out the front door. Before Cpl. Oates left, he told Davis to "consider himself confined to quarters...in the event he was needed."

At length Davis was left alone. His head was splitting, and the lights in the house blinded him. He turned them off and moved through the house from room to room by the light from the streetlight outside the windows.

Even in the dark he could feel Celeste's presence. It seemed to rise like a vapor from her belongings, her toilet articles left by her on the bathroom shelf, her clothes hanging lifelessly on the back of the bedroom chair, her sheet music scattered across the coffee table in the living room.

Haphazardly, he started straightening up in the bedroom. He hung her clothes, picking them up one by one, stirring the smells they held, releasing *her* smell into the air, their soft fabric snagging at his coarse hands. From time to time, he buried his face in the soft folds of the formless clothes and inhaled her odors, realizing the smells would soon fade away.

Next, he moved to the bathroom. He found a shoebox and placed her toilet articles in it. Then he remembered the fifth of whiskey with the two glasses on the bedside table. Panic swept over him. Had Oakes seen them? He didn't ask about them. Another lie Davis would have to tell. He would have to say Celeste picked the glasses for them but he didn't want a drink. He grabbed the fifth and returned it to the cupboard in the kitchen and then washed the two glasses, *twice,* and dried them and put them away.

He walked back to the bedroom and began tearing the bedclothes off the bed. Then he remembered the sheets, pillowcases, too, were on the bed when Vince and Celeste were making love. *Signs of their lovemaking may be clinging to the sheets!* He yanked and jerked, frantically trying to get the sheets of the bed. And when he finally did, he bunched them up and ran back to the utility room and jammed them into the washing machine, threw in soap powders and started the machine. Then he retrieved the fifth of whiskey, got a glass from the back of the cupboard and poured, with hands shaking, a half glass of whiskey. By now sweat was pouring off of him but he didn't stop until he had put fresh sheets on the bed. Exhausted, he fell across the bed.

Sleep would not come. All he could think of was Celeste. Did she die instantly, or did life seep out drop by drop like the blood that stained the towel he had wrapped around her head? Did she cling to life desperately, or embrace death, finally understanding that the life she loved had required more and more from her as time went on? Did she succumb to pain, or did she step forward, in her mind wearing her black velvet gown trimmed with rhinestones, hair rippling across her shoulder, head tilted back revealing her graceful neck, spotlights flashing over her. And did she sing her songs, one by one, in the last performance of her life?

And the most important question of all: in the end did she forgive him for all he had taken from her?

How could he live without Celeste? Nothing mattered without her. He had killed the one thing he had ever really loved.

Celeste's death unleashed a series of events Davis could not halt. His parents hired a lawyer from Jacksonville, Isaiah Pinckney, who appeared on his doorstep at 8 a.m. the morning after her death.

Mr. Pinckney listened to Davis's story and then described what he thought would occur. He explained that in the case of an accidental death to military personnel or a family member, either on or off base, an informal hearing was held by the Judge Advocate General's office. Following the hearing, a recommendation was sent to the Commanding Officer of the camp. In extreme cases, the recommendation might refer a case to a civilian court. He said Davis should strive to avoid a civilian court hearing at all possible costs.

In Davis's case, the first hearing recommended a psychological evaluation. He was told he could either stay in the
hospital during the evaluations, or stay in the brig. He chose
the latter. Celeste had worked at the hospital and he couldn't
stand to be there.

Several days later he was summoned from his room in the
brig and told he had a visitor. The duty guard led him to the
visitors' room, which was located on the left front of the
building. The room was a large, rectangular room with
barred windows running across the front and down the side.
Long tables stretched end to end down the middle of the
room. Chairs faced each other across the tables to allow conversations.

The duty guard opened the door for Davis and followed
him into the room, locking the door behind them. He stood
at attention, guarding the door.

Davis instantly recognized his visitor. Vince was sitting in
one of the chairs in the center of the room. He was sprawled
back with one arm on the table and his legs stretched out. He
was drumming a pencil on the table.

Davis walked the length of the room on the other side
from Vince. He pulled out the chair opposite Vince and sat
down leaning toward his visitor, "What the fuck are you
doing here, you sleaze-bag," he seethed.

Vince pulled himself erect and pulled his chair closer to
the table.

"You didn't have to kill her, you bastard!" Vince hissed
through his clenched teeth. Then he glanced down the length
of the room to where the guard was standing at attention.

When Vince glanced away, Davis leaned over the table
and grabbed him by his tie. He wrapped his fist around the
tie and twisted until Vince was choking. Still clasping the tie,
Davis pressed his fist hard against Vince's Adam's apple.
Vince's eyes rolled toward the guard and his mouth opened
as if he were struggling to speak. Davis tightened his hold.

"Don't you dare try," Davis whispered. "You feel my knuckle on your wind pipe? You call the guard, and I'll push that knuckle you can feel, along with the rest of my fist, into that scrawny neck of yours. I have to live with knowing what I did, but I want you to live with knowing you caused it."

"Put me down, you maniac," Vince croaked.

"I told you to stay the fuck away from me 'cause if I ever get out of here, I'm gonna kill you. You better watch your backside, wherever you go, everyday of your life, 'cause one day I'm gonna be there and when I am, you're dead." Then he dropped Vince, stood up and walked the length of the room to where the guard was standing and signaled to be let out.

Vince called after Davis, "You're crazy! You know that, you crazy bastard!" Vince was coughing and rubbing his throat while trying to straighten his tie and smooth his hands over the ducktail that had not been there in ages.

Several days later, Mr. Pinckney returned. Davis had been expecting him. "I don't have good news for you, Davis," he said adjusting the chair under him.

"Yeah?" Davis asked. Over the last few days, Davis had noticed a change in the attitude of the doctors and nurses toward him. At first they were nice enough to him. Lately, they seemed annoyed. During his psychological evalua-tions, the questions posed had become more and more per-sonal. Initially, they gave him Rorschach and standard tests. Next they started asking him about the school he had attended in New Jersey, and then they wanted him to describe the battle in the Korean War when Mace was killed and how Davis had taken out the North Korean soldier. Plus, every other battle in which he fought and how he had performed. They jumped from subject to subject, including questions about how he and Celeste got along, then moving quickly to something else before he could answer. Gradually, he understood the process had moved from eval-uation to interrogation. One day the questions went on so long his head was splitting, and he was forced to ask for medication.

"I don't know exactly how to say this to you," Pinckney said.

"Just say it. I'm ready."

"They want to make a deal"

"A deal? The Corps doesn't make deals."

"They want you out. They think you're one of those soldiers who can't adjust when we aren't at war. They talked about how you performed in Korea and a fitness report somebody named Russet gave you."

"Yeah, Russet didn't like me. Said I was too gung-ho. If they throw me out because of Celeste, fine. I deserve it. But because I'm too gung-ho? Nothing doing. They taught me everything I know about fighting."

"They said there was a risk factor where you were concerned. Couple of other things came up. Said you went to some mental institution for high school and college."

"It was a school for kids with behavior problems, not mental problems! It was *not* a mental hospital."

"Well, they believe you were not honest about that period of your life. You had mental problems as a young person and did not disclose it on your enlistment application. It's a felony to falsify information on an application for military service. They asked for a report from the school. On the report, there was a notation that you had seizures as a young person."

"They cleared up! Christ, I outgrew 'em after they put me on a regular medical routine. Is it against the law to have seizures?"

"More than likely, you would have been Four-F if they'd known. Something else, a marine from your outfit named Vincent came forward and said you'd threatened him on two separate occasions."

So, Vince figured out I didn't tell he was there, Davis thought.

"Couple of other things," Pinckney continued. "things that *could* be looked into. From the M.P.'s report, for instance, was anyone else there that night?" Pinckney figured it out, too. "Also, people from Ft. Bragg are asking questions on behalf of Celeste's father and mother."

Davis shook his head. "Well, I guess I know what your advice is."

"I wish it were different, son, but I'm afraid the results would be even tougher in a civilian court," Pinckney said.

"What's the deal they'll make?" Davis asked.

"If you'll agree to go to High Meadows Institute near Bishop..."

"I do *not* want to go back to Bishop. I'll go anywhere but there. I don't get along with my father."

Mr. Pinckney shook his head. "I don't think they'll give on that one. It was the recommendation of the psychiatrist who interviewed you. They want you to be near family. Anyway, if you agree to stay in the institution for six months, they will rule Celeste's death accidental. Otherwise there will be a full investigation, which could lead to an immediate court martial as well as referral to the local judicial system. If you accept their offer, they will pay for your care until your enlistment is up. Six months, I think. At the end of six months, you'll be discharged from the Marine Corps on a section eight, mentally unfit."

"Why are they willing to pay for my care if they're throwing me out of the Corps?"

"I'm not sure, son. Maybe loyalty. Maybe pride. Anyway, they don't like to admit they're wrong about anybody they accept in the Corps. They said you performed admirably in Korea, and they want to see you through this problem."

Davis sighed. There really was no choice. "What happens at the end of six months?"

"From that point, it's up to High Meadows. If all goes well and they agree you are mentally fit, you are free to leave and go on with you life."

"Okay," Davis said evenly. "I have three stipulations of my own: I want it in writing, signed by somebody in the Corps, Sgt. Wilbur accompanies me to High Meadows, and we stop in Fayetteville so I can see Father Kirkpatrick, the priest who married Celeste and me. I want him to know it was an accident. I want Celeste's parents to hear my side."

Davis never returned to "Roach Villa #1." That part of his life was over. But not Celeste, he would never be over Celeste.

Sgt. Wilbur did pick up a few personal articles for Davis before he drove them to Fayetteville in a military vehicle. There, they met Father Kirkpatrick, who told them Celeste had been cremated. Before they left, Davis handed Father Kirkpatrick the keys to Roach Villa #1 and asked him to pass them on to Celeste's parents.

"Tell them to take anything they want but please return the key to the landlord when they're through. It's rented until the end of the month."

After they left Father Kirkpatrick, they drove the long distance across the state to High Meadows, some 375 miles.

When they drove through the iron gates and up the sweeping driveway, Davis stared in disbelief at the collection of brick buildings. *So this is High Meadows Institute for the Criminally Insane,* he thought. Was it a haven or a prison? He didn't know. Perhaps a little of both.

Contrary to Mr. Pinckney's prediction, at the end of six months, Davis's life at High Meadows was just beginning.

CHAPTER TWENTY

"How did she die?" Josephine asked in the waning light of her living room. Their nightly conversations had become a ritual.

Davis replied sharply. "An accident. That's all I can say." The color had washed from his face. What was he hiding, Josephine wondered? But she changed the subject, pretending she didn't notice.

"How did you end up at High Meadows?"

"Sent by the Marine Corps. I was supposed to stay six months, only I gave in to the craziness." What he didn't tell Josephine—what he was too embarrassed to admit—was that he had believed at first he could lick it. Everyday he followed a rigorous workout, which included jogging around the fenced perimeter of High Meadows. But after five months, five long months, the loneliness and isolation overtook him. The thoughts in his head pooled together. His brain felt constricted—like a safe in which the tumblers on the lock had fallen into different places. Scenes and characters shifted. He couldn't quite sort things out. What had he done and to whom? When he visualized in his mind shooting Josephine, Celeste fell to the ground. When he pulled his knife across the North Korean soldier's throat and tilted back his head, he looked into the face of Mace. And when Celeste lay dying, his arms were around Uncle Jack.

He did tell Josephine how Mace died. His descriptions were vivid—so real she could feel the fear rising off of him. As he talked, she could see the face of the young North Korean soldier as Davis ripped the knife across his throat. When he told how he was wounded, she felt the trip-wire strike his legs. In her mind she saw the tank turret swing around toward him, watched as the quick blast of gunfire raced toward him. She felt the bullet knock him to the ground and saw him motionless, sprawled in the dirt, bleeding.

When he had finished his stories, she rose and put her arms around him. "Why didn't we help you?" she sighed.

"A person has to find his own strength," he replied.

She answered. "It's almost impossible to conquer a mountain alone."

She couldn't explain the surge of strength she felt, even to herself. The cool lavender evening was surrounding them. She looked beyond Davis and the room in which they were standing and saw the navy blue mountains rising like monuments on the horizon.

He took her hand and turned it over as if to read her palm. "Josephine," he said to her, "whose name means powerful woman."

"How can you remember that?" she asked.

"When we were kids, you used to say it if we called you Jo."

"I hated my name. When I complained about it, that's what Momma used to say."

On Wednesday, Josephine and Josie stopped at the post office to pick up the mail. Inside their box was a long, slim envelope with Michael's name and a return address of McDonough Hotel, McDonough, N.C.

Josephine turned the letter over in her hand with puzzlement. Why was Michael writing her? His style was to pick up the phone and call. If it were serious, his instinct would be to wait and discuss it when he arrived in the mountains.

Josephine slipped the letter out of its envelope and unfolded it, uneasiness settling over her. *"Dear Josephine,"* The usual greeting was *"Hi, honey?"* Something was definitely wrong.

Josie was tugging on her mother's jeans. "Do I have a letter, Mommy?"

"No, Punkin. It's from Daddy to me."

"From Daddy! I wanna see." She reached for the letter.

"No, Josie," Josephine answered sternly, pulling the letter out of Josie's reach. "Let me read the letter. I'll tell you what's in it."

She settled Josie in the car and read through the letter.

Dear Josephine,

I am going to get away early on Friday and should arrive in Rocky Ridge by three o'clock. Please get a baby sitter for Josie and make a reservation at a restaurant. There's something I want to talk to you about.

Love,
Michael.

"What's Daddy say, Mommy?" Josie asked innocently.

"He says he's coming up early Friday afternoon." Josephine mulled over in her mind what the letter implied, trying to read between the lines. *"Something…to talk…about."* Had he found out about T.J.? Her mind raced forward to that possibility. What if she had to discuss T.J. with Michael. Did the letter imply the threat of divorce?

She turned to her daughter. "Dad and I are going out for dinner Friday night. I'll call Maylynn Eberhardt to stay with you. Would you like a pizza?"

"Oh, boy! Cheese and hamburger on it. That's what I want."

Josephine was so distracted by the letter that she barely heard her daughter. She steered the car out of the parking space and pulled off in the direction of home.

Later, while Josie was having a peanut butter sandwich on the front stoop, Josephine placed a call to Angie. When her friend answered, Josephine glanced at Josie to see if she was occupied, then plunged into her suspicions about Michael's letter.

"Angie, I just got a letter from Michael. I think he knows about T.J. He *never* writes. He's coming up early Friday and says he *wants to talk!* What am I going to do?"

"Jo, get hold of yourself. Just because a man wants to talk to his wife doesn't mean its bad news. Maybe it's the prowler you had. Or his job."

"You don't know Michael. He's a play-it-close man. Anyway, he wants me to get a sitter and make a reservation at a restaurant. You think that isn't a clue? Going off some place where Josie can't hear us?"

Angie interrupted, "Stop it, Josephine. You're going to drive yourself nuts before he gets here. You brushed T.J. off. You didn't do anything! Now quit worrying. You have nothing to apologize about."

Josephine ignored Angie and bantered on. "I let T.J. kiss me! I broke the trust between Michael and me when I did that."

"Listen, I've seen it all. Believe me, I have never heard of anyone breaking up over a kiss. You're overreacting."

"If I kissed somebody, he could, too. Or he could actually be having an affair."

Angie raised her voice. "Just stop it. Go vacuum your house. Make a cake. Get your mind under control."

Josephine sighed. "Okay, okay. You're right. At least I'll have a clean house."

For the next two days Josephine made the arrangements Michael requested and cleaned. She vacuumed her house from top to bottom, dusted, scrubbed and mopped the bathrooms, cut fresh flowers, made a pan of brownies, and cooked a hen and fresh vegetables. In addition, Sister Agnes called to remind her of her commitment to create a special display of memorbilia for the residents at Our Lady of the Hills.

Every time Josephine sat down to take a break, her mind raced forward. But the overriding thought that continued to return to her was that Angie was right. She had not done anything wrong, at least not seriously. She and Michael loved each other. When they were first married, their love was all they needed. A touch of a hand, a quick, knowing glance and they exploded into each other's arms. That love was still there. All she needed was more affirmation from Michael. This summer she had reexamined her life—her inner self— reconnected with her past. The results were that she was stronger, more unified. Even to the point of talking with Davis, something she had been certain she would never do. The results were that she had found a new determination in herself, which had become such a vital part of her that she couldn't give it up, not even for Michael.

On Friday Michael arrived a little after three carrying a handsome potted plant for Josephine and coloring books and crayons for Josie. Josie immediately headed for the dining room where she spread out her crayons, opened her coloring book and began coloring.

Josephine took her gift, admiring it. The plants were tastefully arranged in a willow basket. The center plant, a large red geranium, was surrounded by feathery ferns, ageratum and baby's breath. Ivy twinned up the handle.

"Michael, this is gorgeous. To what do I owe this gift?"

"It's my peace offering. I was a jerk the other night when you had the prowler."

Josephine laughed, "Yes, you were and thank you very much. Apology accepted, but it did raise some issues I want to talk over with you later." He nodded and said he wanted to unpack.

Josephine followed him into the bedroom where they chatted pleasantly without mentioning any controversial subjects. Josephine told him about the dinner arrangements, and Josie, who had joined them in the bedroom, told him that Maylynn Eberhardt was going to teach her to march "just like a big girl that very night."

After Michael had settled in, Josephine suggested they take a short hike to Wilderness Falls. "I'd like you to see it," she said. "It's spectacular. Sometimes Josie and I explore there."

Michael nodded. "It would be good to stretch my legs," he replied.

While Josephine began collecting items they needed, Michael stood in the hall, observing all the activity she was generating. Once when she passed through the hall, she paused, glancing at his feet. "You brought sneakers, didn't you," she asked. Without waiting for a reply, she added, "Better put them on. We'll drive to the creek and park. Josie can hike from there on her own. We won't have to carry her."

"You and Josie hike?" Michael asked. His eyes were wide with disbelief.

"Yeah, we go on short hikes. She's doing great. The first of the summer I used to trail ride on horseback, but Josie couldn't go because of an age minimum. One day Angie asked us to hike with her, and we've been going ever since."

"Angie knows all the good trails," Josie piped in.

"Isn't that dangerous? I mean Josie's so young," Michael interjected.

"Heavens, we don't do anything dangerous. No cliffs or ledges. If she gets tired, Ang or I carry her on our backs."

They loaded the station wagon with their gear, and Lady jumped in.

"Okay if I drive?" she asked, climbing behind the wheel.

He shrugged. "Sure."

They pulled out of their driveway and left the blacktop just beyond Davis's, making a sharp right turn onto Wilderness Trail. Josephine was not traveling fast, but the station wagon bounced and slid over the dirt road, and Michael clung to the armrest nervously. The road led in front of Davis's and Josephine's properties, then bent sharply to the left, following the natural curve of the mountain around and down. It was covered with rock-sized gravel, which spewed out from the tires and occasionally struck the inside of the fenders. They passed through a hairpin turn to the right, then back left and continued traveling down the mountain. At length they reached the stream.

"This is where we'll park," Josephine said, an eagerness in her voice. "Wilderness Trail was an old Indian trail. Braves served as lookouts up on our ridge near Lover's Leap. I never realized it before, but we have the best view on the entire mountain. Every movement in the valley shows up. The main tribes camped down in the valley by the Boone River where buffalo grazed."

She left the car and opened the door for Josie and Lady, both of whom headed for the creek.

"Wait for us, Josie," Josephine called. "I don't want you to get wet." Josie waited for her parents, but Lady was already splashing water in all directions.

"The falls are about three quarters of a mile. They're stronger than usual this year because of heavy spring rains." She swung Josie up on her hip until they crossed the creek. Michael followed. "I wanted you to see this, Michael," she said over her shoulder. "We're in virgin forest this very minute."

He gave a cursory look around. "Yeah, looks great,"

They passed through dense green forest, lush with moss and galax leaves, which reminded Josephine of green pools of thick water plants. They came across deep streams where they bent to watch speckled trout glide and swim through the water. Once, Josephine stopped them in a glade of meadow grasses and wild flowers. "Shh," she cautioned, whispering. "Hear that?"

"Couple of blue jays," Michael answered nonchalantly.

"Deeper. Over there in the weeds. That sawing. Grasshoppers. And the 'chee'? A chipmunk."

Josie said, "Angie says Mama hears bugs where there are no bugs."

Josephine laughed and added, "In a minute you won't be able to hear yourself think. The falls will drown everything out."

She paused momentarily, then continued slowly as if she were sorting out what she wanted to say. "Can't you feel the 'rightness' of this place? Nature is so *balanced*. The flowers are perfectly symmetrical. Leaves duplicate themselves on either side of a limb. And there's a perpetual rhythm that keeps everything moving forward toward endless possibilities. It all makes such good sense." She took a deep breath and moved on toward the falls.

Around the next bend, the falls came in view. They were located where several steams merged and crested. The accumulation of water plunged some sixty feet over cliffs and rocks. A fine spray rose from the water, dampening everything in sight. Here and there jagged out cropping of rock diverted the water, causing it to gush in a new direction. At the base where the water struck the rocky ground, it shot back skyward like a geyser.

Lady barked and tried to bite at the water. Josephine and Michael both dashed for her, grabbing her collar to keep her from sliding over the edge. Their presence seemed to urge her on and she thrashed and struggled against their restraints. Finally they managed to get her under control and decided they needed to return to the car.

When they were home, Josephine asked Michael what he thought of the falls.

"The falls were dangerous," he said emphatically. "Lady could have plunged over the side. If it could happen to Lady, it could happen to Josie. That's the possibility I saw." Then he turned and walked into another part of the house.

"I should have taken a leash," Josephine yelled after him sarcastically.

That evening Maylynn and Josie were practicing in the garden when Josephine and Michael left for dinner. They said their goodbyes and Josephine gave instructions to Maylynn on where they would be.

As they drove away, Josephine could see Michael out of the corner of her eye. He looked so handsome. He was wearing a white, open collared shirt and a brown sport coat. The color brought out his eyes. The only mention of the tension between them was the two-line apology Michael made when he arrived. Neither of them mentioned the hike.

Josephine continued to watch Michael until he turned toward her and smiled. "You look pretty tonight."

"Thank you," she smiled back. "This afternoon we didn't talk about your work. What's going on with the Bank? Have they decided which bank they want to purchase?"

"Yes, I'll tell you about it when we get to the restaurant."

They drove on in silence until they reached the Mountain Trout.

In the restaurant the hostess greeted Josephine warmly, and Josephine introduced her to Michael. As they sat down, Michael remarked, "I keep forgetting you have a complete life up here."

Josephine laughed nervously, "Angie introduced me to the Mountain Trout. I know it's been hard on you for me to be up here this summer, but I can't tell you how important I feel it's been for me and Josie."

He shrugged, conceding, "It's probably best. I've been on the road most of the time."

Changing the subject, Josephine asked again about the Bank merger.

"They're making an offer this weekend for a bank in this region. Wilkes. In fact, they've asked me to head the region at quite a salary increase. That is if the merger goes through."

"How much increase?"

"Thirty-five percent."

"Honey, that's huge. Congratulations."

"Well, a lot of things have to happen. The bank we're trying to buy has to accept the offer. Then, of course, we have to
decide if we want to move."

Josephine's heart sank. Another move! Their drinks
arrived, and she took a big swallow of hers. She said, "We
have to start thinking about what's best for Josie. She's
enrolled in kindergarten in Matthews. She needs to grow up
in one place. On the other hand, I've always told you I'd do
what was best for your career."

That was not what she was feeling. Move if they had to,
but she longed to say no. She added tentatively, "It does
bring up something else."

"What?"

"We need to make decisions together."

"That's what we're doing."

"Is it? After all the hoopla, do I really have a choice?"

He flinched and started to say something. Then he shook
his head and reached across the table to take her hand. "Of
course, you do. You don't want to go, just say the word."

She squirmed in her seat. "Tell you what," she said. "Let's
talk about it after the banks make their decisions, okay?" He
nodded, downed his drink and signaled the waiter for
another. "Want another?" She shook her head, remembering
the night she drank too much brandy.

They chatted during Michael's second drink. When their
food came, her mountain trout sat on a white plate swimming in butter, a sprig of parsley on the side. Tomato wedges
garnished her tossed salad, which was smothered with thick,
blue cheese dressing. The minute she looked at it she lost her
appetite. She picked up her roll and began tearing off bite
size pieces and eating them.

She tried to listen to Michael while he prattled on about
"due diligence" and "asset ratios." These new developments,

a move and job change for Michael, made her issues seem small. What could new-found respect and standing up for her convictions mean compared to a thirty-five percent salary increase? How could "reconnecting with her past, reaching her full potential and leading a fulfilling life" stack up against being part of the management team of an up and coming bank? Clearly they didn't. Michael's career had to come first. The futures of all three of them depended on it, she thought with resignation.

Michael finished his meal while Josephine ate her roll and pushed her food around. After they paid the check, they rose to leave the restaurant. On the way out the hostess spoke to them again, "Nice to have you and your husband, Josephine. Come back soon." Josephine blushed, surprised the hostess remembered her name, and a lump rose in her throat. Her summer was slipping away. Soon she and Josie would be leaving Rocky Ridge. With the first cool snap, a few leaves would turn yellow. No more long conversations with Angie over wine and dinner. No more talks with Davis, which despite earlier reservations, she was beginning to enjoy. No more digging for quartz rocks or looking for arrowheads or exploring the mountains with Josie. The day after Labor Day, Josie would be having her first day at kindergarten. The decision about the bank and their future—whatever it was— would have been made.

They walked out of the restaurant under the quirky trout sign that Josephine had come to love. Thunder was rumbling in the distance.

"Better hurry. Looks like a storm's coming," Michael said.

Josephine nodded, concern spreading over her face. "Maylynn needs to get home before the storm."

They dashed for the car and sped for home.

It was still light when they reached home. The thunder they could hear was rising from a distant ridge. They considered having Michael follow Maylynn home, but she insisted she could beat the storm home and left.

Josephine checked on Josie, who was fast asleep, and then she went to the kitchen to make coffee. Michael settled down in front of the TV to watch a baseball game.

"What did you want to talk to me about?" he yelled to her from his place on the sofa.

She was surprised by his remark. She had assumed they would continue to hold controversial subjects in abeyance. She returned to the living room, holding a china cup in her hand, her finger looped through the handle. "You sure you want to get into this now?'

"Now's as good a time as any."

"Let me get our coffee first." She left the room, returning in minutes. "I'm glad you told me about the bank offer," she began. "Of course, we can't decide until the offer has been accepted."

"Right, but that's not what you had in mind the night the prowler was here."

"No," she replied slowly, measuring what she should say to him. That she wanted to live life all the way to the edge. That she wanted to take risks like Laura, even if it meant making mistakes. That she couldn't accept simple hymns to life anymore. Rather that if life were a symphony, she wanted to be a kettledrum—hearing, feeling, being every drumbeat. Would he understand a statement like that? Should she say the land possessed her? That she wanted to know the mountains intimately, hike the trails, run the rivers, fish the streams. Or should she say she wanted to be like her mother? To wear her hair twisted around "rats" into sweeping rolls on either side of her head. That she wanted to wear a USO uniform and commit to the "war effort" by working at the USO day after day, literally serving thousands of soldiers each week. Even if it meant she would spend the last years of her life in a cloudy haze of being nowhere.

She sat down slowly on the sofa. Thunder was still rumbling in the distance. Now and then a crack of lightning sizzled across the sky. Her voice was low when she spoke. "I don't want to be on the fence anymore. I don't want to play it safe. I want to commit completely to the things I believe in. And I want you to be more positive about the things I want to do. I'll fight for them if I have to."

"Fight for what?" he asked, tilting his head quizzically.

"I'm not sure. Things I believe deeply. People's rights. The right to be respected, to be educated, to go to bed with a full stomach, to be loved. I don't know what."

"That's all?"

"No, it's not *all*," her irritation rising. "I'm not the same person I was. I can't go back to being that person, even after I go home. For one thing, I'll never keep a checkbook the way you want. I'm going to open my own account. And I'm not going to iron shirts anymore."

He leaned back in his chair just as a clap of thunder shook the house and rattled the dishes in the kitchen. "I'm not sure what it all means, Josephine, but I guess I can live with taking my shirts to the laundry. I've been doing it all summer. And the checkbook? Well, the money you inherited is your money, and you need to do with it what you want. I understand that."

A severe thunderstorm warning flashed across the bottom of the TV screen. When the regular program returned, a sports announcer was saying that women are beginning to demand equal money for women's athletic programs in colleges. Michael said that was going to ruin college athletics. Alumni give money to college football and basketball programs, he said. If women take half the money, the "real" programs will go down and alumni will quit giving.

Josephine answered, forgetting for the moment the discussion they had been having. "What do you mean, 'real programs'? The point is women should be given an equal chance. Right now they aren't."

"That's ridiculous. Women have every chance men have!" Michael fired back.

"Michael, you know that's not true. If the NCAA doesn't

require it, less than a third of a college's athletic budget will go to women's athletics."

"Men's programs bring in revenue. Women's don't," he retorted.

"Don't you understand!" Josephine jumped up from the sofa and threw a dishtowel she was holding on the sofa behind her. Then she began pacing across the living room. "It's not about money. It's about your daughter! I don't want her to have to play half-court basketball the way I did.

"We could only bounce the ball *once!*" She emphasized every word with an appropriate hand gesture. "Guards couldn't cross the center line. Nobody wanted to play that game. Only one girl in my high school, Evie Tate, ever stuck with it."

He was saying something about the answer is to change the rules.

"It's *not* about rules," she answered. "It's about what's right! College is the time to experiment and learn." She had paced down the room for the third time and stopped to face him.

Michael turned his hands up. "Hey, don't get so huffy. We're just having a discussion. This isn't a fight."

"This *is* a fight," she insisted, stomping her heel on the floor. "You *have* to take my concerns seriously and not simply sweep them away! You cannot analyze this until it just vanishes. *I will not let you do that!* Women have to have the same opportunities as men, or you are undermining half of the population! Don't you get it? To make this country great we need *all* the people!"

A clap of thunder followed an explosion of lightning. Everything in the living room turned momentarily white. A mournful whistling, which started in the upper end of the valley, followed and worked its way toward them.

"What's that noise?" Michael asked, jumping up.

"The storm's coming down the valley. I think the river draws it," she replied nonchalantly. "When you hear that sound, it's time to move. It'll be here in no time."

"What do we do?"

"Look in the front hall closet for candles and flashlights in case we loose electricity," Josephine ordered. "Matches, too. I'll get extra blankets. We need to put Josie in our bed. Lady, too. She's going to start howling any minute."

They sprang into action, rushing in different directions, and assembled back in their bedroom with their collection of supplies. "The rain will start any minute," Josephine said, "and you won't believe how hard it will be. It'll feel like the storm is right over our heads."

Lightning and thunder were exploding around them. Lady started howling. "I'm going to get Josie," Michael was saying.

"I'll make sure the windows are tight," Josephine called out as she headed for the living room where she checked the windows and pulled down the shades.

Lightning flashed every few seconds, and thunder came so fast it shook the foundation of the house. A crack, louder than the others, ripped somewhere close to them, followed by an explosion. The lights went out.

Michael had brought Josie from her bedroom. She was whimpering. Lady had crawled under the bed and Michael was trying to coax her out.

Outside the wind howled through the trees. They tossed and swayed in the strong wind, their shadows whipped across the window shades. The rain was coming in torrents, pounding on the rooftop, gushing out of the gutters, splashing against the windows.

Michael had managed to get Lady up on the bed where she was howling and shaking. They all crawled under the covers and huddled together.

Josie was snuggled against Michael's chest on one side, Josephine on the other. When the storm began to subside, Josephine fell asleep with her head on his chest, where she could hear his heart beating.

The argument had been forgotten in their struggle with the storm.

The next morning when Josephine awoke, Michael was already up. She could hear him rumbling around in the kitchen. "What's going on?" she called from the bedroom. "We're fixing your breakfast, Mommy," Josie called to her.

Michael and Josie entered the bedroom with a cup of coffee. "Your treat today," Michael said, handing her the coffee.

"You're dressed," Josephine replied with surprise. "How did I miss all that?"

"You were exhausted," Michael answered. "We decided to let you sleep. Then we got this great idea to serve you breakfast in bed."

Josie nodded. "I picked the flowers, Mommy."

"That's very sweet, honey."

"By the way," Michael added, "I was very proud of you last night. You're a take-charge kind of person. And now, how do you want your eggs cooked, Madam?"

"Two, over light. And thank you."

CHAPTER TWENTY-ONE

When they finally landed in Wonsan, the North Koreans had left and the South Korean Army occupied the city. Captain Russett called in Park Kwon-mi, their interpreter, to arrange a beach party for all his surviving troops.

"These men have fought hard, Kwon-mi. We'd like to give 'em a party. Can you get us some fresh meat?"

"No meat, Captain. Pig gone."

"Fowl's okay. Chicken maybe."

"No chicken. Pheasant," Kwon's hands drew circles in the air, "till guns go boom, boom, boom. Pheasants fly! No fowl."

"Fish's okay."

Kwon-mi's head bobbed up and down. "Aaah, plenty good fish. Squid. Octopus."

"Hell, no!" Russett reared back on his heels. "Yanks would starve before they'd eat squid or octopus! Just fish with two eyes. Whatever you catch in the bay."

"Plenty two eye. Ell two eye. I get. Make good Korean food. Cabbage, onions, turnips, radishes. Good vegetables. We fix kim chee. Very good."

"No eel. You hear? No eel and no kim chee. Yanks want American food! White fish with barbeque sauce, vegetables and fruit." He paused, balling up his fist and drumming with it for emphasis. "You know what, Kwon-mi? You and I are going to make a real Yank family reunion out of this. Can you handle that?"

Kwon nodded but he looked worried. He was not sure that he understood American parties.

❧

For two days before the storm, Easy had been traveling in that thin space between fantasy and clear headedness. It all began when Davis asked him to open the *entire* puppet play by playing a song on his harmonica. At first Easy had been pleased, but as the days passed and the event approached, he began to think better of the idea. What if that teacher from the second grade, *miss-what's-her-name*, showed up, the one who sent him home to stay? What if she started asking him numbers? They always mixed him up. If she wanted to asked him, for example, how many turns it took Bessie the Mule to plow the cornfield, or how many gunnysacks were needed before the entire apple orchard was picked, he could answer straight away.

Besides playing his harmonica, Easy had another problem. Last night's storm had knocked out his electricity. He had no way to iron his shirt. Mama wanted him to be clean and neat and orderly. He understood that. But it wasn't all that easy without her. He had managed to wash his shirt and dry it in the sun. Then the storm came.

It was too much, he thought miserably. He balled up his shirt and headed for his pickup truck. He was going to tell Davis he was dropping out of the show. And he was going to tell him this very minute.

It was 7:15 a.m. when Easy burst into Davis's kitchen. Davis and Eula Mae were sitting down to breakfast.

"'At harmonica you wuz wanting me to play?" Easy said. "Cain't do it. Mama don't want me in the puppet play 'cause I cain't arn this-yere shirt." He tossed the shirt onto the table.

"Easy, your mama's dead," Davis chided. "Besides,

nobody'll know your shirt isn't ironed. We're all wearing smocks."

"Don't matter. She ain't gonna like it if my shirt ain't arned."

"Lemme see that thing," Eula Mae piped in, snatching the shirt off the table. "I'll iron it. Reckon your mama'd like that all right." She put the shirt on the counter and passed a plate and fork to Easy. "Eat some breakfast. I'll do the shirt when we finish. Wash your overalls, too, if Davis'll find something for you to put on."

"Well," Davis said, rubbing his hands together, "we settled that problem. Now let's talk about the harmonica. Are you getting stage fright?"

"'At harmonica sounds like a screech owl."

"You'll do fine. You play in the park all the time."

"Ain't no walls in the park. Jest birds."

"I can't think of a more critical audience. If you want, you can close the puppet show instead of opening it. Your nerves will be settled by then."

"Adopt-a-Grandparent Day" at Our Lady of the Hills was scheduled for 4 p.m. on Tuesday. The event began with a reception, complete with punch and cookies, and tours of the home.

By the time Josephine and Josie had dressed and rounded up Lady to put her in the kitchen, they were running late. Once they arrived at the parking lot, they were delayed further by having to hunt for a parking space. After driving through the entire lot several times, Josephine pulled on the grass at the end of a row and hoped her wagon wouldn't get sideswiped. She grabbed her pocket book, and Josie picked up the bag containing her costume, and they rushed inside.

By then, Josephine was hot and frustrated and anxious. She was thinking how hard the residents had worked on the memborbilia posters for their doors. What if nobody paid any attention to them? Or what if Josie forgot her dance and just stood there while the piano played? And how was she going to keep from crying the way she always did when she watched Josie perform?

Once inside, the building was cool and the atmosphere festive, and Josephine began to calm down. People were milling about the halls, laughing, and to Josephine's relief, they were talking to residents while admiring their displays.

Sister Agnes passed them in the hall and called out, "The door decorations are a great success, Josephine. And your dance, Josie. You'll be lovely, dearie."

Sister Michael Anne, who helped Josephine organize the doors, ran up to her. "Everybody loves the doors! We ended up with so many professions represented—teachers, nurses, engineers, storeowners, mothers, even a lawyer! Oh, I can't think of all of them," she chortled happily.

The door of each resident's room was crowded with mementos, giving a view into each life. Photographs of men blasting through solid rock to build the Blue Ridge Parkway. WW II pictures of soldiers with pretty girls, or standing in front of famous, foreign landmarks, or preparing for battle. There were newspaper clipping of residents who had marched in civil rights demonstrations, and articles featuring people who helped bring financial and educational development to the entire Blue Ridge Mountains. One woman had a sign of "Rosie the Riveter" taped to her door. Another, a navy nurse, wore her blue cape and cap.

Josephine and Josie found Angie and Maylynn. Josephine had insisted they come to see Josie dance. The four of them walked together through the halls, admiring the memorbilia and chatting with residents.

Some time had passed when Josie grabbed her mother's skirt. "Mommy, I hear singing," she said. Josephine was engrossed in a conversation, "Just a minute, honey," she answered, waving Josie off. Josie insisted. "The program's starting, Mommy. I gotta get my costume on."

The sound of music rose from the activity room, where

the program was being held. "Oh my gosh," Josephine declared. "I almost forgot you're dancing! Excuse us, please."

She grabbed Josie's hand and the two of them dashed down the hall, looking for a rest room. They hurried inside. Josie squirmed into her fluffy yellow duck costume which Michael had brought the weekend before while Josephine held her ballet shoes for her. Then Josephine pinned the yellow feather headdress in her hair, but the bobby pins wouldn't hold.

"Drats, you're hair's too thin," Josephine sighed. The hair band kept slipping forward over Josie's forehead. "Honey, if this slides off, just hold it in your hand, okay?" Josie nodded, ready to leave the rest room. "Wait," Josephine said, holding up a shinny tube of lipstick. "Want some lipstick and rouge?" Josie's eyes gleamed with excitement. When the makeup was in place, Josephine hugged her daughter. "You look wonderful. Now, break a leg."

"What's that?"

"Good luck."

"Oh," Josie replied, looking at her mom like she was nuts. And she pushed through the door.

Josephine left Josie in the hallway and went to find Angie and Maylynn. Her stomach was doing flip-flops. When she found them, they were lining up across the back of the room with the puppeteers, where they could see every move Josie made.

The furniture in the activity room had been removed and replaced with folding chairs. The puppet theater was placed against the back wall and large potted plants were lined up down the sides, marking an area for a stage.

Residents and guests were milling about looking for friends and settling into their seats. Sister Agnes began the program by welcoming everyone and thanking them for their participation. She gave a brief explanation of "Adopt a Grandparent Day," then introduced Sister Michael Anne as the one who would introduce the program.

A clown who made animals out of balloons was first. His

act ended with three other clowns running into the activity room passing out animal balloons.

Josie was next. Josephine could hardly breath as she watched Josie emerge from the hallway. She walked with her head up, hands out to the sides like a real dancer. She was smiling broadly. When she reached the middle of the performance space, she turned toward the audience and made a sweeping bow. Her right foot was pointed and her arms extended behind her back like a butterfly. Josephine and Angie giggled.

"If she isn't adorable?" whispered Maylynn. "I want a bunch of kids."

"I have no idea where she got that," Josephine declared, shaking her head. "At that age, I was scared of my own shadow."

"Not so," interjected Angie. "As I recall, you were game for anything!"

Josie had turned toward the pianist, a nun, and nodded. The nun played a few bars, and Josie began to dance. She started into her routine smoothly. About halfway through, her headdress began to slip. She pushed it back several times, but it continued to slide onto her forehead. Finally, she yanked it off and held it, just as her mother had suggested. Toward the end of her dance, she must have realized she needed her hands to be free for the duck walk. So she stuck the headband back on her head and went into her popular duck walk, squatting down with her hands under her armpits. The audience went crazy. They loved her.

She exited briefly into the hallway, then returned and curtsied. She looked around the room for her mother. Instead she spotted her new friend Daisy, who was clapping and cheering loudly, and Josie ran and hugged her. By then her mother had come to meet her.

"You were wonderful," Josephine whispered in her daughter's ear as she lifted her up. "I am so proud of you. How did you remember all of those beautiful dance steps."

Angie, Maylynn and the puppeteers had followed

Chapter Twenty-One

Josephine and were swarmed around Josie, congratulating her.

Just then the room lights switched off and the stage lights on the puppet theater came up, pulling every eye in the room that way. The theater itself was the height of a man and looked to be portable. Black curtains surrounded the bottom section. The upper part, where the stage was located, was painted glossy black and trimmed around the edges with golden scrolls and lines. A red velvet curtain was pulled across the front. The effect was handsome, Asian and mysterious.

At the sound of a Chinese gong, Darlene stepped in front of the theater. She wore a kimono of blue silk with a red obei sash around her waist. Her hair was styled like a geisha girl and her face was painted white. She spoke in a formal, ceremonious voice.

The Un-Less
By Davis E. Williams

The story here-in is about to begin
A warrior who loves, a Princess she was.
The fates may smile, the gods may bless,
Unless, of course, unless...

She continued by naming the troup: Eula Mae Dysart, Blackie Statton, Davis, Easy Highfill and Darlene Adams, narrator. Easy was to conclude the performance by playing the harmonica, Darlene said.

The gong sounded again. A hush came over the audience. The curtain opened revealing a backdrop of light blue sky and darker blue ocean. The sound of Oriental wind chimes rippled through the activity room. A ship with the princess and oarsman inside appeared. The ship and puppets moved in tandem with the waves. Through clever use of lighting, sound effects and staging, Davis had created a unique setting. His rod puppets gave an illusion of realism. Easy had attached similar rods to props such as waves, a boat and a palace so that they also moved realistically.

Darlene continued:

> *Once upon a time a beautiful princess sailed from far across the sea to the mysterious land of Korea. The princess' name was Celestial Star of Beauty, Star for short.*

Darlene exited.

The audience oohed and aahed as the play progressed. Josephine was surprised at how striking the puppets were. They were hand-carved and handsomely dressed. The warrior and oarsman both had Asian features with dark hair, while Star was fair and blonde. They were smartly painted with black eyes for the men and deep blue eyes for Star. Their hair looked almost human, and bright red circles were painted on their cheeks.

A warrior entered from stage left. He spoke to the audience, gesturing toward the boat with the princess in it.

> *"Who is this beautiful princess who approaches the shores of my native land, Korea? She must have come from some distant land."*

> *The princess' boat lands on the shore and she steps out. The warrior greets her. "I have never seen such beautiful hair. It is like spun gold," he says. They fall in love, but alas, a fire-breathing dragon captures the princess and locks her in the tower of a palace. The warrior tries to rescue her. "Throw down your golden hair and I will climb it to save you." he calls to the princess. She answers, "No way, Hose! There's not a beauty parlor in this entire tower. Climb up that vine." With great difficulty, the warrior manages to climb the vine and rescues the*

*princess, but as they are running away, the dragon
reappears and tries to capture Star again. A donny-
brook ensues with Star running from the dragon, the
dragon chasing Star, and the warrior chasing them
both. Round and round the stage they go until the
warrior fires an arrow at the dragon. The wise
dragon ducks and the arrow flies passed him into
Star. Star falls on the stage. The warrior runs to her
crying, "Oh, my beautiful Celestial Star of Beauty,
please do not die!" Star raises her head and says.
"What an incredibly bad shot you turned out to be,"
and slumps back on the stage. The warrior, weeping,
believes she is dead and says, "I have killed the only
thing I will ever love. However, this life is only an
illusion. I will join you in Nirvana where our hearts
will be united for eternity." The princess raises her
head again and says, "I can hardly wait," and she
dies.*

When the curtain fell, the audience cheered and
applauded, but Josephine was puzzled. Clearly the audience
loved the play, but she wondered if there was a deeper meaning within it.

Just then Easy came forward from behind the puppet theater and took the position where Darlene had stood. He
removed his black smock, folded it neatly in front of him and
placed it at his feet.

"Wonder why he did that?" Darlene whispered to Eula
Mae.

"He better. I ironed that shirt for him this morning," Eula
Mae proclaimed.

Easy's mind was locked on his performance. His harmonica was in the deep pocket in the right leg of his overalls.
When his hand reached down and touched the cool metal,
when his fingers hit the small perfectly formed rectangles
where the music was made, when the sharp dent on the corner pricked his thumb—during those brief moments he

remembered he had brought Mama to Our Lady Nursing Center when she became sick. First, he had taken her to the hospital. After a week, the doctor said she should be transferred to a nursing home and recommended Our Lady Nursing Center. At the time, Easy believed she would stay a short time. What he couldn't possibly guess was that he would never bring her home.

In those darting moments in which his fingers were wrapping around the harmonic and pulling it from his pocket, he remembered two important things. The Sisters had been good to him and Mama. They had fed him, walked with him up and down the hall, prayed with him in the tiny chapel where everything was colored by shimmering red and blue glass. And when they comforted him, their arms were boundless.

The other thing he remembered was how he had wanted to play his harmonica for Mama at her funeral, but he was too scared. What if he made a mistake in front of all their kin and the brethren of Truelight Baptist Church? What if the music came out wrong? And so he kept quiet, sat there on that cold, hard pew, listening to the preacher and wanting to touch Mama's hand one last time.

He looked down at the shiny musical instrument no bigger than two fingers. He turned it on edge and rubbed it across his coverall. And when he touched his lips to it and began to play, he played notes he didn't realize he knew. A song he heard while he was at the nursing center, something he associated with the nuns. The notes were full and melodious as he breathed in and out over the tiny reeds inside the harmonica, cupping his hands just so to cradle or release the notes. *Aah-ve Mah-re-ee-ah. Aah-ve-mah-ha-ha-re-ee-ah.*

People in the audience began to recognize the song. Sister Agnes stepped forward from the back of the room and began to sing in a rich contralto voice. A member of the choir stood up and started singing, too. Other choir members joined. Nuns began arriving from various halls that fed into the activity room. They began moving among the patients, singing. Patients who could, stood-up singing or humming.

Angie grabbed Josephine's hand and squeezed. "Can you belief this?" She swiped a tear away. "I'm so glad you've come back in my life."

"It's been a hard summer, Angie," Josephine replied with a sigh. She felt confused by Davis's play. "The play. Davis. I don't know what to make of it. But I do know this. I feel I've found another sister in you. I'm very grateful for that."

Whatever concern Josephine might have been feeling, the audience was putty in Easy's hands. His music echoed down the halls of the nursing center into patients' room and floated out the door.

It caught a breeze and traveled skyward.

Chapter Twenty-Two

"You didn't tell me Davis was so good-looking," Angie said to Josephine as they drove away. After the program, Josephine, Davis and their friends decided to go to Pizza Hut for dinner.

When Josephine heard her, she almost slammed on her brakes. Angie's tone was unlike her—almost sweet. "What!" she bellowed. "You can't be serious."

"Of course I'm serious." Angie was staring straight ahead, her pert nose tilted. "His baby blues are gorgeous."

"Angie, he's been in a state institution for the criminally insane!" She hissed her words, not wanting Josie and Maylynn, who were talking in the back seat, to hear her.

Angie continued, "You just got through telling me, not an hour ago, the two of you had worked through your difference."

"Well, yes, but I never imagined anybody—especially not you—would look at him—well, you know—romantically!" Josephine sneaked a glanced at Angie. She was still looking straight ahead. "He'll be on medication all his life," Josephine added.

"Good grief, who cares about that? People in the mountains accept you the way you are. Like Easy. No big deal. He's just *slow*. But also gifted in unique ways." She had glanced at Josephine and then settled back with her arms folded.

They drove on in silence. After several blocks, Josephine opened the conversation again. "There's a tragedy with Davis, Angie. I don't know it all but I think clues were in the puppet show. Didn't you think it was strange that a blonde heroine was in an oriental play? And that her name was Celestial Star of Beauty? His wife's name was Celeste. That was no accident, believe me. "

"Okay, so he wrote the play about his dead wife."

Josephine answered, "He's a very complex man. Smart, but complex." By then they were pulling into Pizza Hut parking lot.

"Let's drop it," Angie said. "When we get inside, I want to hear about Michael."

"Ah, yes, Michael." Josephine turned off the motor and slumped back in her seat. "I haven't told you my big news about Michael." She dropped her keys in her purse and opened her car door.

Davis and his puppeteers had not arrived. The restaurant was dim with heavy tables and booths stained dark brown. Red and white checked curtains had been pulled to keep out the oblique afternoon sun. Delicious smells of rising dough, melting cheese and sizzling pepperoni rose from the kitchen, where a collection of young people, students no doubt, were performing various organizational steps in the preparation of pizzas.

Angie and Josephine selected a table large enough for everyone, and they each ordered wine.

"Can I have a Coke, Mommy?" Josie asked.

"Milk, hun. You'll be up all night if you drink Coke," her mother replied.

The waiter, a pimply-faced teenager, was watching Maylynn, who pretended she hadn't noticed. She and Josie were coloring the children's placemats. They were bent over their mats, intent on what they were doing. Their hair was hiding their faces.

The waiter cleared his throat and spoke to Maylynn. "Miss, would you care for a glass of wine?" Maylynn giggled and lifted her eyes to the young man, her eyelashes fluttering.

"Who, me? Heavens no. Just Coke."

Josie imitated her. "I'll have some wine, please, waiter."

Maylynn slapped at her arm. "You! Listen to you." Then Maylynn's face came up again and she stroked her long hair. "She'll have milk."

Angie and Josephine laughed.

"What about Michael?" Angie asked, turning to Josephine.

"His bank's made an offer to a bank in Wilkes. If it comes through, they've offered Michael the job of managing it and developing the entire western region. It means a huge salary increase."

"Hey, that's just sixty-five miles away! You can come up whenever you want!"

Josephine smiled tentatively and shrugged. "We've moved so much. I was hoping Matthews would be the last one. Josie starts kindergarten right after Labor Day."

Davis and his group entered the restaurant and began settling at their table. Pizzas and beer were ordered, and the conversation moved back to the program, rehashing every detail and congratulating everyone involved.

When their food came, everyone settled down to eating but continued talking and laughing. Josephine felt like crying. She told herself it was because Josie performed. She was always emotional after Josie did well, but there may be more to her feelings. Snatches of conversation from other tables swirled around her, clouding what her own friends were saying. She felt an urge to protect the good time they were having, to keep outsiders from disturbing them.

The program at Our Lady of the Hills had been a marker for her and Josie. Their summer was almost over. Soon they would be returning home. Everything would be changing. The evenings would turn chilly. Hydrangea bushes would flush with pink, and hardwoods would turn reds, yellows and oranges. Fall would come, and she and Josie would be back with Michael in Matthews, or some new place.

She looked around the table at the assortment of people. Her friends, some new, some old. Their lives would change, too. Eula Mae, recruited by Sister Agnes, was going to conduct gospel sing-alongs at the nursing home. Davis, who had managed to sit down by Angie and now had his arm around her, had promised to do another puppet show at Christmas. Angie—*heavens above*—was batting her eyes at him like crazy. Maylynn, under Angie's coaching, had been elected head drum majorette for her high school. Easy had gotten an order for a hundred paddle toys from a convenience store. Josephine's summer—her soul searching, all she had learned about herself and her relationships with her family—was it going to be forgotten when she went home? Could she continue to feel strong when she couldn't look at the mountain, that she felt had become a source of strength for her? Could she face her future with courage?

Their evening together was winding down. People were taking one last bite of pizza and emptying their beer glasses. Pizza pans, still holding remaining slices, littered the table. Cups, glasses, used napkins were cast aside.

Josephine leaned over toward Angie and whispered. "I've been thinking. If you think you might be interested in Davis, go for it. It *could* be very good."

Angie squeezed her hand.

Josephine and Josie drove Angie and Maylynn back to their car. Then they said goodnight and headed for home. It was twilight after a bright sunny day and the sky was cast with pink. In the altered evening light, the road, the houses that ran beside it, the foliage of trees behind glowed with iridescent colors. Ordinary items, such as rakes, and fences, and dahlias assumed new characteristics. They were mysterious

as if they held some special knowledge or secret understanding.

Josie, still excited from her day, was bouncing on the car
seat beside her mother. They were singing "She'll Be
Coming Around the Mountain." They entered, Valley View
Trail, and passed the first string of small houses, passed the
dirt road leading down to Wilderness Trail, passed Davis's
house and commented that his jeep was already parked in
the carport. They drove by the entrance to Lover's Leap, and
Josephine steered her wagon over the bump at the summit
of her drive.

She paused to looked down at the driveway and her
house and the mountains beyond. The evening was beautiful.
The sky had slipped to gray, and the night insects, cicadas
and crickets that lived in nearby trees and bushes, were
sounding an insistent, metallic tone. But as she looked about
her and listened to the evening—an evening meant to be
calm and peaceful—she realized it was not. Something was
different. Some adjustments of unknown proportions had
shifted the natural order of this evening. Everything was
about to move to a new place.

In a low, tense voice, she reached her hand out to Josie
and spoke slowly to her. "Honey, stop singing. Is that Lady
barking?" Just then Lady let out a series of vicious barks.

"Yep, that's Lady all right," Josie nodded.

"Josie," her mother said more cautiously, "didn't we leave
Lady inside?"

"Yes'um," Josie nodded. She paused momentarily, then
added with surprise, "Hey, how'd she get out? We put her in
the kitchen. 'Member?"

"That's what I thought."

Josephine allowed the car to roll slowly down the drive.
At the hairpin turn Josephine noticed a pickup truck. It was
partly concealed in the bushes beside her neighbor's house.
Why was a pickup truck there? No one had used that house
all summer. Could one of the owner's grandchildren be
checking on things? As her car passed the turn, Josephine

looked through the trees for lights in the house. It was dark.

They passed the rear of the truck. Josephine thought she saw the flash of movement inside. At the same time, Lady began another bout of barking.

"Something's wrong," Josephine said. She steered the car passed the truck to the end of their drive and came to a stop. Her daughter's eyes widened and her lower lip formed into a perfect "O," and Josephine realized it would be impossible for Josie to believe anything could go wrong on such a wonderful day. A day when she had danced her duck dance and had been admired by so many people and had the time of her life. Everything was right on such a day.

By now Josephine was sizing up the situation. She thought she recognized the truck hidden in the bushes as belonging to T.J. And really, if she were honest with herself, didn't she have unfinished business with him? Had she really thought he would accept a simple brush-off? Once she came to that understanding in her mind, once she accepted that she had started something she must finish, a calm came over her. Her thoughts became uniquely clear. She must get Josie out of any danger, and she must get help.

"I want you to listen carefully to Mommy and do exactly what I tell you," she said to Josie. Josie's eyes were wide with fear, but she nodded. "Even if it doesn't seem right, I want you to do it." Josie nodded again. "I'm going to get out of the car and I want to you follow me."

As Josephine left the car, she called to Lady, who was still barking in the vicinity of the back door. The dog rushed around the rose bush at the bottom of the stairs and sprinted up the steps. As soon as she reached the top, Josephine grabbed the dog by the collar and pulled her to Josie, who had climbed out of the car as her mother had instructed. Josie was pointing up the driveway and said, "Look, Mommy. It's just T.J."

T.J. had climbed out of his truck and was leaning against the tailgate. Josephine stooped down beside her daughter and spoke quietly. "I know it's T.J.," she said, "but he's not our friend like we thought, Josie." She glanced up at T.J. who was still in the same place. "I need you to be a big girl and go to Davis's for help."

"T.J.'s not our friend?" Josie asked. "He taught me to ride."

"No, sweetheart. Even though he taught you to ride and acted like our friend, he isn't." She glanced up the drive. T.J. was still leaning against the truck. "You and I are going to play a little game," she continued. "Can you do that?" Josie nodded. "My part is to keep T.J. from doing something bad like go in our house. Your and Lady's part is to run to Davis's for help. Lady knows the way because she gets scraps from Eula Mae. Can you do that with Lady?" She nodded again. "Tell Davis and Eula Mae I said to call the police, okay?" Josie looked at her mother and started to cry. "Baby, don't cry. Now be a big girl and do what Mommy says."

Josephine hurried Josie and Lady to the catwalk. She gave her daughter a quick kiss and urged her on the catwalk. Then she commanded Lady, "Take Josie to Davis's, Lady. Go!"

Josie took several steps on the catwalk with Lady and turned around. "No, Mommy," she said firmly. Her little foot came down with a thud on the wooden planks. "I don't wanna go. I don't wanna play the game."

"Go, Josie! Run! Quick!"

Josie turned away from her mother and ran down the catwalk with Lady beside her. Josephine watched until her daughter disappeared in the bushes that lined the catwalk.

Once Josie was out of sight—once Josephine turned back to face T.J.—she focused more clearly on him. He was sauntering down the driveway toward her. As he came toward her, Josephine suspected he was trying to look seductive. His blue jeans were skin tight, and the top of his shirt was unbuttoned to reveal a tuft of reddish blond hair on his chest. He had a beard that was several days old.

"That was real smart getting rid of the kid like that," he said. His voice was hoarse, and Josephine judged he had been drinking.

Chapter Twenty-Two

"Don't come any closer, T.J. Why did you break into my house?"

"Looking for my yellow gloves. Jeeter said you took one of them."

"Oh, so you *were* the one who dropped the other glove on the catwalk."

He smirked. "It was me all right. Bet you didn't know I live right below you on Wilderness Trail. I know every inch of this mountain. Anything moves, I know it. Anyway, all I had to do was park my pickup at the bottom of your lot and step on the catwalk. Easy as pie. Been watching you and that kid since you first got here."

Josephine's back stiffened, and she spoke harshly. "There are two things that are not going to happen here, T.J. One is that we are not going into my house either to get the gloves or for any other reason. And the second is that Josie is not going to be involved. She's gone. This is between you and me. As for the gloves, I'll take them to the barn and leave them. You can get them there."

T.J. started toward her, swaying as he moved.

Josephine ordered, "Stop right there. I want you to get off my property now. There's nothing here for you."

He continued down the driveway. "Well, la-dee-dah. That's where you're wrong, sweetheart. You been sending me messages all summer, and ol' T.J.'s gonna collect."

"You're drunk. Go home."

"Oh, I'll go home all right, but you're coming with me. Now, you can come nice, or I can force you. Believe me, I have ways. Wouldn't you rather come peaceful-like?" He puckered his lips as if for a kiss.

"I'm not going anywhere with you." She gripped her pocketbook, glancing around for something heavier with which to defend herself. Across the drive was a row of mid-size rocks. If she could dash for one, she might be able to hit him with it.

But T.J. appeared to have sobered slightly, and he was advancing on her so fast he would grab her before she could reach one of the rocks. Her only choice was to rush him first.

With that thought in mind, she garnered all her strength and ran toward him, slamming into his chest. His arms were grabbing at her but she managed to swing her pocketbook with all her might into his neck. It must have winded him because he staggered slightly; and during that one second, she tossed aside her bag and grabbed his belt with both hands. Then she bashed her right knee into his groin so hard that he collapsed on the ground, groaning. Then she dashed across the driveway toward the rocks. By the time she reached them, he had followed her and grabbed her around the waist. They tussled, rolling over and over on the rough asphalt and gravel drive. Bits of crushed rock dug into her arms and legs, but she managed to hold on to the rock she had picked up.

They stopped near a boulder on the edge of the driveway. Seizing the opportunity, Josephine raised her arm high enough to bring the rock down on T.J.'s head. She felt the weight of the rock pound into his skull, heard the crunch of rock on bone, felt his chest sink with a groan, felt his arms slip away. Still, she raised the rock again—this time with both hands, raised it high above her head—and brought it down again. She was sobbing, crying out, "No, no!" The rock was heading down again when something stopped her. Someone behind her had grabbed the rock.

"Don't, Josephine." It was Davis. "You've got him. That's enough." He took the rock and put it aside and pulled her away from T.J.

Josephine began crying harder, "I've killed him."

Davis answered, "No, but he's gonna have one hellava headache. I brought some rope to tie him."

"Where's Josie?"

"With Eula Mae's. She's okay. Scared but okay."

Davis tied T.J.'s hands behind his back and leaned him against the boulder. Then he tied his feet. T.J. was moaning and swaying.

"I was going to kill him," Josephine sobbed. "If you hadn't come, I would have killed him."

"You were trying to stop him," Davis said. "You were trying to stop whatever evil he had in mind."

"That's what happened to you and Celeste, isn't it. That's what the puppet play was about. You accidentally killed Celeste, but if I had killed T.J., it wouldn't have been an accident. I was capable of killing him, and it wouldn't have been an accident."

"You were capable of protecting yourself and your daughter. Nothing more." He helped her rise and steered her to the stairs to her house.

"We'll call Josie when the police come," he was saying to her. "She's going to want to know you're okay."

He folded his arms around her as they sat down on the steps to wait for the police.

CHAPTER TWENTY-THREE

Josephine did not hear the soft rain that started during the night. Around two o'clock she failed to hear Michael's car bump onto their driveway, or his tires crunch over the place where she and T.J. had rolled across the road. Nor did she hear the car come to rest near the spot by the side of the drive where T.J.'s blood had left a quarter-size stain in the dirt.

Michael had driven down the drive through the darkness and into what should have been the sanctity of their parking area and its adjacent turn around. Instead part of the drive was still taped with fluorescent police tape. He stepped out of his car onto the asphalt drive, walked to the tape and peered over it at the ground. Seeing nothing but crushed weeds and scuffed dirt, he moved on, a fine coating of rain clinging to his face and chilling him. He hurried—perhaps too fast—down the stone steps, across the stepping stones and up the porch steps, and tapped on the glass panes in the front door.

In no time Davis was there, letting him into the quiet of the sleeping house.

"They're all right," Davis said from the dark living room. The two men shook hands, and as if that weren't enough of a greeting, Davis grasped Michael by the arms and squeezed. "They're okay," he repeated.

"Thank you for helping them. Josephine told me you called the police. Then came to help her. Thank God you were home."

"Of course," Davis acknowledged.

"If you'll excuse me, I'm going to check on Josephine now." Michael left the living room, and Davis returned to the front bedroom where he was staying.

Josephine was sound asleep. Michael took off his slacks and shirt and crawled in the bed beside her. He began stroking the soft hair at the nape of her neck and kissing her ear.

"Umm," she mumbled, arousing. "Is it morning?"

"I couldn't wait 'til morning."

"What time is it?"

"Around two."

Abruptly, fully awake, she sat up in bed and threw her arms around his neck. "I'm so glad to see you. Michael, it was horrible." Then she disentangled herself from him and continued. "The whole thing was so strange. I can't explain it, but I felt as if I knew exactly what to do. When I realized Josie and I were in trouble, I knew I had to get her away, to protect her, but also to get help. At first I thought of running to Davis's with her. But I kept thinking if he caught us, he'd have Josie, too. I realized I had to stand him down."

"Go on," Michael urged from beside her in the darkness.

"This man from the barn—T.J.—started walking down the driveway. He acted like he'd been drinking. I decided my best chance was to rush him and hit him with my pocket-book. Then I kneed him as hard as I could. He was doubled up, but he managed to grab me and wrestle me to the ground. We were rolling across the driveway. When we got to the other side, I grabbed a rock and hit him. I kept hitting him over and over." She stopped as abruptly as she had started.

"What happened then," Michael asked.

"Davis came and stopped me. And the police came. When they left, Eula Mae brought Josie home.

"There's more, Michael," she continued. "While Davis and I were waiting for the police, I had this startling realization—out of the blue—as if I'd always known it, but never understood. Momma and Daddy and Laura knew it. Maybe they always did. *Life is worth dying for because it's worth living.* One validates the other. I was perfectly willing to risk dying on the one chance that I could go on with our life just as before. It made Momma and Daddy and Laura's hard years so much easier to take because of their good times. Even Momma not knowing who she was, and Laura battling cancer and Daddy knowing he was going to die when he still wanted to live. That's it. That's what I knew from some place inside myself."

Michael took her hand and kissed it. Then he spoke, "I'm so relieved you and Josie are all right. Thank God your strength brought you safely through."

For a moment they were silent. Then Michael said, "I've been a self-centered jerk this summer. You and Josie mean the world to me, Josephine. On the way home last weekend, I realized I enjoy hiking and I love the woods. I'm proud of you for everything you've done this summer. I don't have any excuse for how I've acted, but I do owe you an explanation. I missed you both and felt left out of the life you were leading up here. But I promise you this. I will never leave you and Josie alone again. Never."

Josephine nodded, "Thank you for saying that, Michael, but can we talk about this in the morning? I can't keep my eyes open."

"We can talk about it for a long, long time, except I have to tell you one part before you go to sleep. I've asked the bank to let me run the western region from Rocky Ridge. What do you think?"

Josephine pulled Michael to her and slid her arms around his neck. "Michael, of course, I want to do it. I love it here, but we'll have to put heat in the house."

"Done and we'll manage some other improvements, too."

They kissed, a long, tender kiss.

Josephine snuggled back under the covers. Michael rose and put on his pajamas. Afterwards, he rambled in the dark through the house, checking on Josie, looking in on Davis, examining the front door where T.J. had broken in and Davis and Josephine had rigged a makeshift lock, checking the windows and making sure all the lights were out. Then he returned to the bedroom and climbed in beside Josephine.

"Is that rain I hear?" she asked.

"Yes," he answered.

"Nothing like a soft mountain rain for a good night's sleep," she said, pushing her back into the curl his body made around her.

During the night, the light rain continued.

Night animals, raccoons and opossum, creatures that travel long distances searching for food, interrupted their foraging long enough to accept a new, slower rhythm to the night.

At Lover's Leap the red fox, whose den was just below the rock, tilted her long, slender nose to catch the smell of fresh, damp earth. She pulled her pups closer to her underbelly and fluffed her tail around them.

Field mice scurried to their nests and ground hogs burrowed deeper into their tunnels. A spider, feeling its way across a slim thread to the outer reaches of its web, took shelter under a leaf.

The starlings roosting above the rock shook their wings and huddled together for warmth.

And the gentle patter of rain settled over the mountain like a lullaby.

EPILOGUE

Daddy liked late summer afternoons best. He used to say, "Josephine, my dear, for direction look to the sun. On a summer eve, you can chart a true easterly course. If there are no obstacles between you and the sun, and the sun is at your back, your shadow will run directly in front of you. For a time, you can hold past and present in tandem as if in each hand. The future lies before you."

"What happens if you go in another direction?" Josephine laughed, her eyes twinkling.

"Well, of course," he replied, "that changes everything."

It is October in the Blue Ridge Mountains, and the tourists are arriving to see the fall leaves. The old people on the mountain claim, as they do each year, that *this* is the best leaf display ever. The hardwoods—birches, maples, beeches, red oaks, and sycamores—have never been so rich. Their yellows, scarlets and oranges look even more vibrant against the background of evergreens—spruce, firs, hemlocks, pines and cedars.

The swallows that roost at Lover's Leap are giddy with the fresh air. They fly off the high rocks in tandem, or side by side in pairs, dipping and swaying until they catch a gust of wind and ride it into the valley.

The park in the center of Rocky Ridge is almost deserted. Older children are in school, and the swings they pumped with such vigor during the summer hang empty, their heavy chains stirred only by the wind.

Dust and leaf funnels dance across the park frightening younger children, who cling to their mothers' hands as they hurry by. The little ones have listened to tales their older sisters and brothers tell about the funnels. *Haints,* they say, who have come back to claim their dead and who had been known to snatch a little brother or sister by mistake.

Old-timers who understand the ways of the mountain know better. They say the wind swirls are Indian medicine men from the spirit world who have returned to prepare the mountain for winter.

In late August the Scarboroughs moved from Matthews to Rocky Ridge in time for Josie to enter kindergarten. They are settling into the cottage on Valley View Trail. Their new furnace has been installed and the kitchen is under renovation.

Michael was appointed western regional director for the bank and established his office in Rocky Ridge. He is working hard learning about the area and its potential for growth. Town leaders are already discussing him as a future candidate for councilman.

Josie loves her school and insists she can already read. For her first show-and-tell, she took a hawk's feather she and her mother had found on a hike. The feather, she told the class, was a gift from the hawk, information from the Indians that her mother had passed on to her. The class oohed and aahed with envy.

Josephine has been researching famous women throughout history and women in her own family, looking at both groups to see what qualities of leadership each possessed. If the research proves her theories, she plans to write a book about how the times make heroines of ordinary women.

Angie and Davis have been on two "real" dates. Everyone feels it is a happy combination but one complication has already surfaced. Angie has to drive because Davis's medications restrict driving. He finds this humiliating.

In September, Eula Mae began her gospel sing-alongs at Our Lady of the Hills Nursing Center. Darlene and Blackie, both of whom have nice voices, join her.

Eula Mae also continues her Sunday lunches every week after church. "Family Reunions" she insists on calling them. Davis protests, fussing that the Scarboroughs are the only family in the entire bunch and he and Josephine, of course, are cousins by marriage, which probably doesn't count.

"This is the '70's," Eula Mae always declares when the discussion comes up. "We're the family of man."

When Angie happens to be standing by, she pipes in, "And woman, and don't you forget it either."

One Sunday, Davis took Josephine aside. "Could you break away with me to Lover's Leap? There's something I'd like to share with you."

"What's going on?" Josephine asked, as they made their way to the rock. They were walking between a thin stand of hardwoods and a solid rock ledge. Beyond was the Blue Ridge Mountain range.

"I have something I'd like you to witness, but I'd rather tell you about it when we reach the top." He was carrying an urn.

They walked on in silence until they reached the summit, where rock outcroppings marked the edge of the mountain on which they stood. They were overlooking a corridor of deciduous forests, Northern conifers and Southern evergreens, which ran on either side of the Boone River. The Blue Ridge Mountains towered above like a benevolent parent. The rim was interspersed with rugged cliffs and hardy undergrowth.

"Josephine," Davis began slowly, "I've held Celeste in my heart too long. Her spirit deserves to be part of the universe.

Lover's Leap is the most spiritual place I know. It's the right place to free her. I want you to be my witness."

Josephine nodded, reaching out her hand to Davis. Together they stepped out to a flat indention in the rock. The end of the rock protruded over the gorge some two or three feet like the point of an anvil. Beneath them was a straight drop to the floor of the valley. The wind swirled dead leaves below them.

"This is the hardest thing I've ever done," Davis said, removing the top of the urn. "I envisioned that after being held in this thing for sixteen years, she'd just rise out of the urn." He tilted the urn, spilling out the ashes. The wind carried the fine cloud of ash over their heads. "Celeste," he began, with a tear in his eye, "I release you to become part of an obstinate universe that will never complete its life cycle."

A lump rose in Josephine's throat. She stepped closer to Davis and he slid his arm around her. "I wish I'd known her," she whispered. She reached up toward the ashes. They dusted her arm and hand.

"She sang like a bird," Davis said. "When she performed, she wore this remarkable black dress with gleaming rhinestone straps."

As they watched the ashes merge into the wind, Josephine felt as if a burden was lifted, not just for Davis, but for her as well. Their mourning was over, his for Celeste, hers for her family. All the questions, the uncertainties, the doubts would never be answered. Somehow knowing them seemed less important now.

For in this broad stretch of land, which held rivers as if they were ribbons, forests that were testaments to past ages, and cliffs no man could conquer, in this place time was superfluous. She looked out across the Boone River Gorge to the mountains beyond and knew her family would be with her forever.

ACKNOWLEDGMENTS

It is difficult for me to trace exactly how I came to love writing. Certainly my mother is the one who introduced me to books and allowed her modest library to become my playground. She also is the one who taught me to love words for their rhythm and cadence as well as their meaning.

My father and his relatives, however, were the real storytellers. Our family gatherings were replete with colorful stories, and I soon learned that if I had something to say I needed to exaggerate and speak loudly. I also learned to listen to the quieter relatives to hear seldom told stories.

If my relatives and neighbors provided the emotional background for my writing, other important people provided the technical aspects.

- Barbara R.Thompson, my editor, taught me how to access my deeper feelings.
- Mena F. Webb, a writer, has been my mentor and friend for many years. We attended creative writing classes together at the University of North Carolina during the sixites. Early in the writing of Portals, she gave me suggestions on the plot.
- Jean Fox O'Barr, another mentor, founding director of Duke University Women's Studies, helped me believe in myself to the point of taking action.
- William J. Spiesel, Col. USMC Retired, Korean War Veteran, provided information about the Korean War.

- James Laney, former Ambassador to the Republic of Korea and his wife, Berta, graciously arranged a tour for my husband and me in Seoul and a trip to Panmunjon for a military briefing of the Demilitarized Zone.
- Harald R. Hansen-Pruss, Col.USMCR Retired, my husband, who served 30 years in the Marine Corps' active and reserve programs, was my advisor on weapons and warfare.
- Our son, Ed, provided final edits, and our daughter, Brandon Frein, provided ongoing encouragment for the project.

ABOUT THE AUTHOR

BETSY GAMBLE HANSEN, a native of High Point, NC, is a graduate of Duke University with a Bachelor of Arts degree in English. Her lifetime enthusiasm for storytelling provided great encouragement to family and others to document these memories resulting in a sizable collection of insightful descriptions of both personal lives and experiences.

Betsy's professional writing career began as a staff writer for the *High Point Enterprise* and special edition editor for the *Beaufort Gazette*, Beaufort, SC. In the 1960's she wrote and directed puppet plays for the Durham, NC, Children's Museum, a natural science museum.

Throughout her life and writing career she has devoted much of her energy toward issues that positively affect both children and women. She has served on the National Board of UNICEF, and been President and National Board Member of ARCS (Achievement Awards for College Scientists) and is a former secretary of the Georgia Center for Nonprofits.

She has served on the Council on Women's Studies at Duke University since 2001 and is currently organizing a Women's Network at Oglethorpe University in Atlanta to support the Women's Studies Program associated with that liberal arts college, as well as raise awareness in the metropolitan community of women's concerns.

Betsy is married to Harald (Pucho) R. Hansen and they have two grown children, Brandon and Ed.

Portals is Betsy's first book of fiction.

Printed in the United States
1023600004B

9 781930 897120